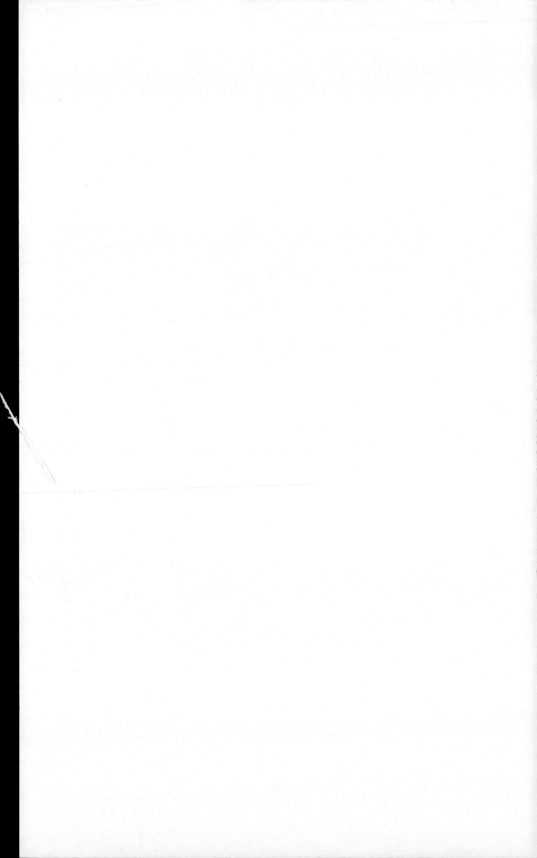

In this study John Bowlin argues that Aquinas's moral theology receives much of its character and content from an assumption about our common lot: the good we desire is difficult to know in particular, and difficult to will even when it is known, because of contingencies of various kinds – within ourselves, in the ends and objects we pursue, and in the circumstances of choice. Since contingencies are fortune's effects, Aquinas also assumes that it is fortune that makes good choice difficult. And since it is the virtues that perfect choice, Aquinas finds he must treat a number of topics in light of this difficulty: the moral and theological virtues, the first precepts of the natural law, the voluntariness of virtuous action, and the happiness available to us in this life. By noting that Aquinas proceeds in this way, with an eye on fortune's threats to virtue, agency, and happiness, Bowlin places him more precisely in the history of ethics, among Aristotle, Augustine, and the Stoics.

CAMBRIDGE STUDIES IN
RELIGION AND CRITICAL THOUGHT 6

CONTINGENCY AND FORTUNE IN
AQUINAS'S ETHICS

CAMBRIDGE STUDIES IN
RELIGION AND CRITICAL THOUGHT

Edited by
WAYNE PROUDFOOT, *Columbia University*
JEFFREY L. STOUT, *Princeton University*
NICHOLAS WOLTERSTORFF, *Yale University*

Current events confirm the need to understand religious ideas and institutions
critically, yet radical doubts have been raised about how to proceed and about
the ideal of critical thought itself. Meanwhile, some prominent scholars have
urged that we turn the tables, and view modern society as the object of criticism
and a religious tradition as the basis for critique. Cambridge Studies in Religion
and Critical Thought is a series of books intended to address that interaction of
critical thinking and religious traditions in this context of certainty and conflicting claims. It will take up questions such as the following, either by reflecting on
them philosophically or by pursuing their ramifications in studies of specific
figures and movements: is a coherent critical perspective on religion desirable
or even possible? What sort of relationship to religious tradition ought a critic to
have? What, if anything, is worth saving from the Enlightenment legacy or
from critics of religion like Hume and Feuerbach? The answers offered, while
varied, will uniformly constitute distinguished, philosophically informed, and
critical analyses of particular religious topics.

Other titles published in the series

CONTINGENCY AND FORTUNE IN AQUINAS'S ETHICS

JOHN BOWLIN

*Department of Philosophy and Religion,
University of Tulsa*

CAMBRIDGE
UNIVERSITY PRESS

PUBLISHED BY THE PRESS SYNDICATE OF THE UNIVERSITY OF CAMBRIDGE
The Pitt Building, Trumpington Street, Cambridge CB2 1RP, United Kingdom

CAMBRIDGE UNIVERSITY PRESS
The Edinburgh Building, Cambridge CB2 2RU, United Kingdom   http://www.cup.cam.ac.uk
40 West 20th Street, New York, NY 10011–4211, USA   htt://www.cup.org
10 Stamford Road, Oakleigh, Melbourne 3166, Australia

© John Bowlin 1999

First published 1999

Printed in Great Britain at the University Press, Cambridge

Typeset in Baskerville 11/12.5 pt [VN]

A catalogue record for this book is available from the British Library

Library of Congress cataloguing in publication data
Bowlin, John R., 1959–
Contingency and fortune in Aquina's ethics/John Bowlin.
p.   cm. – (Cambridge studies in religion and critical thought; 6)
Includes bibliographical references and index.
ISBN 0 521 62019 8 (hardback)
1. Thomas, Aquinas, Saint, 1225?–1274 – Ethics.   2. Contingency
(Philosophy) – Moral and ethical aspects – History.   3. Fortune – Moral
and ethical aspects – History.   I. Title.   II. Series.
B765.T54B65   1999
171'.2'092 – dc21   98-35103   CIP

ISBN 0 521 62019 8 hardback

For Mimi

While the earth remaineth, seedtime and harvest, and cold and heat, and summer and winter, and day and night shall not cease.

Genesis 8.22

Contents

Contents

Preface

One might imagine Aquinas regarding this effort with suspicion. It too easily tempts confusion and scandal. Fortune is a pagan matter. Things that happen *a fortuna vel casus* are imaginable features of the world only if we restrict our inquiries to proximate causes. They vanish as attention is fixed upon higher, distant causes, and Aquinas, no doubt, would encourage us to keep ours fixed upon Divine Providence. Of course, given our short views and fallen nature it is unlikely that we can, and thus it comes as no surprise when Aquinas admits that in this world the effects of chance and fortune seem to abound. Still, he insists that appearances deceive, and insofar as they do we might expect him to borrow Augustine's advice to the person who speaks of fate and means Providence. The person who speaks of the fortuitous and contingent affairs of this world while at the same time conceding their demise in the Divine intellect should "retain his thought, but correct his language" (*sententiam teneat, linguam corrigat*) (*De civ.Dei* v.1; cf. *ST* I.116.1).

But without qualification this hunch misleads, and the fact that Aquinas himself neither corrects his language nor holds his tongue is the best evidence that it does. Repeatedly he insists that we must refer to things subject to fortune's unexpected twists and turns if we are to understand the contours of the moral life, its origins and problems, its rules, virtues, and customs. And yet even as he admits that as moralist he must speak of fortune Aquinas hesitates, he resists. He strains against the necessity, not because it concedes too much to mere appearance, but rather because he yearns for longer views and perfect nature. He longs for a kind of moral life, and in particular a kind of virtue, that can disregard contingency, that fortune can neither constitute nor unsettle. It follows that Aquinas's suspicions are not so much with the resort to talk of contingency and fortune, but with the virtues we praise in this life and that we explicate in these terms. Above all, it is this eschatological setting of his remarks about the moral life, about

xi

virtue, fortune, and contingency, that I hope to make plain in what follows.

This book began as a dissertation, and I would like to thank the two advisers who guided my first efforts. Victor Preller's enthusiasm for Aquinas's moral theology sparked my interest in a project of this kind, while his mastery of Aristotle's ethics and the Latin Stoics saved me from mistakes both venial and mortal. Jeffrey Stout's uncanny ability to pose the questions that I needed to address, to ferret out doubtful arguments, to distinguish lean from fat, and to determine which bit should lead and which should follow focused my efforts and sharpened my prose. Both remain steadfast mentors, critics, and friends. Fellowship support from Princeton University made my graduate career possible, and the Charlotte W. Newcombe Foundation funded an additional year of research and writing. I am grateful for their generosity.

Along the way from dissertation to book, I received a faculty development fellowship from the University of Tulsa that enabled me to write chapters three and four. My thanks goes to Dean Thomas Horne. I also benefited from countless conversations with my colleagues in Philosophy and Religion: Jane Ackerman, Jacob Howland, Russell Hittinger, and the late John Carmody. John Taylor gave careful attention to drafts of a number of chapters. Scott Davis sent on pages of commentary and criticism that were indispensable for my revisions. Stanley Hauerwas and Gene Rogers read the penultimate version and replied with many helpful suggestions. Russ Hittinger also read through the typescript toward the end and gave special attention to my discussion of Aquinas's treatment of the natural law. He saved me from a number of careless missteps in argument, translation, and expression. On exegetical matters our differences remain, and yet after many hours of conversation, we found that they are subtle, more a matter of emphasis and sentiment than substance. To these colleagues and friends, I am happily indebted. For their assistance and encouragement, I am grateful. I share credit for the virtues of this effort with them. Its vices are mine alone.

My series editors, Wayne Proudfoot, Jeffrey Stout, and Nicholas Wolterstorff, guided the project through its initial stages with wise counsel and cautious optimism. My editors at Cambridge, Camilla Erskine, Ruth Parr, Kevin Taylor, and Audrey Cotterell, were patient with my many delays and provided invaluable assistance along the way.

This book includes reworked material from the following essays: "Aquinas on Virtue and the Goods of Fortune," *Thomist* 60:4 (October 1996) 537–570, © Dominican Fathers Province of St. Joseph; and "Rorty and Aquinas on Courage and Contingency," *Journal of Religion* 77:3 (July 1997) 402–420, © The University of Chicago; and "Psychology and Theodicy in Aquinas," *Medieval Philosophy and Theology* 7:2 (Fall 1998), © Cambridge University Press. This material appears by permission.

To my family, Mimi, Nicholas, and Isaac, the debt I owe exceeds all measure. Their love and friendship, faith, and encouragement are gifts for which I am daily grateful.

List of Abbreviations

De ente	*De ente et essentia*
De malo	*Quaestiones disputatae De malo*
De pot.	*Quaestiones disputatae De potentia*
De verit.	*Quaestiones disputatae De veritate*
De virt. card.	*Quaestio disputata De virtutibus cardinalibus*
In Ethic.	*In decem libros Ethicorum Aristotelis expositio*
In Metaph.	*In duodecim libros Metaphysicorum Aristotelis expositio*
In Perih.	*In libros Peri Hermeneias Aristotelis expositio*
In Phys.	*In octo libros Physicorum Aristotelis expositio*
SCG	*Summa contra Gentiles*
ST	*Summa Theologiae*
Super Iob	*Expositio super Iob ad litteram*

For classical texts I use the *Oxford Classical Dictionary*'s list of abbreviations; for other medieval texts I follow the standard abbreviations.

Introduction

The contemporary legacy of Aquinas's account of the moral life is perplexing. Irony abounds. Consider the following.

In recent years many moral philosophers and moral theologians have looked to Aristotle to help them bypass the sterile debate between Kantians and consequentialists. Since Aquinas is one of the more able interpreters of the Aristotelian moral tradition we might expect them to consider his efforts a resource for theirs. Some, of course, do, principally Alasdair MacIntyre, and yet most do not. In fact, many of these reformers in moral philosophy and theology suspect that Aquinas is the theological ancestor of their contemporary rationalist and rule-obsessed opponents.[1] Others insist that his desire to deduce concrete moral guidance from abstract principles of natural law obscures those features of praiseworthy practical judgment that in fact deserve accent: its flexibility, its attention to particulars, and thus its resistance to simple characterization, to descriptions that resort to legal generalities.[2] Others still conclude that rationalism in morals, whether Aquinas's variety or some other, prevents us from acknowledging a feature of the moral life most of us consider obvious and ordinary: its intractable conflicts, its tragic dilemmas.[3]

These are textbook distortions, false charges. This much is obvious. But then why have they remained so prominent, so easy for so many to accept? Perhaps because too many of Aquinas's defenders offer interpretations of his account of the moral life that either goad his detractors or confirm the caricature. The ironies here are delicious. Those who wish to convince us that Aquinas's treatment of practical judgment, for example, is more attentive to particulars, complexity, and conflict than most suspect, have, more often than not, transformed him into a

---

[1] Baier (1985a, 232–236).   [2] Nussbaum (1978, 168–169).
[3] Williams (1973) lodges this complaint against moral rationalism in general.

I

consequentialist of one kind or another.[4] Dismayed by this conclusion, still other friends and exegetes dash in to rescue Aquinas from his rescuers, hoping to restore that law-obsessed and rationalist moral theorist his contemporary critics love to loathe. They don't find him. Or, rather, the most prominent among the anti-consequentialist rescuers – John Finnis, Germain Grisez, and Joseph Boyle – concede that Aquinas's treatment of the natural law must be supplemented with Kantian arguments, alien to Aquinas, in order to advance an account of the moral life that the critics consider stereotypically Thomistic. Defending Aquinas against his defenders, Finnis, Grisez, and Boyle insist they can succeed only as they regard his own treatment of the moral life as inchoate and incomplete Kantian rationalism, thus inadvertently perpetuating the erroneous image.

Much of the confusion here follows from the inordinate attention all parties give to Aquinas's remarks about the natural law in the *prima secundae* of the *Summa Theologiae*. In this Aquinas's foes merely follow the lead of his friends, many of whom regard his remarks on the first precepts of the natural law as the centerpiece of his efforts, and, as we have noted, too many find there either some variation on Kant's ethics, where the demands of practical reason specify the morally obligatory, or some variety of consequentialism, where prescriptions, prohibitions, and exceptions to each are derived from the basic features of the natural human good. The problem with this approach is two-fold. First, it is unlikely that Aquinas offers a medieval antecedent to this or that position in the modern metaethical debate. Indeed, both friends and foes of modern moral philosophy have noted that its largely secular sources and its consistent attention to doubts about the origins of obligation mark a significant departure from the sources and concerns of the moral theology that came before.[5] Here the irony is obvious. Those contemporary interpreters who fail to take note of this difference cannot say why Aquinas's account of the moral life deserves attention. If his concerns and conclusions are roughly equivalent to those found in this or that modern view, then he reproduces what we already know while providing few resources for understanding what we do not, few challenges to our settled convictions. Second, the vast majority of Aquinas's remarks about the moral life in the *secunda pars* regard human actions and passions, and the virtues that perfect them. Remarks about the natural law are scant; one question (*ST* 1–11.94) amid only eighteen

---

[4] For a good example of this effort and outcome see Fuchs (1983).
[5] See Schneewind (1993) and Anscombe (1981).

on law as a whole (*ST* i–ii.90–108).[6] By contrast, the remarks about action, passion, and virtue in general require eighty-nine questions (*ST* i–ii.1–89). Those about specific virtues and vices require many more (*ST* ii-ii.1–189). Once again the irony is obvious. Interpreters who regard the treatise on law as the main event have in fact been concentrating on a side show. They contend that Aquinas's treatment of the natural law deserves our careful consideration, and yet our attention is directed to that which he considers only briefly. There are, of course, dissenters, exegetes who resist unproductive comparisons between medieval and modern morals and who look beyond Aquinas's treatment of the natural law to his remarks about other matters,[7] and yet few of them have been able to show how the preponderance of his efforts – those that regard action, passion, and virtue – hang together with his discussion of the natural law in a more or less coherent view.[8] Indeed, if it is a mistake to think that Aquinas's remarks about the first precepts of the natural law represent a medieval antecedent to this or that position in modern moral philosophy, then what exactly does he hope to accomplish with those remarks, and how do the intentions that motivate his efforts in the opening questions of *de Legibus* line up with those that motivate his remarks about action and virtue?

These questions press upon us all the more once we notice that still others give special attention to Aquinas's remarks about the natural law in order to muster critical leverage against certain social and political arrangements in the modern period. Dissatisfied with this or that aspect of modern life, dismayed by institutions and practices that refuse to provide moral guidance, and appalled by the inability of modern moral philosophy to offer stable foundations and compelling warrants for those institutions and practices that deserve to be sustained, friends on both the left and the right look to Aquinas for aid, hoping his appeal to nature can yield the prohibitions and prescriptions that these troubled times need. Still, it is not at all clear that Aquinas's remarks about the first precepts of the natural law can bear this burden, largely because (as I shall argue in chapter three) he has something else in mind as he discusses the *principiis exterioribus actuum* (*ST* i–ii.90.prologue), something other than providing moral guidance for humanity as such, something

---

[6] Unless discussion is required, reference to Aquinas's works will be included in the body of text. For the most part of I have made use of the available English translations. When I have not, this is so indicated.

[7] Recent efforts include: Cessario (1991), Harak (1993), Hibbs (1990), Wadell (1992), and Westberg (1994).

[8] Notable exceptions include: Nelson (1990), MacIntyre (1988b), McInerny (1982), Pinckaers (1995).

other than securing legitimacy for some institutions and practices but not others.

We are left wondering what kind of resource Aquinas might be for our own reflections on good and evil in human action and on the virtues and vices of modernity. If he is to help us make sense of the moral life we lead, then we will have to determine how his efforts compare with ours, how his puzzles and concerns line up with our own. This is not simply a matter of specifying his contemporary relevance and justifying our interest, but of necessity. There is no activity called "understanding Aquinas's account of the moral life" that does not include mapping the relations, the identities and differences, between his views and ours and assessing the truth-value of each. In fact, there is nothing we can know about that account apart from those relations and assessments. It follows that anachronism *per se* is not an exegetical vice.[9] Nor is it a charge that sticks to those interpreters who regard Aquinas's efforts in the treatise on law as a resource for our contemporary metaethical debates. Rather, the complaint must be that they have not determined how his interests and concerns can be usefully related to ours. They have not made the right comparisons across time. This is, of course, a moral judgment about the interests and concerns worth having, the comparisons worth making, and it is confirmed retrospectively. If we assume that our inquiries into the character of the moral life are best motivated by a certain collection of interests and concerns, and if we assume that Aquinas's efforts can be a resource for our own precisely because he shares many of those interests and concerns, then our assumptions will be confirmed only if we in fact make better sense of his account, and only if the interpretation that results in fact provides useful resources for our own inquiries.

Every effort to understand Aquinas's account of the moral life will begin with assumptions of this kind. Let me make mine plain. I do not believe that doubts about the content of our most basic moral obliga-tions should motivate our inquiries into the character of the moral life. Nor should doubts about the warrants that justify acting in accord with the basic obligations we do accept. Why? Because in each instance the doubt is more apparent than real. I am not suggesting that skepticism is unimaginable here. Nor am I implying that there is perfect agreement among us about the content of obligation. However, I am convinced that skepticism about fundamental moral matters is not a real option, at

---

[9] For a fuller treatment of the irrelevance of anachronism see Rorty, Schneewind, and Skinner (1984, 8–11).

least not for most of us. For the most part, we do not need to be told
what our most basic obligations are or how they are justified. Most of us
consider moral guidance of this kind unnecessary, if not insulting, and
most of us regard with suspicion those whose doubts about obligation
are such that they welcome the aid that action-guiding moral theories
provide.[10] Of course, we may not be able to say much about the origin of
the obligations we do recognize, but no matter. This inability prevents
few of us from thinking that there are some things we should do, others
we should not. By contrast, we can be genuinely confused about what
our basic obligations require of us in concrete circumstances. Basic
obligation aside, we can be puzzled about the character of the good and
the best in some particular instance. Knowing it is difficult, and willing it
because of that knowledge is no less so. It is my assumption that these
difficulties generate our most fundamental puzzles about the moral life.
Why is it that the good that obliges (i.e., the best) is difficult to know?
How is it that the will at times fails to desire the good that is known to
oblige? And notice, these are not questions motivated by puzzlement
about what we should do, at least not principally. They are, rather,
questions about the causes of our everyday moral difficulties, questions
that will be answered only as the arduous character of knowing and
doing the good is explained. I also assume that Aquinas can be a
resource for our contemporary efforts to address these questions, in part
because I find no evidence that he intends his inquiries in the second
part of the *Summa Theologiae* to dissolve basic doubt about good and evil
in human action or to provide rules that guide conduct in the particular,
in part because I believe that his efforts there are, in large measure,
designed to address our more ordinary puzzles about the causes of
moral perplexity and weakness. Since the vast majority of his remarks in
the *secunda pars* regard human agency and virtue I also assume that he
addresses these puzzles as he treats these topics.

His reply can be put simply. The good is difficult to know in particular, and difficult to will even when it is known, because of contingencies
of various kinds, within ourselves and in the circumstances of choice. It
follows that the moral life described in the *secunda pars* receives much of
its character and content from the ability of the virtues to confront these

[10] If I know what I am obliged to do, wouldn't we regard my effort to locate reasons for acting as I
know I should as senseless? If I continue to press the inquiry, wouldn't we suspect that I am trying
to avoid acting in accord with the obligation? My hunch is that most of us would, and for good
reason. For the best explication of these reasons see Davis (1992). For evidence that most moral
philosophers in the modern period have disregarded them see Darwall (1995).

contingencies.[11] By "moral life" I mean what Aquinas does (*ST* I–II.I.3): the life of human action, its causes, both intrinsic (intellect, will, and virtue) and extrinsic (law and grace), and its character, either good or evil. By "contingency" I mean the states of affairs in the world and in ourselves that fortune can alter.[12] Restated with clarifications: Aquinas's account of our agency – caused by intellect and will, made distinctively human by the natural law, corrupted by sin, and perfected by virtue and grace – is best understood in light of his remarks about the contingencies, the difficulties, in the world and in ourselves.

It follows that Aquinas's treatment of the moral virtues is largely functional. Their significance, he insists, lies in their ability to cope with those contingencies that hinder our achievement of the good and the best. Indeed, above all, the virtues work. This is what they do, this is what distinguishes them, and this, according to Aquinas, is why we praise them. Their intelligibility and their goodness follow from their efforts, and their efforts are needed precisely because our pursuit of the good is hounded on all sides by contingencies of all kinds, difficulties great and small. This is my principal exegetical conclusion, and it is not the one found in most treatments of Aquinas's remarks about the virtues. A number of reasons account for this, and first among them must be the fact that Aquinas leaves the conceptual connections between the virtues, various contingencies, and the fortuitous events that generate them largely undeveloped. What he does say he locates in remarks about other matters, scattered throughout a variety of questions and articles. Perhaps more to the point, even when gathered together it is not at all clear that they can be used to make sense of his account of the virtues. Indeed, there are at least two reasons for thinking that they cannot.

First, Aquinas says very little about those things that happen by chance or fortune and what he does say comes largely in his discussion of Providence (*ST* I.116). Little mention is made in his discussion of the moral life's general features, even less in his treatment of the virtues. Second, it appears that Aquinas uses his brief remarks about chance and Providence in order to dismiss the very idea of the former. He argues that what happens here by accident, both in the natural world and in human affairs, can be reduced to a preordaining cause, to divine

---

[11] I will also discuss passages from the *prima pars*, as well as from the smaller *summa*, the commentaries, and the disputations, as needed, in order to fill out my findings.

[12] Thus my topic is *not* the centerpiece of Thomistic metaphysics: the contingent being of all things created. See *De ente*, especially chapter 5 and *SCG* II.30–31.

Providence (*ST* 1.116.1). Thus, fortune, it seems, can be explained away, both as event and as object of interest, by referring to God's command over how things go. How can we reply?

To the objection that Aquinas says very little about virtue and fortune, we can note that he does, nevertheless, say quite a bit about contingency as he develops his account of the moral virtues. The moral virtues perfect choice (*ST* 1–11.58.4; 65.1), choice is normally preceded by deliberation about what is to be done, and deliberation regards those singular and contingent things that make choice difficult (*ST* 1–11.14.1). Contingent things are, therefore, the matter that the moral virtues regard (*ST* 1–11.60.1.1), and, following Aristotle, Aquinas insists that chance and fortune make contingency possible (*In Perih.*1.13.9). That is, all events would be necessary, happening always and unavoidably when their sufficient conditions were in place, if the causes of at least some events – call them contingent – were not periodically subject to accidental disruption. Chance and fortune, according to this view, divide the contingent from the necessary, creating that part of the world – contingent happenings – that is virtue's concern.

Both Aristotle's remarks (*Int.*18a34–18b16) and Aquinas's commentary indicate that what is at stake here is the character of the concepts and the relations among them, with defeatability and frequency setting the terms of each. The causes of necessary events cannot be defeated and thus always produce their effects. The causes of contingent events can be defeated. Disruptions by chance or fortune can prevent them from producing their effects. And yet, because these disruptions happen infrequently, contingent events happen for the most part. Thus, it is that which happens rarely – the disruptions of chance and fortune – that distinguishes that which happens always from that which happens for the most part. Turning gray, for example, comes with age, and for the most part most do. But there is no necessity here. With good fortune, this fate can be escaped (*In Perih.*1.13.9; cf. *Ph.*196b10–196b17, and *In Phys.*11.8.209–210), and indeed, it is by showing us how this can be so, how seemingly uninterruptible causal chains can be interrupted, that Aristotle displays what chance and fortune are and how they generate contingent events.[13] We speak of an event of chance or fortune when,

---

[13] Fate is the right word, for it is the causal necessity the Stoics feared that Aristotle addresses in *Metaph.*1027a28–1027b16; 1065a6–14 and *Ph.*196b10–198a13. There is no vicious anachronism here. Aristotle has something to say about a worry that gained greater prominence later on, and there is no harm in saying with Aquinas (*In Perih.*1.14.10) and Sorabji (1980, 70–88) that Aristotle's arguments respond to the Stoics' worries about fate. I am indebted to both commentaries for my understanding of Aristotle's arguments and conclusions.

apart from the intention of any agent, two causal chains collide, disrupting the course of each. I go to the market and run into a debtor. I neither intended nor expected to meet him there. He is equally surprised. Our meeting was an accidental coincidence, good fortune for me, bad for him. From examples of this sort (*Ph.*196a2–5) Aristotle draws two conclusions: chance events of every kind have no cause, and, as a result, we can speak of contingent events, events that are caused without necessity. Aquinas concurs (*In Perih.*1.14.11; *In Metaph.*vi.3.1191–1202; *ST* 1.115.6; II–II.95.5).

The argument turns on an assumption about causation. Both Aristotle and Aquinas insist that when we ask for the cause of a thing we are asking for reasons that explain its occurrence and character (*Ph.*194b16–195a26; *In Phys.*II.5.176–181).[14] In fact, both contend that causation has more to do with rational explanation than with constant conjunction, antecedent necessitating conditions, or exceptionless regularity. Aristotle's phrasing captures it best. Understanding the primary cause of a thing is equivalent to "grasping the 'why' of it" (*Ph.*194b19–20; cf. *In Phys.*II.5.176), and of course, why questions are answered when compelling explanations are offered.

What then is the "why" of our meeting at the market? It is precisely that which explains why this fortuitous coincidence occurred, and it is not at all clear what that could be. One might be tempted to reply that a combination of decisions, my own and my debtor's, does the explanatory work, but this would be a mistake. These decisions explain why each of us went to market; they do not explain why we went to market *at the same time*. And of course, this latter coincidence is what we want explained when we ask for the cause of our meeting.[15]

With Aquinas in step (*In Metaph.*vi.3.1201; *In Perih.*1.14.11; *ST* 1.115.6), Aristotle concludes (*Metaph.*1027b12–14) that it is a mistake to say that all things that happen have a cause. Fortuitous happenings do not. Our meeting in the market did not, and thus the world is not as the Stoics imagine. It is not an uninterrupted causal nexus. Causes produce effects that converge for no reason and when they do the web of causal connections is broken. It follows that a cause located, even a sufficient cause, does not necessarily yield its effect, since most can be interrupted by coincidence with another (*Metaph.*1027a30–2; *In Metaph.*vi.3.1192–

---

[14] For an excellent discussion of the relation between causation and explanation in Aristotle and others see Sorabji (1980, 10–12, 26–44). The relation is difficult for us to imagine, largely because we assume that causes must be active. They must do something to produce an effect. For the historical origins of our assumptions see Frede (1980).   [15] Sorabji (1980, 10–11).

1193,1200; *In Perih*.1.14.11). My ship and crew may in fact be sufficiently readied to make the voyage from A to B, and yet it is surely possible for a storm to happen upon us and interrupt our progress. Interruptions, of course, are infrequent, and yet insofar as they are possible – insofar as the movement from cause to effect can be thwarted in this accidental way – we are justified in speaking of contingent causes, those that produce their effects for the most part but not always (*In Perih*.1.14.12; *ST* 1.115.6).[16]

It is this possibility that, above all, permits Aquinas to develop an account of the moral virtues that highlights our relation to contingencies, to things subject to fortune. Aquinas distinguishes chance and fortune as Aristotle does (*Ph*.196b10–198a12). A chance event is any happening that affects the character of something else by accident. A fortuitous event affects the happiness of rational agents alone. Thus when an aged satellite falls from the sky striking and killing a tree we say that its death was by chance, in part because satellites are not made for the sake of killing trees, in part because a tree is not a rational agent. However, if it turns out that the tree is my prize-winning walnut, and if in sorrow and anger I exhaust my health and my bank account seeking compensation, bringing misery to myself and to my family, then we would say this event was also my misfortune. It affected my happiness by transforming my agency. And since the happiness that fortune affects is largely a consequence of acting well – that is, a consequence of acting in a manner that is both virtuous and successful – "it follows that fortune pertains to the actions in which one happens to act well or is impeded from acting well" (*In Phys*.11.10.229). That is, fortune pertains to accidental happenings that affect the character of one's virtue.

But of course it is one thing to notice that Aquinas brings together virtue and fortune as he accounts for each, quite another to insist that these conceptual connections make sense once we assume, as he does, a world governed to the ground by Providence. Indeed, Aquinas insists that while there are no proximate causes of fortuitous events, there is an ultimate cause. When I encounter my debtor at the market we assume

[16] *Ibid*., 12–13, Sorabji makes note of the obvious: at some point in every causal chain the effect becomes necessary, its cause uninterruptible by others. Happily, nothing of much significance follows. Some causes are necessary, some are not. Aristotle and Aquinas, I suspect, would contend that most are not, if only because in most instances it is difficult to distinguish the necessitating conditions of some effect from the effect itself. If we bracket the possibility of intentional reversals, at what point are conditions such that my ship must reach its destination? At what point have I escaped fortune's reach? Most probably when the voyage is over and I am safe in port. In that event, the cause of my getting to port was contingent all along, or very nearly so.

that our meeting was accidental insofar as it occurred apart from any intention we can locate. However, we must also assume that the Divine intellect that orders all things brought our paths to cross. Like two servants sent to the same place by their master, we must consider our meeting fortuitous, "but as compared to the master, who had ordered it, it is directly intended" (*ST* 1.116.1). Should we conclude, then, that Aquinas considers fortune and contingency mere appearances, mere phantoms of our ignorance?

No. Despite appearances to the contrary, Aquinas does not consider fortune and Providential certitude incompatible, precisely because he regards the assumption about divine knowledge that generates the worry false. By his lights we cannot assume that God's mode of knowing is equivalent to ours, and thus we cannot conclude that God knows contingent things – those things subject to fortune – as we do (*In Perih.* 1.14.18). We know them "successively, as they are in their own being" (*ST* 1.14.13). They have a future when they are not yet actual, a present when they are, and a past when they are no more, and our knowledge of them follows this historical progression. If God knows in this mode, then contingencies seem to vanish in the necessity of God's knowledge. God knows all things, not only the past and present, but also the future, and since God's knowledge is necessary, if God knows that some contingent event will be, then it will be (*ST* 1.14.13.obj.2). However, God does not know as we do, as a creature in time, but rather as the eternal Creator who transcends time. As such, all things that have been and will be are simultaneously present to God all at once, in one simple intuition (*In Perih.*1.14.20). From this angle of vision contingent things are known, not successively according to their mode of being, but simultaneously according to the mode of the eternal knower (*ST* 1.14.13). As such, it is misleading to speak of God knowing the contingent future, for God does not know in this historical mode. There are no future events that can be foreknown from God's perspective, just as there are no past events to remember. It follows that we cannot fear that God's knowledge of the future fixes its character. Rather, we can only say that God knows what we know as future contingents, together with all other things past and present, in a glance, in a flash, in a timeless instant (*In Perih.*1.14.20).[17]

---

[17] The secondary literature on Aquinas's treatment of these matters is vast. A representative sampling includes: Burrell (1984a; 1986, 92–113; 1988; 1993, esp. 95–139); Incandela (1986); Verbeke (1974); and Wippel (1988). For doubts about the necessity of God's knowledge that generates the problem in the first places see Mavrodes (1984). For doubts about the incompatibility of God's certain knowledge of the future with certain kinds of contingencies, see Zagzebski (1985).

The visual metaphor is indispensable here. It enables Aquinas to say that God's knowledge of contingencies is necessary, as it must be, and yet innocuous to the contingent and temporal character of the thing known. Since God sees all things all at once, the divine mode of knowing contingent things is equivalent to the human eye that sees Socrates sitting (*In Perih*.1.14.20). Equivalent effects follow. To see Socrates sitting does not affect the modal character of what he does. His sitting remains contingent (*In Perih*.1.14.21). And yet while he sits, it must necessarily be the case that he does sit, and our knowledge that follows from seeing him sit must have an equivalent necessity (*ST* 1.14.13.2). As a result, Aquinas can say that the necessity that attaches to contingencies and accidents is conditional, not absolute; conditioned upon God's mode of knowing, not built into their causes as a consequence of being known (*ST* 1.14.13.3).

And yet, it would be a mistake to say that Aquinas considers God's knowledge inconsequential for the character of the thing known. God's knowledge of created things is practical. It brings them into being and accounts for their modes of existence (*ST* 1.14.8). Thus to say that God knows things according to the diversity of their modes is equivalent to saying that God wills some things to be done necessarily, some contingently, and some by chance or fortune. Hence contingent events and chance occurrences are features of the world, not because their proximate causes are contingent, not because casual chains can cross each other, disrupting the course of each, at least not principally. Rather, contingency, chance, and fortune are features of the world because God has willed them there (*ST* 1.19.8; *In Perih*.1.14.22).

With this conclusion Aquinas believes he has shown the conflict between the necessity of God's knowledge of all things and the contingency of some to be merely apparent. It should be noted that his solution is hardly original. Both Augustine (*De civ.Dei* xi.21) and Boethius (*De Consol*.v.2–6) advance similar arguments. Nor is it without its problems. For once Aquinas asserts that God transcends history it is not at all clear how he can continue to maintain, as Christians must, that God redeems by acting in time or responds to petitionary prayer.[18] Aquinas's critics insist that he cannot, that he has made God a prisoner of eternity, and that as a result his attempt to secure a place in creation for contingency, chance, and fortune comes at too high a price. Still others believe that he can and defend him in a way we would expect given his insistence that

---

[18] See Pike (1970) and Wolterstorff (1975).

God is the primary cause of temporal contingencies. They argue that while it indeed makes little sense to speak of an eternal being acting in time, nothing prevents us from speaking of the temporal effects of an eternal agent.[19] Nevertheless, it is not at all clear how we can speak of an eternal agent at all, since all of our talk of agency is tensed. He does this, she did that. For us, at least, agency is unavoidably historical.

Happily, we need not solve this philosophical debate before exegesis can proceed.[20] All we need is evidence that Aquinas thinks he has good reason to find contingency, chance, and fortune in creation. With that in hand we can ignore those who say that fortune can have no place in Aquinas's account of the moral life, and we can ask whether he in fact develops his treatment of the moral virtues by specifying their relations to contingencies within and without.

However, even if we conclude that exegesis can proceed, the truth remains that it has not. Aquinas's remarks about contingency and fortune, virtue and difficulty have been largely ignored, and I suspect it is because, as I have noted, most contemporary exegetes assume that fundamental doubts about obligation should mediate our interest in his efforts. With this assumption guiding interpretation, Aquinas's treatment of the natural law receives undue attention, while his remarks about virtue as a perfected power of the soul are emphasized at the expense of his remarks about the difficulties the virtuous overcome as they know and will the good. These are related exegetical moves and it would not be inappropriate to call them Stoic, for together they remove the moral life from fortune's reach. Once the most basic precepts of the natural law are regarded as the specific prescriptions and prohibitions of our common human nature, our access to the concrete content of moral obligation is freed from fortune's whim. Virtue is similarly liberated insofar as the natural law provides universal standards of virtuous conduct that all can know and have good reason to honor. It follows that the virtuous differ from the rest of us only as they are habitually disposed to act as the natural law prescribes. The success of their efforts, their ability to effect in the world what principle demands, is secondary. In fact, the actions of the virtuous can be described quite apart from their effectiveness in the world. Virtue is nothing but a good faith effort to act according to principle. Indeed, virtue *must* be described in this way

---

[19] Stump and Kretzmann (1988). Other defenses of Aquinas's view can be found in Alston (1985); Burrell (1984a); Hasker (1983, 1985).

[20] In fact, Burrell (1986, 104) contends that we couldn't anyway, if only because the relation between time and eternity defies formulation.

precisely because effectiveness is largely a matter of good fortune and thus cannot be assigned to the virtuous. It cannot be what we regard when we speak of their virtue.[21]

Resisting these Stoic tendencies in Thomistic exegesis and spelling out his remarks about virtue and fortune are thus largely equivalent tasks. If Aquinas in fact insists that the moral virtues cope with contingencies of various kinds, and if he in fact believes they become intelligible and desirable precisely because they do, then it is unlikely that he thinks they withdraw us from the world we inhabit. Better to assume that he praises them because they allow us to live well where we find ourselves, notwithstanding the world's many difficulties, its twists and turns of fortune. Similarly, if Aquinas's treatment of the first precepts of the natural law is designed neither to dispel basic doubts about obligation, nor to provide warrants to act in accord with an obligation that is known, then it is unlikely that he thinks those precepts secure our moral knowledge against fortune's buffeting. And note, these exegetical conclusions will compel assent only if Aquinas can answer the worries about the affects of fortune upon virtue, agency, and happiness that motivate Stoic accounts of the moral life and Stoic interpretations of Aquinas. If a virtuous life engages the world that fortune, at least in some measure, commands, then virtuous habits and actions run the risk of being subject to fortune's whim. The acquisition and exercise of virtuous habits, the success of virtuous choices, and the happiness that success is thought to bring may all be threatened with fortune's taint. If we assume the threat is real, then how can we be confident that virtuous actions are voluntary and praiseworthy? Indeed, how can we excuse God, who controls fortune and thus also the happiness that virtue yields? T. H. Irwin suggests that it is this collection of worries that encouraged the Stoics to pursue accounts of the moral life that insulate virtue from fortune.[22] Julia Annas contends that it is their modern equivalents that precipitated solutions in the modern period – what we have come to call

---

[21] According to T. H. Irwin (1986, 229–230; 1990a, 63–65) it is the worry that fortune divides virtuous choices from the end the virtuous seek that, above all, precipitates Stoic rethinking of Aristotelian virtue. It is a similar worry that goads Kant to locate the human good in the character of the will, not in its objects. It couldn't be in the latter, he argues, because our practical reason, our ability to link means to ends, is so incompetent that successful achievement of the will's objects is as uncertain as it is infrequent. How then can we insist that reason and will are best suited for pursuing success of this sort? Indeed, by Kant's lights, we cannot, which in turn implies that we must rethink the character of each apart from their sporadic success in achieving the ends they together pursue. See Kant (1985, 395–396). For Kant's affinities to, as well as differences from, the Stoics see Annas (1993, 432–433, 448–450).
[22] Irwin (1986); Irwin (1988, 1990b).

Kantian ethics – that bear a remarkable resemblance to those advanced by the Stoics.[23] It comes as no surprise then that so many contemporary interpreters approach Aquinas's account of the moral life with Stoic assumptions about the problems that should be addressed in that account and Stoic expectations about the kind of solutions that will satisfy.

This brings an additional exegetical challenge into plain sight. If Aquinas considers the moral life enmeshed in the world that bears fortune's marks, can he answer the Stoic's worries about fortune's influence upon virtue and happiness without significantly modifying his account of either? Since he does not explicitly address these worries, our question should be: can *we* locate resources within his account of virtue and happiness that give him good reason to disregard fortune's threats, good reason to refuse Stoic withdrawal? We will find that we can. We will also discover that when Aquinas does at last resort to a Stoic account of virtue it is in order to express his theologically charged discontent with the virtue and happiness available to us *in via*. On this reading, Stoicism offers Aquinas very little as he explicates the character and content of human virtue in this world, while it becomes indispensable as he imagines a life of virtue that transcends our own.

This borrowing should come as no surprise, in part, because Aquinas proceeds pragmatically throughout, adopting new moral languages as needed to respond to antinomies in his account of the moral life, and in part, because Stoic virtue is so well suited to respond to antinomies of just this kind, to discontent of just this sort. We expect virtue to yield happiness, and for Aquinas, expectations are especially high. God made us for happiness, for the perfect operation of our highest powers (*ST* I–II.3.2–4). The virtues – with the assistance of nature, law, and grace – make that perfection possible (*ST* I–II.4.6; 55.1). Unfortunately, in this life East of Eden, misfortune too often intervenes, rupturing the connection between acts of virtue and human happiness. Stoicism offers Aquinas a moral language that can express these expectations of his theological inheritance, while at the same time providing resources to reassess the character of both virtue and happiness, healing the rupture between them, at least in some measure.

Situating Aquinas in relation to the Stoics should enable us to place him more precisely in the history of ethics as a whole. It is, of course, commonplace to notice that he draws on a variety of authorities – principally Aristotle, Augustine, and the Stoics – as he develops his own account of the moral life and the moral virtues. However, it has been difficult to say with any confidence how he uses his mixed moral inheritance, explain why he switches languages when he does, or tell us which *auctoritates* are best suited for which tasks. With little confidence here, saying how Aquinas's views stand in relation to alternatives, both ancient and modern, has become a hopelessly muddled enterprise.

By insisting that his account of the moral life cannot be read aright without attending to his remarks about contingency and fortune, virtue and difficulty, and by refusing to believe that he intends his remarks about the first precepts of the natural law to answer the skeptic and provide moral guidance for the rest of us, I assume his efforts are largely Aristotelian in character. Here I rest on the authority of others. Aquinas admits that the moral life *in via* is best described in Aristotle's vocabulary (*ST* I–II.3.2.4; 3.6.1), while Aristotle's contemporary interpreters have come to agree that an Aristotelian treatment of the moral life must have something significant to say about virtue's relation to fortune.[24] What that relation entails in Aristotle remains a matter of dispute. I will not enter that fray. I will, however, suggest how Aquinas conceives that relation, which in turn will enable me to indicate where he stands among the possible interpretations of Aristotle's legacy.

Placing Aquinas in relation to Augustine is far more difficult. Not only is there the question of compatibility between Augustinian and Aristotelian aspects of Aquinas's thought,[25] but there is the more fundamental question of which parts of Augustine's legacy Aquinas inherits. The latter puzzle is not as simple as it seems, if only because Augustine's treatment of the moral life in general, and of the virtues in particular,

---

[24] See Cooper (1985; 1987); Irwin (1986; 1990b); Kenny (1992); Kraut (1989, 150–151, 170–175, 253–300); Nussbaum (1986); Reeve (1992, 139–189); Sherman (1989); and Yack (1989).

[25] Disagreement abounds among the commentators. Jaffa (1952) argues that Aquinas's efforts to bring Aristotle's treatment of the virtues within Augustine's theological framework, though noble, do not bear fruit. The two traditions are incompatible. By contrast, MacIntyre (1988b, 167–168, 402; 1990, 105–126) contends that as a result of a providential education and rare gift of empathy, Aquinas mastered both traditions, which enabled him to "accommodate Augustinian claims and insights alongside Aristotelian theorizing in a single dialectic." How? By showing that Augustine's theological commitments are needed in order to resolve puzzles Aristotle leaves unanswered (MacIntyre 1990, 105–126). Jordan (1990) rejects both conclusions. By his lights we find neither incompatibility among Aquinas's authorities, nor Augustine supplying the answers to antinomies of the Aristotelian tradition. Rather, we find one authority, Augustine, dominating all others including Aristotle: amending, transforming, and conditioning what he offers in nearly every instance. Bradley concurs (1996). My own view, as will be soon apparent, departs from each of these, largely because I am not convinced that Aquinas regards the authorities he appeals to as competitors. Nor am I convinced that deciding which of Aquinas's authorities wins is equivalent to understanding why he appeals to this one or that, in this context and not that, and in conjunction with this authority but not others. It is this latter understanding that we want.

changes considerably, early to late. What we can say with some confidence is that Augustine's treatment of the virtues is more or less Stoic; more in early works such as *De libero arbitrio*, books I–II and *De moribus ecclesiae catholicae*, less in *De civitate Dei*. It follows that when Aquinas appeals to both Aristotelian and Augustinian accounts of the virtues, compatibility will be determined in large measure by his ability to bring together Aristotelian and Stoic treatments.

Everything depends upon how we imagine the coming together. If we assume that a single view of the moral virtues issues from Aquinas's artful blending, prospects for compatibility look dim right from the start. It seems unlikely that Augustine's Stoicism can be grafted to Aquinas's Aristotelian commitments without transforming the latter into something altogether different, if only because the Stoics believe their treatment of virtue makes a significant advance over Aristotle's.[26] If, however, we assume that Aquinas regards his mixed moral inheritance as a collection of tools, each suited for different tasks, then we will find the compatibility that Aquinas achieves to be thoroughly pragmatic. Our question must be: at what points in his Aristotelian account of the moral life does Aquinas find Augustine's Stoic treatment of virtue useful, appealing, even indispensable in ways that it could not be for Aristotle? The advantage of asking this question is that we are prevented from rushing too quickly from judgments about incompatibility to conclusions about incoherence. It is, of course, undeniable that many of the theological commitments that Aquinas inherits from Augustine cannot be expressed in the language of virtue that he borrows from Aristotle. In this sense there are incompatibilities among the sources that Aquinas employs. Nevertheless, if we regard that inheritance as so many tools, each suited for different tasks, we will in fact discover that he resorts to different aspects of his inheritance in order to deal with conflicts among its parts. Indeed, we will find that he turns to Augustine's Stoic treatment of virtue precisely when his theological commitments present demands that his Aristotelian moral language cannot meet.

But of course, we not only want to know how Aquinas stands in relation to his ancient past, we also want to locate him among moral philosophers and theologians who come after. In fact, unless we have antiquarian motives we read Aquinas either because we hope to find our own puzzles about the moral life addressed, or because we hope to uncover points of view that will challenge our settled habits of thought.

---

[26] Irwin (1986, 1990b).

Both hopes are normally pursued by comparing what we find in Aquinas with what we find in others, and, as I have indicated, many foes and some friends regard Kant as Aquinas's modern progeny.[27] I have also indicated why this lineage is unlikely. Indeed, if I am right to conclude that his account of the moral virtues emphasizes their usefulness in our human form of life, their work upon the contingencies we confront day to day, then his efforts bring him closer to Hume than to anyone else in the modern period. If this alliance is difficult to imagine (indeed few have imagined it), consider how Aquinas's doubts about the virtues of the blessed track Hume's doubts about the usefulness of justice apart from ordinary human difficulties.

Aquinas argues that we cannot imagine the blessed possessing moral virtues of the sort that we know and praise precisely because the obstacles that call for their labors will be absent in their life. He writes, "there will be no concupiscence and pleasures in matters of food and sex; nor fear and daring about dangers of death; nor distributions and communications of things employed in this present life" (*ST* I–II.67.1). In a similar fashion, Hume asks us to imagine,

that nature has bestowed on the human race such profuse *abundance* of all *external* conveniences, that, without any uncertainty in the event, without any care or industry on our part, every individual finds himself fully provided with whatever his most voracious appetites can want, or luxurious imagination wish or desire. His natural beauty, we shall suppose, surpasses all acquired ornaments: the perpetual clemency of the seasons renders useless all clothes or covering: the raw herbage affords him the most delicious fare; the clear fountain, the richest beverage. No laborious occupation required: no tillage: no navigation. Music, poetry, and contemplation form his sole business: conversation, mirth, and friendship his sole amusement.[28]

Hume concludes that in this kind of life the "jealous virtue of justice would never once have been dreamed of," never once considered useful, and for largely the same reason that Aquinas refuses to assign justice to the blessed (*ST* I–II.67.1).[29] The distribution and commutation of things, let alone the perfection of these activities by habit, would concern no one in such a frictionless form of life.

For Aquinas and Hume alike the moral virtues become intelligible

---

[27] Perhaps I should say "Kantian ethics," in part because it is this creature that Aquinas's efforts are most often compared to, in part because Korsgaard (1985), Herman (1985), O'Neill (1989), and others have quite successfully distinguished what has traditionally been called Kantian ethics from the account of the moral life Kant explicates and defends. It follows that saying how Aquinas stands in relation to Kantian ethics tells us very little about how he stands in relation to Kant. [28] Hume (1975, 183). [29] *Ibid.*, 184.

and desirable as a result of their efforts, as a consequence of the
assistance they provide as we struggle to achieve the good in spite of our
human frailties and in the face of the world's resistance. Both regard the
relation between the virtues and our human form of life roughly transcendental. Both concede that the virtues would have no point – at least
not the virtues we know and praise and desire – without the concrete
conditions of the life we know and the world we inhabit.[30] If we ignore
their disagreement about the origin of those conditions, they differ only
in this: unlike Hume, Aquinas must also speak of the virtues of those
who live apart from the conditions that make virtue intelligible to us –
Adam in Eden and the blessed heaven. Yet he remains Hume's ancestor
even in this, for he admits we can speak of their virtues only as we leave
behind, if only in this instance, the transcendental connection between
human virtue and our shared human form of life in this world.[31]

A final word: It is philosophical reflection on Aquinas's moral theology
that yields these historical benefits. This is hardly surprising. At the very
least, philosophy entails spelling out the warrants and implications of
this or that account of how some corner of human life hangs together
generally, and historians of philosophy are obliged to pursue this labor
as they explicate texts and situate figures in context.[32] But this means
that at times historical payoff comes only as I treat Aquinas less as a
historical figure and more as a contemporary conversation partner. The
requirements of philosophical assessment occasionally create curiously
ahistorical demands. In some instances I describe Aquinas's views in
language that is not his own, pursue the implications of his views in
directions that he does not, ask him to address questions that he forgoes,
or provide warrants when he remains silent. This indifference to the
historical integrity of his efforts, this disregard for the disciplinary
boundaries that divide philosophy from history, will probably satisfy
few. Philosophical readers may grow impatient with my exposition of
Aquinas's views and wish for more analysis. Historians may doubt the

---

[30] Thus Hume writes (1975, 188), "the rules of equity or justice depend entirely on the particular
state and condition in which men are placed, and owe their origin and existence to that utility,
which results to the public from their strict and regular observance. Reverse, in any considerable
circumstance, the condition of men: Produce extreme abundance or extreme necessity: Implant
in the human breast perfect moderation and humanity, or perfect rapaciousness or malice: By
rendering justice totally *useless*, you thereby totally destroy its essence, and suspend its obligation
upon mankind." He concludes that in fact, "the common situation of society is a medium amidst
all these extremes."

[31] For a preliminary account of the common treatment that Aquinas and Hume give the virtues see
Bowlin (forthcoming).   [32] I am indebted to Schneewind (1984, 174–175).

accuracy of my exposition and the nuance of my interpretation. Both
may become annoyed by my willingness to place Aquinas's arguments
in conversation with contemporary authors and by my desire to reinter-
pret and reappropriate his views for use in philosophical debates,
ancient and modern.

To these complaints I can only say that I see no other way of
proceeding. For the most part, philosophical and theological inquiries
are pursued in response to something written earlier.[33] Our interpretations of completed inquiries require a similar kind of response from us,
and thus it is not at all clear how historical understanding can be had
without philosophical and theological effort. Surely, philosophically
minded historians are not doing their job well if their explications of
Aquinas's treatment of the moral life fail to tell us whether his views
have anything interesting to say *to us*, given our concerns and our beliefs.
If they refuse to be anachronistic in this harmless manner on the
grounds that it would distort the integrity of Aquinas's views, then they
have ensured that his work will be of little interest to those of us who
wish to make sense of our own lives.

If this reply does not satisfy, then perhaps we can find comfort in the
fact that as a practical matter there is a significant difference between
historical exposition and philosophical reconstruction, and I do my best
to keep these tasks separate. Further consolation still comes as we
recognize that Aquinas himself provides the historical precedent for my
procedures. Aquinas was a master at recognizing the resources of his
predecessors and recasting them for his own theological purposes.[34] At
times I subject him to similar treatment. I doubt he would object.

[33] I am indebted to Kilcullen (1988, 3).
[34] MacIntyre (1988b, 164–182; 1990, 105–126) makes this plain. Aquinas's willingness to put his
intellectual inheritance to work in novel contexts has an Augustinian precedent. The truth is
God's wherever it is found. When it is encased in pagan falsehood it can be lifted from its place of
origin and set among other truths, just as Israel secreted gold out of Egypt for use in the temple
(*Conf*.vii.ix.15). Aquinas follows suit, with two differences. He treats both pagan and Christian
authors in this fashion, and he rarely indicates that he is putting his *auctoritates* to uses that exceed
or conflict with their intentions. At times he even dissembles. He appears respectful of the
integrity of their positions, even as he self-consciously makes use of one bit and ignores another
or makes additions to their views that they would not allow. For an example of Aquinas's
reconstruction of Augustine, one so vigorous that it tempts creative misreading, see his treatment
of Augustine's insistence that the soul's knowledge of itself is both substantial and immediate (*ST*
1.87.1 and ad 1). For an excellent discussion of this article see Jordan (1986, 126–129).

CHAPTER I

Virtue and difficulty

To explicate Aquinas's treatment of the moral virtues one must begin somewhere, presumably in the middle, with one of the cardinal virtues. Any one of them will do. This follows from their unity, or what is better referred to as their mutual dependence or *connexione*. The claim is a rather simple one. When one virtue is in place the work of the others is made easier. In fact, without this mutual assistance the perfect exercise of any one virtue would be impossible (*ST* I–II.65.1). Thus, for instance, an agent cannot choose just or courageous or temperate courses of action without prudence, the virtue that makes every sort of choice good. Similarly, she cannot choose prudently without justice, since justice orders her practical deliberations to the ends that deserve pursuit. And finally, without courage and temperance, her prudent deliberations would be disrupted by unruly passions that direct her attention to ends that she ought to avoid (*ST* I–II.65.1). It follows that attention to any one of the cardinals will direct us to the rest.

Each are willing guides, and yet scholars normally give special attention to either prudence or charity, and for good reason, for so too does Aquinas.[1] The priority of prudence follows quite naturally from his insistence that virtuous action of any sort is dependent upon sound prudential judgment (*ST* I–II.58.4; 65.1) and from his belief that prudence brings us into conformity with the rule of reason, which is the proximate standard of goodness in action (*ST* I–II.60.5; 64.1). The priority of charity follows from its influence upon prudence. Charity allows prudence to deliberate over actions that direct us to our ultimate end by graciously disposing our will to God (*ST* I–II.65.2; II–II.24.1). Because of the priority of prudence, the good works of all the other virtues are, in turn, referred to this last end, and therefore through

---

[1] For examples of each approach see Nelson (1990) and Wadell (1992).

charity, "all the moral virtues are infused together," whole and connected (*ST* I–II.65.3).

Nevertheless, the connections among the virtues ensure that the priorities of prudence and charity do not rule out other renderings. Moreover, the fact that Aquinas's reflections on the moral life can be viewed through the lens of any one of the cardinal virtues does not imply that each will yield identical interpretations of his views. In fact, we should expect that different virtues will direct our attention to quite different nuances, emphases, and problems. And it is precisely because the virtues are connected that we should expect to find Aquinas using the concepts and categories that apply to any one of the virtues in particular as he explicates the virtues in general. Indeed, this is how Aquinas proceeds throughout the *Summa Theologiae*: interpreting a number of its topics and concerns in relation to a number of others, redescribing some pieces in light of other pieces, and thus showing how the moral life can be regarded whole.[2] It follows that interpretations of his efforts that begin with either prudence and charity, while important and necessary, leave us with an incomplete picture of the virtues and of their place within the moral life as a whole. We can be more precise. Aquinas tells us that a virtue is properly defined by its matter and object (*ST* I–II.55.4; 67.1). Attending to the place of prudence and charity in a virtuous life directs us to the object of virtue, which is the good simply. The same can be said of justice (*ST* II–II.136.2; 157.4). Attending to the place of courage or temperance directs us to the matter that virtue regards, an aspect of the moral virtues that Aquinas considers indispensable for their proper characterization and yet is easily overlooked when attention is directed to prudence or charity alone.

In order to explore this neglected aspect of Aquinas's treatment of the moral virtues, and thus to see what his account of the moral life looks like from the perspective of its matter, I want to attend to some of his remarks about courage. More specifically, I want to consider Aquinas's functional account of the virtues that becomes prominent when attention is given to those remarks, and to the topics and problems that emerge with them.

By assigning a functional account of the moral virtues to Aquinas I mean to imply he is struck by the fact that many human goods can be known, loved, and achieved only with great difficulty and thus only with the assistance of the virtues. Providing this aid, they fulfill their function

---

[2] For an excellent treatment of Aquinas's effort to regard the moral life whole see MacIntyre (1990, 135).

in our form of life. I also mean to imply that he refuses to believe that the
goodness of our virtuous habits and actions can be divided from their
effectiveness, from their ability to provide this aid and fulfill this function. Beginning with courage brings these functional features of
Aquinas's account of the virtues into relief. Taken together, they allow
us to regard that account as a kind of human moral ecology, as a
description of our species in its natural environment.[3] Above all
Aquinas's concern is to characterize our ability to flourish in the world
according to our kind, given our various powers and frailties and in spite
of the various difficulties we confront. Think of his description of our
agency – built on nature, assisted by virtue, and perfected by grace – as
the product of his fieldwork. Think of the difficulties that obstruct our
agency and threaten our flourishing as the matter that captures his
attention in the field. Think of his treatment of courage and the other
virtues as his description of our response to the threat.

I .

Courage, or fortitude (*fortitudo*), resides in the irascible appetite, the
power of the soul whose objects are sensible goods difficult to achieve
and sensible evils difficult to avoid (*ST* i–ii.56.4; 61.2). Aquinas writes,

But, since the soul must, of necessity, experience difficulty or struggle at times,
in acquiring some such good, or in avoiding some such evil, in so far as such
good or evil is more than our animal nature can easily acquire or avoid;
therefore this very good or evil, inasmuch as it is of an arduous or difficult
nature, is the object of the irascible faculty. (*ST* i–ii.23.1)

A good is difficult (*bonum arduum*), in a manner that calls for courage,
when moving to achieve it endangers some other good that we love (*ST*
i–ii.123.3). In the standard cases, this prospect arouses fear, and fear
tends to make us withdraw from the dangerous and difficult good (*ST*
ii–ii.123.3).[4] This is when courage is needed: when fear discourages us
from pursuing some good made difficult to achieve because its pursuit
endangers some other good. Courage allays fear, strengthens us to

[3] The image is adapted from Jordan's (1986, 143–145) remark that when Aquinas does moral
psychology he shuns introspection and instead proceeds like "an observing naturalist" who
describes the soul "as if from the outside." He catalogues the soul's actions in the world and from
this data makes inferences about the nature of its powers.
[4] A good causes fear, and therefore becomes difficult to achieve, only when its pursuit threatens
another good that we love. Thus Aquinas concludes that "all the irascible passions terminate in
the concupiscible passions" (*ST* i–ii.23.1.1), and that "fear is born of love" (*ST* ii–ii.123.4.2).

endure difficulties and dangers, and enables us to pursue the good that right reason dictates (*ST* II–II.123.3, 6).

Of course, not all cases are standard. For some, the fearless and the daring, dangers and difficulties do not elicit enough fear. They stand firm when they should flee, attack external threats when they should retreat (*ST* II–II.126.2; 127.2.3). For them training in courage corrects this deficiency. It does not allay fear but rather elicits it, enabling the formerly fearless and daring to fear the right objects, in the right circumstances, and to the right degree, and to withhold aggression in the right contexts. It enables them to respond to difficulties and dangers with passion that tracks the judgments of right reason (*ST* II–II.123.3; 127.1; 127.2.3). Thus Aquinas writes that "it belongs to fortitude that man should moderate his fear according to reason, namely that he should fear what he ought, and when he ought, and so forth. Now this mode of reason may be corrupted either by excess or by deficiency" (*ST* II–II.126.2). Aquinas contends that courage principally strengthens us against the gravest dangers and evils, those that create the greatest difficulties precisely because they incite passions most likely to withdraw us from the good with the greatest intensity (*ST* II–II.123.2, 4, 5). For Aquinas, death is the greatest of dangers, particularly death that threatens in battle (*ST* II–II.123.4–5; 124.2; 125.2.2). Fear of death that combat elicits is the passion most able to withdraw us from the demands of right reason (*ST* II–II.123.3), while the goods that just courses of action hope to secure are those most likely to present the greatest difficulties, the gravest, most deadly, dangers. Each point requires some explanation.

First, death is the greatest danger, the fear that it elicits the most intense, because life is our greatest love (*ST* II–II.123.4.2; 124.3). Life is loved above all, in part because Providence inclines us to it simply and absolutely (*ST* I–II.94.2), in part because the other goods that we are naturally disposed to love cannot be had without life (*ST* II–II.123.4). Second, Aquinas insists that courage principally regards death that threatens in battle, not because he finds courage among warriors alone. This he explicitly denies (*ST* II–II.123.5). Rather, the point is that courage, like the other virtues, brings perfection to human action, which by definition tends to the good (*ST* I–II.1.1). As such, the deadly dangers that courage regards must attend the pursuit of some good, whether the common good that soldiers pursue in a just war or the private good that individuals pursue in circumstances that threaten life or limb (*ST* II–II.123.5; I–II.55.1.4). Of course, the courageous will also respond well to dangers that arise apart from intention, "sickness, storms at sea, attacks from robbers," and the like (*ST* II–II.123.5). Nevertheless, accidental dangers, even deadly ones, cannot be a part of courage simply, if only because they do not regularly arise as a consequence of pursuing any good in particular, but come and go as misfortune does, with fickle disregard for our intentions. Lastly, the courses of action that the just pursue are most often the most life threatening, because they regard those "external actions and external things" that we can owe one another as we forge a life together (*ST* II–II.58.9; 58.1). Since we tend to dispute over these externals, at times even violently, justice frequently offers the most dangerous course. Thus Aquinas writes: "though dangers of death are of rare occurrence, yet the occasions of those dangers occur frequently, since on account of other good deeds, man encounters mortal adversaries" (*ST* II–II.123.11.3).

Some, I suspect, will wonder whether Aquinas exaggerates the connection between courage, justice, and deadly dangers. They will notice that the demands of justice rarely generate deadly contests, that our public roles and private duties rarely put life and limb at risk. Aquinas, no doubt, would reply that his remarks refer to great acts of justice, acts that most of us exclude from our daily routines precisely because they come packaged with life-threatening harms and therefore cannot be done well without a significant measure of courage – desegregating the public square during the heyday of the civil rights movement, working in an inner-city emergency room, exposing corruption in a great and powerful institution, rescuing a neighbor from a genocidal tyrant, and so on.

But that said, courage also has to do with more ordinary courses of action, with difficult goods of a lesser order, goods whose pursuit neither threatens bodily evil nor generates stupefying fear. For Aquinas these lesser things that courage regards are difficult activities of great importance and typically entail "the best use of the greatest things" (*ST* II–II.129.1). He has in mind "perfect works of virtue" and the "use of any other good, such as science or external fortune" for some great and noble end (*ST* II–II.129.3.4). Both activities are of sufficient difficulty to demand that honor be given to those who complete them well (*ST* II–II.129.2), and although their arduousness does not threaten life or limb, the toil required to achieve them and the fear of failure they incite can diminish hope. Magnanimity is the part of courage that principally deals with flagging hope in the face of difficult goods of this sort.

The magnanimous "intend something great in every matter,"

whether willing an act of virtue or making (*faciendo*) something in external matter. This distinguishes their actions from those of the magnificent, which only regard great works that can be done in external matter and through large expenditures (*ST* II–II.134.2.2; 134.4). Magnanimity is immediately about hope, which tends to the difficult good, and mediately about honor, which is owed to those who do or achieve something great and difficult (*ST* II–II.129.1.2). Accordingly, magnanimity is also about hope for honor and therefore must regard two things: the attempt to accomplish some great deed as its end, and honor as its matter (*ST* II–II.131.2.1). The trouble here, at least for Aquinas, is that unlike Aristotle, whom he follows in these matters, he cannot recommend honor as a good that may be desired and hoped for as virtue's reward.[5] For Aristotle, those who wish to accomplish great things also desire honor, and they justly claim it for themselves in accordance with the greatness of their achievements. This is why he refers to them as the proud (*EN* 1123b16–26). By contrast, Aquinas declares that desiring honor for oneself is nothing but vicious ambition, and this is true even if one is deserving, having pursued some great deed or accomplished some great work. It is "inordinate appetite of the arduous good," what Aquinas calls "pride of life" (*ST* I–II.77.5; cf.*ST*. I–II.84.2; II–II.162.1) because it represents a failure to recognize that great things are accomplished only with God's assistance, and that, as a result, honor is due principally to God, not to the magnanimous. It is also a failure to recognize that God grants excellence to the magnanimous in difficult matters so that they may profit others. It follows that right appetite for excellence must not "rest in honor itself, without referring it to the profit of others" (*ST* II–II.131.1). For this reason Aquinas describes magnanimity as "the best use of the greatest thing" (*ST* II–II.129.1), by which he means using honor, the greatest of external goods (*ST* II–II.129.2), to seek the good of one's neighbor and to revere God.

These distinctions help us draw Aquinas's account of courage with greater precision. Courage properly regards fear of some evil, such as mortal danger (*ST* II–II.123.3), while its part, magnanimity, bears on hope for the difficult good (*ST* II–II.129.6.2). Nevertheless, each regards the matter and object of the other as a secondary concern. Evil is confronted and fear aroused only as one hopes to achieve some "difficult thing" whose pursuit places some other good in danger (*ST* II–II.123.3). Thus, for example, the Freedom Riders hoped for justice

---

[5] For an excellent discussion of Aristotle's treatment of honor and courage see Berns (1984).

between blacks and whites in the American South, a good that was dangerous because pursuing it placed another good, their lives, at risk. This in turn aroused fear and diminished hope, making the good difficult to achieve without the moderating influence of both courage and magnanimity. Similarly, a difficult good whose pursuit does not threaten mortal evil will require not only magnanimity to bolster hope, but something like courage to moderate fear of failure.

This difference in matter and object allows Aquinas to say that although magnanimity agrees with courage "in confirming the mind about some difficult matter," it differs in that,

> it is more difficult to stand firm in dangers of death, wherein fortitude confirms the mind, than in hoping for or obtaining the greatest goods, wherein the mind is confirmed by magnanimity, for, as man loves his life above all things, so does he fly from dangers of death more than any others. Accordingly it is clear that magnanimity agrees with fortitude . . . but falls short thereof, in that it confirms the mind about a matter wherein it is easier to stand firm. (*ST* II–II.129.5)

It is the agreement that this difference assumes that matters here. By distinguishing courage and magnanimity in this way, Aquinas shows us what unites them, which in turn indicates what characterizes courage generally and what features of the moral virtues it brings into special prominence. What distinguishes the two virtues is the degree of difficulty they withstand in order to achieve their respective goods. A good that is dangerous and fearsome is more difficult to achieve than one that presents only toil. But the fact that both virtues regard the difficult good unites them in a single genus of virtue.[6] What's more, it suggests that steadfastness in the face of some difficulty that hinders the achievement of some good is that characteristic of virtue in general that courage and its parts, above all, display. Thus Aquinas remarks, "now one of the general modes of virtue is firmness of mind, because a firm standing is necessary in every virtue according to II *Ethic*. And this is chiefly commended to those virtues that tend to something difficult, in which it is most difficult to preserve firmness."[7]

Aquinas's assertion that endurance is the chief act of courage pro-

---

[6] The difficult good attracts because it is good and repels because it is difficult. Accordingly, courage must both restrain daring and moderate fear. In a similar fashion, humility "temper[s] and restrain[s] the mind lest it tend to high things immoderately," while magnanimity "strengthen[s] the mind against despair and urge[s] it on to the pursuit of great things according to right reason" (*ST* II–II.161.1).

[7] *ST* II–II.129.5: *Inter alios autem generales modos virtutis unus est firmitas animi: quia firmiter se habere requiritur in omni virtute, ut dicitur in II Ethic. Praecipue tamen hoc laudatur in virtutibus quae in aliquo arduum tendunt, in quibus difficillimum est firmitatem servare.* Aristotle's remarks can be found at *EN* 1105a7–13.

vides further warrants for this conclusion. Endurance is the ability to restrain fear, "to stand immovable in the midst of dangers rather than to attack them" (*ST* II–II.123.6), and consequently to "cleav[e] most resolutely to the good" (*ST* II–II.123.6.2). It is the chief act of courage precisely because remaining unmoved in the face of dangers for the sake of the good is more difficult than the alternative, attacking (*ST* II–II.123.6). Aquinas gives three reasons for this. First, endurance implies that the attack comes from a stronger person, while aggression implies that strength is on one's side; and surely it is more difficult to contend with a stronger opponent than with a weaker. Second, those who endure know danger face to face, while aggressors see it as yet to come; and surely it is more difficult to stand unmoved by present dangers than by those of the immanent future. Finally, endurance entails standing unmoved over a considerable span of time, while aggression is normally a sudden and decisive affair; and surely it is more difficult to stand at length unmoved by danger than it is to move quickly toward some difficult good (*ST* II–II.123.6.1). The point of significance is this: by regarding endurance as the chief act of courage Aquinas can draw connections between aspects of virtue that principally belong to courage and the general modes of virtue that must be found in the acts and included in the descriptions of each of the other cardinal virtues. If it is difficult to imagine how acts of prudence, justice, and temperance could be described in the language of aggression and attack, it is another matter altogether with endurance and difficulty. Difficulties are legion, in some manner obstructing the virtuous pursuit and achievement of every good, and therefore it is easy to see how virtuous actions of all kinds normally include something like endurance.

When we turn from the principal act of courage to its various parts again we find that *firmitas* is the mode of virtue in general that courage displays. Perseverance (*perseverantia*), for instance, is assigned to courage because it principally regards firm endurance of "those things which are most difficult to endure long" such as dangers of death (*ST* II–II.137.1.1). Clearly, in this strict sense perseverance applies to the courageous alone. However, Aquinas explicitly draws connections between perseverance *per se* and the long endurance that is needed in every act of virtue. Thus he insists that we can take *perseverantia* to denote any habit that makes us "persist firmly in good against the difficulty that arises from the very continuance of the act" (*ST* II–II.137.3) and any act that is a "long persistence in any kind of difficult good" (*ST* II–II.137.1.1). It follows that any good made difficult because its pursuit requires long suffering and

its achievement long endurance will demand something like the firmness and persistence that characterizes perseverance.

In a similar manner Aquinas notes identities and differences between
strict and generous senses of *constantia*, another part of courage, and thus
once again indicates how standing firm against some difficulty is a
characteristic of every virtue. As a part of courage, *constantia* causes
persistence in those goods that are difficult in two senses: because
pursuing them is dangerous and because of various attending *impedimen-
tis* that are external to the pursuit itself (*ST* II–II.137.3). Thus, for
example, justice is a difficult good since achieving it at times requires
resort to violence. Violence puts life and limb at risk, which generates
both fear and the need for courage. It may also happen that as a result of
pursuing justice by violent means our friends are injured, perhaps
mortally. Sorrow follows in turn and action is hindered. In cases of this
sort, Aquinas regards the causes of sorrow as an external impediment to
the successful achievement of our just aims, an additional difficulty that
requires a distinct act of virtue, one that encourages persistence in a
dangerous good despite this additional difficulty (*ST* II–II.137.3.1).[8] But of
course, external hindrances can be of various sorts and can add a variety
of obstacles to the pursuit of goods that are already difficult in themselves in assorted ways. Therefore we should not be surprised when
Aquinas describes the constant in generous terms and includes in their
company all those who "persist firmly in good against difficulties arising
from any other external hindrances" (*ST* II–II.137.3).[9]

The pattern should now be clear. For Aquinas courage in particular
and virtue in general have to do with standing firm, with endurance and
constancy in the face of difficulties that hinder the achievement of the
good and the best. He borrows the language he employs to describe the
special character of courage – steadfastness in the good whose difficulty
is danger, the good that elicits fear and prompts flight – from the
language he uses to describe virtue generally. Indeed, for Aquinas, the
language of courage is a subset of the language of virtue in general.

Caution is required here. The fact that Aquinas employs a portion of
the language he uses to describe virtue in general as he characterizes
courage does not mean that he finds nothing of substance distinguishing

---

[8] Because it regards sorrow, constancy in this strict sense stands between perseverance and courage
on the one hand and patience on the other (*ST* II–II.137.3.1).

[9] If our concern was metaphysics we would expect Aquinas to say that a thing's incorruptibility, its
steadfastness in being, marks its courage. This is just what we find, as Aquinas refers to God's
immutability as an expression of divine fortitude (*ST* I–II.61.4).

the various kinds of virtuous habits and actions. In fact, he explicitly denies that there is only one moral virtue (*ST* I–II.60.1). This, however, does not close the matter for he nevertheless flirts with the idea. While considering the connections between the cardinal virtues (*ST* I–II.65.1; 66.2) he refers to the account of the virtues found in Gregory (*Moralia* xxii.1) and Augustine (*De trin.*vi.4). Both contend that every act of virtue exhibits discretion, rectitude, moderation, and strength and that the cardinals are distinguished only insofar as each is assigned one of the four characteristics that every virtue shares. The practical result is dissolution of the many into the one. The virtues become virtue.[10]

Aquinas, however, seems to prefer Aristotle's approach, which he recounts immediately after leaving Augustine and Gregory. According to Aristotle, the virtues are distinguished one from another by their object and matter (*ST* I–II.60.1, 5; 65.1; 66.2). Thus, for example, temperance regards the sensitive good *per se*, while courage regards that which is both good and difficult to obtain (*ST* I–II.60.5). Similarly, they are distinguished by the matters about which they are concerned, by the quite different passions of the concupiscible and irascible appetites. What unites them is prudence, which both disposes them to their objects (*ST* II–II.47.6.3) and is disposed by them to the ends that initiate its deliberations (*ST* I–II.58.4; 65.1; 66.2).

Clearly, the distinctive character of each virtue is better secured by Aristotle's account of the connections among them. At the same time, distinction does not yield unqualified difference. Even Aristotle's account assumes certain shared characteristics among the virtues insofar as they are united under a common genus, and as we have seen, Aquinas refers to some of those characteristics as he describes the distinctive matter and object of courage. This does not mean that every virtue regards difficult goods and irascible passions. In fact, the goods of the body that temperance regards are frequently quite easy to obtain, if only because we naturally desire the pleasures they elicit (*ST* II–II.141.1.1; 141.3). And yet it is precisely this ease, along with the intensity of these passions (*ST* II–II.155.2), that makes striking the mean difficult and the need for temperance constant (*ST* I–II.60.5; II–II.129.2; 141.2).

Perhaps the best evidence that Aquinas regards the difficulties the courageous confront as vivid examples of the difficulties implicit in the life of virtue in general comes in his treatment of virtuous actions and

[10] It was the Stoics, of course, who maintained that virtue is one. For discussions of Stoic virtue see Rist (1969, 81–111); Sandbach (1975, 41–45); Zeller (1962, 254–272). For an account of Stoic antecedents in Augustine and Gregory see Colish (1985, 207–220, 252–266).

habits as such. Following Aristotle, he maintains that an action is virtuous if it is done knowingly, by choice, and "from a firm and unchangeable character" (*ST* II–II.58.1; cf. *EN* 1105a30–1105b4). The first two conditions define the voluntary character of virtuous action. The third, which is my concern here, regards the origin of virtuous action in habit. "The word habit implies a certain lastingness," a certain stability in being that yields, over time, a certain constancy of agency (*ST* I–II.49.2.3). It follows that we will not be able to distinguish real from apparent virtue unless we can conclude that the action in question arises from habit, not from chance or coercion, and we will not be able to reach this conclusion without noting this lastingness. Confidence comes when we observe persistence, the dogged ability to function well across a variety of circumstances. Thus for example, we cannot, by Aquinas's lights, conclude that a man acts justly simply because his will is disposed to the just course in some particular instance. Rather, we come to this conclusion when we find that he has "the will to observe justice at all times and in all cases" (*ST* II–II.58.1.3). Since some of those cases, will, no doubt, present some difficult matter, some threat to the perpetual will of the just, it follows that the ability to pursue just courses despite various difficulties will be the gauge of lastingness and the measure of virtue.

Indeed, these conceptual connections between difficulty and habit go to the heart of Aquinas's understanding of virtue. The virtues perfect the soul's powers, and a power is perfected when it can act well at its limit, at the far reaches of its agency (*ST* I–II.55.1). Borrowing from Aristotle, Aquinas writes, "if a man can carry a hundredweight and not more, his virtue is put at a hundredweight and not at sixty" (*ST* I–II.55.1.1).[11] He can, no doubt, carry lesser weights with ease, but when he lifts a hundredweight, he strains at this burden with all his strength, and when he moves it he acts at the limits of his power and thus with virtue. Of course, Aquinas intends this example to tell us something about *moral* virtue, and it is this: we determine that an action originates in a power perfected by a virtuous habit not by observing just any "operation of that power, but in such operations as are great or difficult; for every power, however imperfect, can extend to ordinary and trifling operations. Hence it is essential to a virtue to be about the difficult and the

---

[11] Aristotle writes (*De caelo* 281a13–18), "A thing, then, which is capable of a certain amount as maximum must also be capable of that which lies within it. If, for example, a man can lift a hundred talents, he can also lift two, and if he can walk a hundred stades, he can also walk two. But the power is of the maximum, and a thing said, with reference to its maximum, to be incapable of so much is also incapable of any greater amount. It is, for instance, clear that a person who cannot walk a thousand stades will also be unable to walk a thousand and one."

good (*Et idea ad rationem virtutis pertinet ut sit circa difficile et bonum*)" (*ST*
II–II.129.2).[12] In many instances the limits of our agency must be reached
if the good is to be done, and we act at these limits only with difficulty
and thus only with the assistance of the virtues. Thus Aquinas writes, "it
belongs to the notion of virtue that it should regard something extreme"
(*ST* II–II.123.4). The virtues bring us to choose courses of action that fall
within the potential range of our agency but from which we often retreat
because of the difficulty of acting at our extreme limits (*ST* II–II.123.2.1).
Since it is often the case that the good can be done only when we act at
these limits, the virtues are needed in order to will the good habitually,
with constancy, across circumstances that present difficulties as well as
those that do not.

For Aquinas, this constancy, this refusal to shrink from the good that
is difficult in itself, or from those obstacles that arise from the pursuit of
ends that are good simply, is the part of virtue in general that courage
brings into special prominence. For on the one hand, "standing firm
against all kinds of assaults" is that which makes acting at the extreme
limits of every power possible (*ST* II–II.123.2.2), while on the other,
standing fast against those assaults that are the most arduous and that
arouse fear in the greatest measure and intensity is the special matter of
courage. Indeed, attention to courage helps us see that the moral virtues
have to do with the difficult as well as the good, and that their character
cannot be captured without referring to both the difficulties they are
ordered to overcome and the good they hope to achieve. This in turns
helps us see what the moral virtues *do* in the most general terms: they
cope with the various difficulties that would otherwise prevent us from
acting in a manner that tracks the judgments of right reason about the
good. Attention to courage causes us to take note of this common
function of the virtues, this common work.

Insofar as Aquinas draws upon Aristotle in order to describe the
difficulty we have acting in a manner that enables us to flourish according to our kind he must regard our need for the virtues, the work they
do, and the obstacles they overcome as a fact of our natural history. And
yet, in a sense no natural history *per se* can be found in Aquinas. Human

---

[12] Aquinas attributes this last remark to Aristotle, and yet in the sections he cites (*EN* 1104b4–
1105a17) we do not find the claim put so tersely. Aristotle remarks that good choice is uncommon
because of our propensity to pursue pleasures of various sorts. He finds our desire for these
pleasures unavoidable, as they are with us from infancy. "This is why it is difficult to rub off this
passion, engrained as it is in our life" (1105a2–3). No doubt the connection between virtue and
difficulty is here, and yet distilling it from Aristotle's discussion of pleasure and choice and using
the distillate to make sense of the other virtues, courage in particular, is clearly Aquinas's labor.

beings are creatures, *viators* on the way to a final end that transcends this
life (*ST* I–II.3.8.1; 69.2), and therefore we should not be surprised when
Aquinas refers to our fall from grace in order to explain this natural fact.
Prior to the fall, reason had perfect dominion over the passions and
directed their acts to the ends that it apprehended and judged good.
After the fall, this original justice was lost, and the appetitive powers,
both intellectual and sensitive, were deprived of their perfect order to
reason's good (*ST* I–II.85.1–3). This created our distinctively human
need for the moral virtues: to return the acts of these powers to their
proper subordination to the judgments of right reason. But note, what is
significant here is that Aquinas describes this need in terms of *difficultas*
and *infirmitas*. The wounds affecting the appetitive powers, wounds that
the virtues must heal – malice, weakness, and concupiscence – are
described as various difficulties, "for it is owing to these three that a man
finds it difficult to tend to the good" (*ST* I–II.85.3.5). Similarly, the error
and vexation that infect the practical intellect and that prudence must
combat are characterized as weaknesses in the face of difficulties caused
by concupiscence (*ST* I–II.85.3.5).

Judith Shklar has said that every "moral psychology of any worth is a
scream of disgust," a philosopher's bitter cry against moral failure.[13]
Aquinas's faith in a God who creates only good and who graciously
cares for what He has made prevents moral psychology from being
overwhelmed by disillusioned misanthropy. But that said, it is undoubtedly true that making our moral failings intelligible is one of the
aims that guide his reflections on the soul and its powers. It is to those
reflections that I now turn in order to consider the general character of
those difficulties that demand virtue's labor in reply. Once again I begin
with courage.

2.

A good is arduous in the sense that pertains to courage when pursuing it
endangers other goods that we love, principally life and limb. Danger
arouses fear, and in the standard cases fear causes us to withdraw from
the true good that we normally desire, to change course, and to pursue
some other, apparent good. Fear makes standing firm in the dangerous
good difficult. For this reason acts of courage take the form of constancy,
of steadfastness in those circumstances that might otherwise elicit fear in

---

[13] Shklar (1984, 193).

measure sufficient to subvert reason's judgment about the good and the will's appetite for it. Thus Aquinas writes, "Fortitude of the soul must be that which binds the will firmly to the good of reason in the face of the greatest evils" (*ST* II–II.123.4), for these evils alone are sufficiently difficult to "disincline the will to follow that which is in accord with reason" (*ST* II–II.123.1). Thus the functional dynamic of courage and fear, of virtue and difficulty, is largely a matter of constancy and change, of contingent fear threatening our constant willing of the good and of courage keeping this contingency at bay.

Fear is contingent and thus difficult in a manner that calls for courage when, (1) it is subject to change in intensity and object, (2) its changes are chance-like departures from the rule of reason that normally guides our agency, and (3) when its changes occur independent of our bidding, which of course, is a direct consequence of (2). Fear is contingent when its occurrence – its presence and absence – is out of our control, and when its various changes – both in object and in intensity – are somehow alien to us. When fear is contingent in this way we experience it as an external influence upon action, even as it remains thoroughly our own. On the face of it, this is, of course, paradoxical, and yet Aquinas considers it merely apparent, and observes that contingency in the passions, whether irascible or not, can be noted and explained by giving careful consideration to the sensitive appetite and its response to the world. Four features stand out: (1) the natural and thus necessary movement of the untutored sensitive appetite, (2) the natural disposition of the sensitive appetite to accept reason's tutelage, (3) our fall from grace, and (4) the contingent world of sensitive goods. Woven together they tell a story about the contingent character of our passions and the causes of our moral failings.

"The sensitive appetite is an inclination following sensitive apprehension" (*ST* 1.81.2) and is divided into two distinct powers: first, the concupiscible appetite "through which the soul is simply inclined to seek what is suitable, according to the senses, and to fly from what is hurtful" (*ST* 1.81.2), and which principally regards pleasure and pain (*ST* 1–II.23.1), and second, the irascible appetite, concerned with passions such as hope, fear, anger, and daring, which are aroused when we sense some potential harm or difficulty (*ST* 1.81.2; 1–II.23.1). Both can be considered either in themselves, or as they participate in reason's judgment about the good (*ST* 1–II.56.4.1). In themselves, they are common to us and animals and act according to natural instinct (*ex instinctu naturae*), that is, of natural necessity, "being ordained to one thing even as nature is" (*ST*

I–II.50.3). Because the sensitive power of apprehension does "not compare different things with each other, as reason does . . . but simply apprehends some one thing" (*ST* 1.82.2.3), the sensitive appetite is moved of necessity once its object is apprehended. Thus, for instance, "a brute animal is unable, while looking at something pleasurable, not to desire it" (*De verit.* 25.1). Similarly, "a sheep, esteeming the wolf as an enemy, is afraid . . . and flees at once," naturally and of necessity (*ST* 1.81.3).

However, treating the concupiscible and irascible appetites in this way, by themselves, is usually inappropriate, for "they have a natural aptitude to obey reason" (*ST* I–II.56.4; cf. *ST* I–II.74.3.1), and this occurs in two ways. First, they can obey reason in their own acts (*ad ipsos suos actus*). Thus, reasoning about some matter can modify or excite anger, fear, desire, and the like (*ST* 1.81.3). In this light, passions are so infused with judgment about the world that they cannot be given a con-cognitive rendering. They cannot be considered the sort of raw feelings common to newborns, nematodes, and other creatures unable to use concepts.[14] Nor, however, can their cognitive content lead us to equate passionate feeling with "emotional insight" into the particulars of a circumstance, at least not by Aquinas's lights.[15] The passive response of our bodies to the world remains one kind of thing, practical judgment another, and Aquinas finds no reason to dissolve the differences that divide them simply because the latter shapes the character of the former. Second, the concupiscible and irascible appetites can obey reason in response to an act of the will. Thus, for instance, while a sheep, fearing a wolf, flees at once, human beings are not moved with an equivalent necessity by their passions. Instead they await the command of the will (*ST* 1.81.3). The will follows reason, and reason can consider many different courses of action, compare one with another, and thus may or may not follow the instinctive promptings of the sensitive appetite.

Putting aside this rationalized account of the passions and treating the sensitive appetite in itself is appropriate only when it responds to sensitive apprehensions with passions strong enough to overwhelm reason and will. In these instances the person in question must be considered mad, his movements irrational.

His reason is wholly bound, so that he has not the use of reason: as happens in those who through a violent access of anger or concupiscence become furious

---

14 Borrowing from Wilfrid Sellars, Rorty (1979, 183) notes that the relevant distinction is between knowing what this or that feeling is like and knowing what sort of feeling this or that is.

15 This is Sherman's (1989, 13–55) reading of Aristotle's account of the cognitive aspects of passion.

or insane, just as they may from some other bodily disorder; since such like passions do not take place without some change in the body. And of such the same is to be said of irrational animals, which follow, of necessity, the impulse of their passions: for in them there is neither movement of reason, nor, consequently, of will. (*ST* 1–11.10.3)

Like animals without reason, persons bound by passion lack the sort of knowledge of the end that permits comparison of one thing with another, what Aquinas calls rational inquiry (*ST* 1.83.1; 1–11.13.1.1; 13.2.1; 14.1). Instead they are moved by necessity to the object of sensible apprehension.

That said, Aquinas notes a difference between insanity and animal agency. Because the sensitive appetite is in principle able to follow the commands of reason, it does not have implanted in it determinate responses to specific apprehensions. Rather, it is capable of being moved by all sensible goods (*ST* 1.78.1). Consequently, when reason is lost and the sensitive appetite reigns, the passions, and the movements they cause, are governed entirely by the progression of sensible goods in the world. The movements of the mad, unlike those of animals, follow no providentially implanted rule because reason, which normally provides it, has been overrun. So there is no moral failure here, for there is no voluntary agency, which for Aquinas has its origin in rational judgment (*ST* 1–11.6.2). Similarly, there is no contingency with respect to the rule of reason that normally guides our action, for there can be no chance-like departures from this rule when it is not in play. All that remains are disordered passions that necessarily cause fitful movements in the response to the changing world of sensible objects.

This madness is, of course, unusual, and thus Aquinas contends that our fall from grace did not generate complete independence of the passions from the influence of reason. Instead, the events in Eden merely diminished reason's dominion and brought incomplete freedom to the passions. The souls of the first human beings were made right by grace, which subjected reason to God, and our passions to reason (*ST* 1.95.1). The fall left them (and us) somewhere between this gracious order and the mad chaos of passion unfettered by reason. It overturned this original righteousness and thus enabled the soul's various powers to act according to their various natural and oftentimes, opposite tendencies (*ST* 1–11.82.2.2).[16] Thus the sensitive appetite naturally responds to

---

[16] Augustine sets the precedent here (*De civ. Dei* xiii.13) and Aquinas takes note (*ST* 1.95.1). For a fuller statement of Augustine's views see *De nuptiis et concupiscentia* 1.7; 11.6. For commentary see Brown (1988, 405).

the bidding of reason, and yet at the same time, by itself, it naturally and of necessity moves in response to objects apprehended by sense. Couple this relative independence with the contingency of its objects – e.g., mutable goods that cause pleasure and pain or the changing states of affairs that spark fear, anger, or desire – and a situation is created where the sensitive appetite generates passions that occasionally confront us as contingent responses to a contingent world.

Following Aristotle (*Pol.*1254b2–10), Aquinas uses political metaphors to describe this intermittent contingency of our passions that follows from their on again off again obedience to reason and their natural ability to track the contingent world of sensible objects. Reason rules the sensitive appetite as a king

rules over free subjects, who, though subject to the government of the ruler, have nevertheless something of their own, by reason of which they can resist the orders of him who commands . . . For the sensitive appetite is naturally moved . . . in man by the cognitive power . . . but also by the imagination and sense. Whence it is that we experience that the irascible and concupiscible powers do resist reason, inasmuch as we sense or imagine something pleasant, which reason forbids, or unpleasant, which reason commands. (*ST* 1.81.3; cf. *ST* 1–11.17.7; 1–11.56.4.3)

Notice how the natural obedience of the sensitive appetite makes its departure from reason's rule chance-like. Because the sensitive appetite normally obeys reason, a rule of sentiment is laid down, a law of emotion is established, where our passions regularly and for the most part respond to the world in a manner that tracks the judgments of reason. This rule becomes us. It characterizes the agency of our species in the most general terms. It is our regular manner of acting and relating to the world. Accordingly, when a chance meeting with a particular state of affairs causes our sensitive appetite to resist reason's judgment and depart from this rule, our passions confront us as alien occurrences, as chance-like and beyond our control as the meeting with the world that precipitates them. Aquinas writes, "it happens sometimes that the movement of the sensitive appetite is aroused suddenly in consequence of an apprehension of the imagination or sense. And such movements occur without the command of reason" (*ST* 1–11.17.7). Notice, the emphasis here is not simply on the suddenness of the passionate response or on the fact that it is triggered by the world, but that it happens apart from reason's command and only sometimes. It is only because we normally and for the most part respond to the world with a sensitive appetite formed by rational judgment that our passions can at times confront us as occurrences beyond our control, as mere arbitrary events.

Following Aristotle (*Metaph.*1026b27–1027a17), Aquinas defines a chance occurrence and a contingent thing in precisely these terms (*In Metaph.* vi.2.1182–1188; 13.8–9 *In Perih.*1.8.9;). A chance occurrence is a departure from what happens for the most part. A contingent thing changes in this chance-like fashion. It follows that the sensitive appetite is a source of contingent passions precisely because it is normally (but not always) subject to reason's rule. When a passion is contingent in this manner, when it flares uncontrolled this way and that (*ST* i–ii.85.3), it confronts us as an "obstacle that withdraws the will from following the reason" (*ST* ii–ii.123.3) and as a result "good actions become more difficult" (*ST* i–ii.85.3). If the intensity of the passion is such that it is unable to overrun reason and move us of necessity according to its inclination (if, in other words, it cannot make us slaves to fortune), then there are four typical human responses to its difficulty and our *infirmitas*: species of constancy, species of inconstancy, vice, and virtue.

(i) Species of constancy

Aquinas uses *constantia* to describe three different actions. As we have already witnessed, he uses it in a strict sense to describe the persistence of the courageous when confronted with all sorts of countervailing obstacles and difficulties that result from the pursuit of a good that is already difficult and dangerous. More generously, he speaks of constancy when he refers to that steadfast affection in the face of every difficulty that is the mark of virtuous action of every sort. He also uses it to describe the act of rational resistance to contingent passion that is needed when the moral virtues are absent. In this sense, among the constant are included "the continent and persevering," those who "withstand the passions lest reason be led astray" (*ST* i–ii.58.3.2).[17]

---

[17] Aquinas states that, "continence and perseverance seem to be species of constancy which pertains to reason" (*ST*ii–ii.53.5.3), which implies that there are other varieties. And yet when he describes the general origins of inconstancy he speaks only of the passions and therefore implies that continence and perseverance exhaust constancy. He tells us that inconstancy denotes withdrawal from some good and that its origin is within the appetite, since "a man does not withdraw from a previous good purpose, except on account of something else being inordinately pleasing to him" (*ST*ii–ii.53.5). When asked for further specification he refers to the passions of the sensitive appetite alone: "Envy and anger cause inconstancy by drawing away the reason to something else; whereas lust causes inconstancy by destroying the judgment of reason entirely" (*ST*ii–ii.53.6.1).

Unlike the virtuous, the continent and the persevering are unable to bring their contingent passions into accord with right reason, but they can resist disordered inclination with acts of rational control (*ST* I–II.58.3.2; II–II.53.5.3; 155.1). The continent frustrate pleasure (*ST* II–II.155.2) and the persevering tether pain, sorrow, and fear, and consequently both pursue external actions that track those of the virtuous. Nevertheless, because their passions follow the random progression of sensible goods they happen to meet in the world, and not the judgments of right reason, the totality of their agency falls short of true virtue (*ST* I–II.58.3.2; II–II.155.1).

The best way to see how far the actions of the persevering and the continent fall short of virtue is to consider how difficult it becomes for their practical deliberations to track the good. Their contingent passions distort judgment "because when a man is affected by a passion, things seem to him greater or smaller than they really are: thus to a lover, what he loves seems better; to him that fears, what he fears seems more dreadful" (*ST* I–II.44.2). Consider anger. Anger is the desire for vengeance that originates in a judgment about the unjust loss of some good, normally honor, at the hands of another (*ST* I–II.46.1, 4; 47.2). Without this judgment, anger would lose its object, and yet once passion for vengeance flares contingently against cooler judgment, reason is hindered and "something seems fitting to him, which does not seem so when he is not affected" (*ST* I–II.9.2). Following Aristotle (*EN* 1149b1–3) Aquinas contends that "anger listens somewhat to reason in so far as reason denounces the injury inflicted, but listens not perfectly, because it

---

Of course, it is Aquinas's Augustinian commitment to the corrupted will as an independent source of withdrawal from reason's good that prevents him from saying that continence and perseverance exhaust constancy. By his Augustinian lights there must be a species of constancy that responds to autonomous infirmities in the will, infirmities that arise quite apart from contingent passions. But oddly enough he tells us nothing about the independent origin of the will's infirmities, nothing about the will's autonomous inconstancy.

In fact, the will plays no significant role in his account of the causes of ordinary sinful action. Instead, he locates the remote cause of every sin in our desires for mutable goods (*ST* I–II.75.2; 77.5). And, as we shall see below, it is the contingent character of those desires that enables them to distract reason from its tasks and distort its judgments about the good. Indeed, even the material aspect of original sin is simply the perpetual character of this contingency in the passions (*ST* I–II.82.3; 74.3.2;). To be sure, the will does contribute to every sinful action in so far as a rational desire of the apparent good follows reason's judgment that it is good (*ST* I–II.9.1). Nevertheless, the belatedness of the will in Aquinas's moral psychology, its ultimate dependence upon the judgments of reason, prevents this contribution from carrying any explanatory power.

I take this to be further evidence of a hunch I have spelled out elsewhere: that despite frequent reference to the will Aquinas does not consider it an independent cause of action, sinful or otherwise, this side of Eden. In this respect at least, his treatment of human action *in via* is thoroughly Aristotelian. See Bowlin (1998). For an excellent treatment of the Franciscan response to Aquinas's intellectualism see Kent (1995).

does not observe the rule of reason as to the measure of vengeance. Anger, therefore, requires an act of reason; and yet proves a hindrance to reason" (*ST* 1–11.46.4.3). Anger proves a hindrance precisely because it incorporates a judgment of reason. It distorts when its own distorted judgment about the injury inflicted is brought to bear upon reason's practical inquiries.[18] And, of course, it is this distortion that makes it difficult for the persevering to know and do the good.

The concupiscible passions of the continent can distort judgment as well, but they can also distract (*ST* 1–11.33.3). The desire for pleasure, for example, can cause the continent to ignore their deliberations and attend to the thing that pleases. For,

those who are in some kind of passion, do not easily turn their imagination away from the object of their emotion, the result being that the judgment of the reason often follows the passion of the sensitive appetite, and consequently the will's movement follows it also, since it has a natural inclination to follow the judgment of reason. (*ST* 1–11.77.1)

Aquinas believes that the pleasures of touch, those associated with "meat and drink, and . . . the union of the sexes" present reason with the greatest difficulties (*ST* 11–11.141.4), not because these sensible goods are difficult to acquire, but because our desire for them and the pleasures they elicit have the greatest natural power to distract reason and redirect the will. Bodily pleasures possess this power, according to Aquinas, because they are ordered to the sensible goods directly associated with our animal survival (*ST* 1–11.31.6),[19] because those same goods are well known, frequently close at hand and easy to acquire, and because we tend to pursue them "as remedies for bodily defects or troubles, whenever various griefs arise" (*ST* 1–11.31.5). Imagine living in an apartment that sits above a bakery. Imagine trying to maintain your attention to the grievous task of writing as the smell of bread baking rises through the heating vents and sparks your desires. Reason would be hindered, its deliberations made difficult, and if it does not strengthen itself in an act of continence, its counsels brought to failure.

Concupiscible passions are not alone in this ability. Irascible passions can distract just as well. For example, fear of some "evil to come, near at

---

[18] I am indebted to Dent (1984, 199) for this observation.
[19] Here Aquinas follows Aristotle (*EN* 1118a23–25,1118b1–4) and argues that the sense of touch is the passion most characteristic of animal natures precisely because "the touch takes cognizance of those things which are vital to an animal" (*ST* 1–11.31.6). And it is because we, like other animals, literally, live by touch, that these passions have the greatest ability to turn our desire and attention to their objects.

hand and difficult to avoid" distracts reason by moving its attention from the good that should be pursued to the evil that is feared (*ST* I–II.43.1). Of course, impending evil can make one "willing or anxious to take counsel" (*ST* I–II.44.2), but Aquinas insists that we have no reason to believe that good counsel follows from fear's proddings. For, though fear may invite deliberation, it nonetheless tends to undermine the attention needed to perceive the good in the matter at hand (*ST* I–II.44.2).

In some instances, passions become so strong that distraction is complete, constancy becomes impossible, and the agent slips into madness. This can occur with the concupiscible passions, "as in the case of those who are mad through love" (*ST* I–II.77.7), but Aquinas considers it more common with the irascible. Anger's rage is the best example (*ST* I–II.48.3; 77.7). Quoting Gregory the Great (*Moralia* v.30) he describes the consequences of anger this way: "the heart that is inflamed with the stings of its own anger beats quick, the body trembles, the tongue stammers, the countenance takes fire, the eyes grow fierce, they that are well known are not recognized. With the mouth indeed he shapes a sound, but the understanding knows not what it says" (*ST* I–II.48.2).[20] Other irascible passions can also bring reason to complete distraction. Sorrow over some evil that cannot be repulsed can bind reason's attention so that "it cannot turn aside either this way or that," its deliberation stupefied, its ability to command the will paralyzed (*ST* I–II.37.2). In a similar vein, "the thoughts" of one overwhelmed by fear "are so disturbed, that he can find no counsel" (*ST* I–II.44.2).

Of course, madness of this sort is rare and usually fleeting. For most of us, continence and perseverance are the norm. Contingent passions confound our judgments and incline our wills to ends we know are contrary to the judgments of right reason about the good (*ST* I–II.58.5). We respond to these difficulties with acts of rational resistance. We refuse to consent to the means that counsel has judged suitable to these mistaken ends (*ST* I.81.3). We withhold command (*ST* II–II.53.5). We then pursue inquiries that discover means suitable to those ends judged good by right reason. By choosing these means we act as the virtuous do, but because our passions are divided from our better judgments, because there is a sense in which they simply happen to us, imposing themselves upon us just as the world does, our selves are fractured and our agency as a whole falls short of virtue.

---

[20] Aquinas believes that some sort of bodily change is the best sign of the complete fettering of reason, and he therefore compares it to sleep or drunkenness (*ST* I–II.77.2).

We are now in a position to specify more precisely in what sense the passions of the constant and persevering are contingent, not only at odds with their rational judgments but experienced as fortune is, as events that simply happen. Of course, all passions escape our control just as the world does that causes them, and thus all are experienced in some fashion as mere happenings (*ST* I–II.22.I). Aquinas notes that some passions display this passivity with greater clarity than others. Fear, for instance, entails passivity in the face of dangerous events in the world that we cannot control.[21] We can, of course, choose dangerous and fearsome courses of action, and thus there remains some causal connection between our agency and our fear, but our choice does little to control the impending evil. Our passivity before it remains, as it must, if there is to be something for us to fear.

The logic of pain, sorrow, and anger is similar. Concupiscence also concurs. A sensible good happens our way, elicits our desire, draws us to it, and when achieved gives us pleasure (*ST* I–II.30.2). In this passionate response we are passive before it, moved by its goodness and accepting its pleasures. But there is a difference here, for concupiscence is the desire for a sensible good that is absent, its pleasures remote and yearned for (*ST* I–II.30.2.I). As such, concupiscence encourages us to seek out its object and this tends to reduce our passivity. By contrast, evil, the object of fear, is never sought, and this enhances the sense in which we suffer fear passively.

Nevertheless, the passions of the merely continent and the persevering agent are out of control in an additional sense: they fail to track her own considered judgment about what passionate response is proper in a given circumstance. Consider someone who simply perseveres. She either fears the wrong object, or fears the right object with the wrong intensity. Moreover, she knows her error. If she fears the wrong object, she knows her fear follows from a mistaken estimation of the dangers and difficulties she confronts. If she fears the right object but with the wrong intensity, she knows she has paid insufficient attention to the good that will result from standing firm as compared to the good that will follow from flight. In each case she can do nothing to bring her passion in line with her better judgment, at least not immediately. All she can do is suppress her fear and refuse to command and consent to the actions it favors.

To be sure, the world also causes fear in the virtuous. It cannot,

---

[21] Indeed, Aquinas insists that, "after sorrow, fear chiefly has the character of passion" (*ST* I–II.41.I).

however, cause fear whose object and intensity are contrary to their own considered judgments, and in this respect, the passions of the virtuous are neither contingent nor out of control, but in a real sense their own.[22]

(ii) Species of inconstancy

If the continent and the persevering cannot bridle their contingent passions, if this task proves too difficult, then evil courses of action ensue. As before, the passions that fail to track the judgments of right reason are too weak to chase the agent off the edge of sanity. Rational resistance is still possible. But insofar as the passions bite with greater force resistance becomes more difficult. In one of the standard cases, what Aquinas variously calls *ignorantia malae electionis* or *praevolatio*, the passions that run free of right reason distract the practical intellect and distort its judgments, and in turn influence the course of action that is actually chosen (*ST* 1–11.6.8; 11–11.156.1). This is made possible by the fact that choice, like the passions, bears on things singular and contingent, and follows two successive judgments about what is to be done, one concerned with universal matters, the other with contingent singulars (*ST* 1–11.14.1; 76.1; 77.2).[23]

Consider, for example, the difference between the judgments of virtuous Hoss Cartwright, on the one hand, and Too Slim, a cowboy down on his luck, on the other. Both begin with a general judgment that they know habitually and a good that they will simply and absolutely. Both know that just property claims of others should be honored. Both wish for just states of affairs in the world. But old Hoss not only wills this good simply and absolutely, he intends to pursue it as an end in this instance. This intention leads him to advance an inquiry into the contingent and singular details of the relevant circumstances in order to determine who holds title to the cattle in question (*ST* 1–11.14.1). His inquiry concludes soundly: the cows belong to another, not the Cartwrights. Together, Hoss's general and particular judgments take the first

---

[22] For an excellent contemporary discussion of constancy see Elster (1984, 36–111), who describes a response to contingent passion that stands between constancy and inconstancy. Those who are weak-willed and know it may find indirect means of achieving their ends in the circumstances that elicit the passions that cause their weakness. Ulysses binds himself to the mast of his ship so that he can proceed past the Sirens and continue his voyage home when he knows their voices will bring on passions that he cannot control with an act of constancy.

[23] Thus Aquinas writes, "Universal knowledge, which is most certain, does not hold the foremost place in action, but rather particular knowledge, since actions are about singulars: wherefore it is not astonishing that, in matters of action, passion acts counter to universal knowledge, if the consideration of particular knowledge be lacking" (*ST* 1–11.77.2.1).

two places in his practical syllogism, which in turn yield his decision to leave the cows alone. He then consents to this decision and chooses in accordance with his consent.

Notice, by Aquinas's lights, Hoss proceeds through four different acts of the will. First, he wills to protect the property rights of others simply and absolutely. A simple volition of this sort is the will's response to our most basic judgments about the good as an end, and as such cannot alone produce action or elicit deliberation (*ST* I–II.8.3; 12.1.4; 15.3). The reason for its insufficiency with respect to action follows from the fact that we will the good itself by nature, and consequently we will simply and absolutely all those things that we judge good (*ST* I–II.9.4 and ad 1; 10.1; 94.2). But this hardly means that we actually pursue every object we judge good in every instance. Rather, we acknowledge their general goodness naturally and in every instance without actually intending to pursue them as ends here and now (*ST* I–II.10.1). Next, Hoss intends in this particular instance to pursue one of the goods that he wills simply and absolutely.[24] That is, he not only considers it good to honor property rights, but he wills to have this good by some means (*ST* I–II.12.1.1,3; 12.4.3). He then consents to the means that he believes will achieve the good he intends as an end (*ST* I–II.15.3). And finally, he chooses, which is to say, he leaves the cattle alone (*ST* I–II.13.1–3; 12.4.3).

For Too Slim things turn out much differently. His inordinate desire for beef and profit prevents his actual consideration of the good that he knows habitually and wills simply. As a result, he can neither intend to pursue this end in this instance, nor take counsel about the means that would achieve it (*ST* II–II.156.1.2). His reason "is deceived" by these passions into "rejecting what before it had rightly accepted" (*ST* II–II.53.5). By distortion or distraction they cause him to move his attention from the prohibition against theft to another universal judgment: beef and profit are good and desirable (*ST* I–II.77.2.4). Under the influence of contingent desire he attends to this new judgment, wills this good simply, and eventually intends to pursue it in this instance. He then pursues an inquiry into the relevant details of the circumstances of choice, and determines that these cows will bring beef and profit. His will consents to this judgment and his practical syllogism concludes in the choice to round them up.

Notice, it is not ignorance of the general principle prohibiting theft that causes Too Slim to sin. His knowledge of the good and his simple

---

[24] Aquinas writes: "the will is moved to the end in two ways: first, to the end absolutely and in itself [*absolute secundum se*]; secondly, as the reason for willing the means" (*ST* I–II.8.3).

desire for what it requires remains intact. What crumbles under the distracting and distorting influence of contingent passion is his judgment of what is good and required in particular. As a result, "his soul yields . . . before . . . reason has given its counsel" (*ST* II–II.156.1).

Of course, all of this turns on our ability to know something habitually but not actually and for Aquinas this presents no difficulty. He seems to believe that our natural habits of attention make it impossible for us to consider all that we know and remember all at once.[25] In other words, the intellect can be in potency in two ways: before learning, that is, before the habit of knowledge, and when it possesses a habit of knowledge but does not actually consider it. It follows that self-deception is a regular possibility, just as it is commonplace to intend courses of action that conflict with what we know habitually and will generally. Thus Aquinas writes, "the soul being one, can only have one intention. The result is that if one thing draws upon itself the entire intention of the soul, or a great portion thereof, anything else requiring considerable attention is incompatible therewith" (*ST* I–II.37.1). Perhaps we can say that our habits of attention give some structure to the intellect and memory, but nothing uniform. It is as if the mind is laid out like a medieval city, with streets going this way and that, some connecting with others, some ending in blind alleys, some in pleasant courtyards, and with our attention normally able to traverse only one neighborhood at a time.[26]

For Aquinas, then, it is entirely possible to have general knowledge of what is required in some circumstance that we cannot actually consider. Some passion is pushed upon us when the circumstance obtains, walling off what we actually know from our attention, and consequently creating temporary, partial, and culpable ignorance (*ST* I–II.76.1; 77.2). Thus it is a principal characteristic of this kind of moral failure, this ignorance of evil choice, that because of some contingent passion, "one does not actually consider what one can and ought to consider" (*ST* I–II.6.8).

But what if Too Slim's desire for beef and profit does not prevent him from knowing what is good and required both in general and in particular? What if he knows that theft is unlawful and that rounding up these particular cattle would be theft (*ST* I–II.77.2)? What if he knows that the good of justice would be achieved if he acted in accordance with this knowledge? Would he then choose as Hoss does? Not necessarily, for there is always the chance that he will act incontinently.

---

[25] For a modern equivalent see Rorty (1972, 387–410).
[26] Rorty (1988a, 214) provides this apt image.

Like *ignorantia malae electionis, incontinentia* is a species of inconstancy, but it does not depend on the agent's failure to know and will what the good requires in particular. Thus if Too Slim's sin is one of incontinence, he works with four propositions, two particular and two universal. His unruly and contingent passion for pleasure fetters his reason and hinders it from pursuing an inquiry under the first universal proposition and concluding that theft is unlawful. Instead, he directs his attention and deliberations to the second, that beef and profit are good (*ST* I–II.77.2.4).[27]

The puzzle here is determining just how it is possible for Too Slim to choose against the good that he knows and wills both in general and in particular. How can he in fact do what he wills not to do? Or, as Aquinas puts it, how can reason be overcome by a passion against its knowledge (*ST* I–II.77.2)? The answer follows from the distinction he draws between assent and consent. Assent is an act of the intellect that follows a judgment that some moral principle is binding or that some good ought to be pursued. To assent (*assentire*), says Aquinas, is "to feel toward something [*ad aliud sentire*]; and thus it implies a certain distance to that to which assent is given" (*ST* I–II.15.1.3). Because of this distance, assent is not immediately directed to action. It "does not consist in a movement towards the thing." In fact, in Aquinas's eyes it is so far removed from action that he considers it indistinguishable from those simple acts of the intellect that merely acknowledge the goodness of some object (*ST* I–II.15.1.3).[28] If the agent intends the good assented to as an end, then counsel deliberates over the means suitable to that end. When counsel's work is complete and assent is given to its conclusions, consent follows immediately, at least in most instances. Consent bridges deliberation and choice. It is the will's response to counsel's judgment that a good, either particular or general, ought to be pursued as an end or chosen as a means (*ST* I–II.15.3). Aquinas writes that "to consent [*consentire*] is to feel with, and this implies a certain union to the object of consent." Its act "consist(s) in a movement toward the thing," and as such consent is more directed to action than is assent (*ST* I–II.15.1.3).[29]

With these distinctions in hand Aquinas describes incontinence as an exception to the norm, where the will follows the intellect's assent with consent (*ST* I–II.77.3.3). Too Slim assents to the universal judgment, that

[27] My treatment of Aquinas's account of incontinence has profited from conversations with Victor Preller and is indebted to Kent's treatment (1989, 199–223).
[28] See Stegman (1989, 117–128).
[29] For more on the difference between assent and consent see Barad (1988, 98–111).

theft is unlawful, and to counsel's particular conclusion, that taking these particular cattle would be theft, but he does not consent to either. Instead, his contingent passions direct him to consent to the other two propositions to which he has already assented, that beef and profit are desirable and that these cattle will bring both.[30] To be sure, he has knowledge of the good and of what particular course of action it requires in this instance, but it is the distant and abstract knowledge that is characteristic of assent. Moreover, he remains at this distance precisely because he refuses to consent to the good and draw himself to it. Switching metaphors, when Too Slim fails to consent to the particular course of action to which he has given his assent he "does not stand to what has been counseled, through holding weakly through reason's judgment" (*ST* II–II.156.1). And of course it is this failure to stand firm, this weakness, that best characterizes his incontinence (*De malo* 3.9.4).[31]

At this point some may object that the discussion has strayed too far afield from courage and the irascible passions. It is not fear or anger that brings on incontinence or impetuosity in Too Slim, but inordinate desire. What's more, Aquinas seems to imply that incontinence cannot be a consequence of contingent irascible passions. The incontinent will changes. It desires what it once repudiated. By contrast, "he who acts from fear retains the repugnance of the will to that which he does, considered in itself." Indeed, "the timid man acts counter to that which in itself he desires now" (*ST* I–II.6.7.2, cf. *ST* II–II.53.6.1), while the incontinent act against what they know habitually and to which they actually assent, but not counter to that which they desire now.

This objection, however, misses the mark precisely because Aquinas insists that the irascible passions presuppose the movement of the concupiscible passions toward its object. When the object is good, "movement begins in love, goes forward to desire, and ends in hope" or despair. If the object is evil, movement "begins in hatred, goes on to aversion, and ends in fear" or daring (*ST* I–II.25.4). And of course, a thing is evil, and thus feared, because it threatens some other good already loved; while anger presupposes both desire and hope for some good, principally revenge for an injustice done, and hatred of the "noxious person, on whom it seeks to be revenged" (*ST* I–II.46.2).

---

[30] Aquinas interprets St. Paul's incontinence (*Romans* 7.14–25) in precisely this manner. Insofar as Paul speaks as a sinful man, he "is subjugated to the flesh, consenting to things urged by the flesh" (*Super epistolam ad Romanos lectura*, n.560). This passage is cited by Kretzmann (1988, 185) whose interpretation of Aquinas on incontinence is quite different from the one offered here.

[31] Kent (1989, 205–206).

This dependence of the irascible passions upon the concupiscible allows Aquinas to say "that inordinate desire of good is the cause of every sin," and that most sins of inconstancy, even those of the timid, require a description that includes reference to incontinence (*ST* I–II.77.6). Of course, when a soldier timidly retreats in battle his action is best seen as a lack of perseverance. He wishes to pursue the campaign. He knows that the good will be done if he pursues this end in this instance. Nevertheless, his fear of death prevents him from standing fast in this good and choosing means suitable to this end. He retreats. No doubt, he wishes things were different. He wishes he could stand fast and pursue the end that he has judged good, and thus when he flees he acts in a way that is repugnant to his will and to his original desire. In this sense, at least, he acts unwillingly (*ST* I–II.6.6).

Still, fear alone does not cause his retreat, and timidity is not his only failing. Since his fear of death presupposes his love of life, his retreat is also incontinent. Habitually and generally he knows he is obliged to pursue justice and he knows what he must do in particular in order to stand fast in this good in circumstances of this sort. As the battle begins, he consents to both propositions and chooses accordingly, but as its horrors increase the desire to live generates fear, which in turn, causes him to withdraw consent to each. In turn, the will is directed to two other propositions: the general judgment that his life is good and ought to be preserved, and the particular judgment that standing fast here and now will threaten his welfare, while fleeing will protect it. The conclusion of a practical syllogism is action. He takes flight.

Of course, insofar as we consider his retreat a consequence of fear alone, his action is not incontinent. He acts against what he actually desires and not because his fear has changed his judgment about what is desirable. He acts only with regret and not with love. However, as Aquinas points out, an action that proceeds from fear alone could not be regarded as properly voluntary (*ST* I–II.6.6), and therefore we cannot provide a compelling account of the soldier's flight without noticing that fear changes his will's desire, directing its consent to different goods. It is for this reason that Aquinas always situates fear in a nest of loves and insists that every account of timidity must refer to weakness in the will.

But note, the point of real significance cuts the other way in an inquiry that begins with courage and attends to virtue and difficulty, strength and contingency. Not only does Aquinas describe timorous acts by referring to incontinence, to contingency in the passions that brings contingency to the will. He also refers to incontinence as a sin of weakness, as a failure in strength. In effect he describes *both* timidity and incontinence in the language and concepts of virtue in general that become prominent in his remarks about courage – difficulty, impediment, resistance, strength, and weakness. He writes, "when the concupiscible or irascible power is affected by any passion contrary to the order of reason, the result being that an impediment arises in the aforesaid manner to the due action of man, it is said to be a sin of weakness" (*ST* I–II.77.3). *Infirmitas* is the inability to stand fast and strong in the face of some difficulty, some impediment that threatens the pursuit of some good (*ST* II–II.53.5). Contingent desire for bodily pleasure can act as such an impediment. So can contingent fear. Both require a strong and steadfast act of resistance if the good is to be chosen and pursued. It follows that in general, "every passion can be called a weakness, insofar as it weakens the soul's strength and clogs the reason" (*ST* I–II.85.3.4), and that Aquinas regards incontinence, like the absence of perseverance, as a failure to act with the strength that is characteristic of every moral virtue, not simply courage and its parts. Similarly, he characterizes our need for temperance, a need made compelling by the weakness that distinguishes incontinence, with the same language he employs to describe our need for courage. Temperance, like courage, is a "resisting virtue," needed because concupiscible desire for the greatest pleasures creates "a difficulty," "a power of resistance" to the judgments of reason, that must be opposed with acts of virtue that are strong and great and difficult (*ST* II–II.129.2; cf. *ST* I–II.60.5).

(iii) Vice

The timid and the incontinent have no chronic disposition to sin. The difficulty lies in their passions, which at times oppose reason's judgment and lead them to act against the good that they know and will habitually. It follows that their moral failures are merely intermittent, precisely because their passions are merely contingent and thus, for the most part, follow reason's bidding (*ST* I–II.78.4). In fact, apart from the occasional bursts of contingent passion, choice tracks reason's better judgment, and when it does not, habitual knowledge of the good normally generates regret over this departure from the norm.[32]

Nonetheless, if passionate departures from reason become regular

---

[32] *Ibid.*, 205, 209.

and sins of weakness frequent – that is, if passions gradually become disordered in a fashion that exceeds mere contingency – then a habitual inclination of the will toward apparent good may arise. Inordinate fear, for instance, may become so constant in the face of frequent dangers that the timid perpetually fail to pursue the difficult good that they know and will. Their inordinate fearfulness becomes habitual and allows their concupiscible passions to turn them from perpetually willing the difficult and true good to habitually willing some merely apparent good. A habit infects the will and the timid become cowards (*ST* ɪɪ–ɪɪ.125). Since Aquinas believes that excessive fear comes packaged with excessive desire for some temporal good, the corrupted will normally inclines toward riches or pleasure (*ST* ɪ–ɪɪ.78.1). Of course, the original difficulty might be insufficient fear or some other habitually excessive or deficient irascible passion, but the outcome would be the same: some variety of cowardice and a consequent inclination of the will toward some apparent good. And when the will is so inclined it moves to evil of its own accord, even in the absence of contingent passions.[33] In short, sin is now committed through habit, through certain malice (*ST* ɪ–ɪɪ.78.3).

(iv) Virtue

If inconstant and malicious actions are to be avoided, and if contingent passions are to be effectively diminished, and not merely controlled by acts of continence and perseverance, then the resisting virtues are needed. Aquinas believes that we are inclined by nature to acquire the virtues insofar as we will those goods appropriate to our human form of life by nature, simply and absolutely (*ST* 1.79.12; 1–ɪɪ.63.1; 10.1; 93.6; 94.2). We are not naturally virtuous, but we do have a natural aptitude

---

[33] The incontinent and the impetuous sin "while choosing" (*eligens*) but not, as the malicious do, "through choosing" (*ex electione*). The distinction turns on different causal histories, different explanations of the will's action. In the malicious the will is moved to choice by reason alone, in the incontinent, by reason distorted by passion (*ST*ɪɪ–ɪɪ.155.3.2). Thus Aquinas writes, "he that sins through passion, sins while choosing, but not through choosing, because his choosing is not for him the first principle of his sin; for he is induced through the passion, to choose what he would not choose, were it not for the passion. On the other hand, he that sins through certain malice, chooses evil of his own accord . . . so that his choosing, of which he has full control, is the principle of his sin: and for this reason he is said to sin through choosing" (*ST* ɪ–ɪɪ.78.4.3). If passion is the first principle of their sin why doesn't Aquinas simply say that the incontinent sin through passion? Because he wants to emphasize the voluntary character of their sin, its origin in will and reason while under the influence of disordered passion. Thus he remarks elsewhere that passions "are not the cause of incontinence, but are merely the occasion thereof, since, so long as the use of reason remains, man is always able to resist his passions" (*ST*ɪɪ–ɪɪ.156.1).

for virtue and thus we do possess them inchoately.[34] Unfortunately, most find it difficult to act in accordance with this natural disposition toward the good "on account of some impediment supervening from without" (*ST* I–II.65.3.2). As we have already witnessed, these impediments are, by Aquinas's lights, contingent passions that respond to the contingent world in a manner at odds with the better judgments of reason, making it difficult to pursue and achieve the good that reason commends (*ST* II–II.129.3). It is this difficulty that generates the need for those acquired moral virtues that cope with these contingent and contrary passions, and safeguard the good of reason when the strength of natural virtue fails (*ST* I–II.65.3.2; II–II.123.11.2).

Caution is required here. To say that the resisting virtues stand against actually contingent passions misdescribes their work. Courage, for instance, is needed not so that we might pursue the goods that are difficult and dangerous in spite of inordinate fear, hope, or anger, but in order that our passions might track the judgments of right reason and thus no longer be contingent – that is, no longer be alien influences upon our agency that make it difficult for us to act in accord with our judgment about the good that reason demands. This change comes about through acts of constancy, when reason endorses the judgments implicit in some irascible passions and rejects the judgments implicit in others.[35] Eventually this rational control of the passions transforms the irascible appetite and enables it to respond to dangers and difficulties in a manner that accords with the judgments of right reason. And Aquinas considers this transition from rational control to habitual response quite natural, at least in part, since both the irascible and the concupiscible powers have a natural aptitude to obey reason (*ST* I–II.56.4).

With virtue established the soul is restored to a semblance of the original justice found in Eden's inhabitants before the fall. Hamlet puts the point well:

> . . . bless'd are those
> Whose blood and judgment are so well co-mingled
> That they are not a pipe for Fortune's finger
> to sound what stop she please.[36]

This co-mingling is, of course, imperfect. Indeed, Aquinas insists that the virtues available to us in this life cannot completely replace lost grace, that contingent passions will disrupt even the most virtuous

---

[34] *ST* I–II.63.1: *Virtus est homini naturalis secundum quandam inchoationem.*   [35] Dent (1984, 162).
[36] From *Ibid.*, 213.

among us in some circumstances (*ST* I–II.65.2; 74.3.2). Nevertheless, by diminishing the effects of the fall, virtue suspends, at least in part, one of the four elements needed to generate free and contingent passions.

Returning again to Aquinas's political metaphors, we can say that courage diminishes the original freedom of the irascible appetite from reason's influence, freedom that was expressed in periodic anarchy in the passions that enslaved us to fortune's whim. Courage tutors the irascible passions in the good that the practical intellect recommends and thus brings them under reason's dominion. Indeed, insofar as the irascible passions direct us to those ends that we would normally pursue after a cool hour of reflection, and to those means that we would choose following reason's careful counsel, we can say that courage brings the passions under the strict control of reason. Perhaps it is inappropriate to say that in the truly courageous reason rules the passions like a despot, and yet surely it is their master.

Some exegetes resist this conclusion. They do not deny that Aquinas situates the passions in cognitive contexts, but they doubt he would call reason's dominion over affection virtue. If he did, they reason, how could he preserve what we praise in the passions: their ability to oppose and correct our mistaken judgments about the good. It will be impossible, for instance, for the upright affection I have for my son to overturn my arrogant judgment that he deserves punishment over a trifle.[37] So, they conclude, Aquinas must praise free passion and bury despotic reason. Indeed, he must consider the relative freedom the passions secure from reason's domination a mark of genuine virtue.[38]

This, however, misrepresents Aquinas's actual view. The passions, he insists, have political freedom and thus "something of their own," only insofar as they "can resist the commands of reason" (*ST* I.81.3.2). This means that passions with some measure of political freedom from reason are actually prevented from causing good and harmonious action, for, as Aquinas repeatedly reminds us, human actions are good only insofar as they follow from the judgments of reason (*ST* I–II.18.5). Consequently, the agent whose passions possess some measure of political freedom stands between the virtuous, whose passions are wholly subject to reason, and the mad, whose passions are entirely free of reason's influence. Frequently at odds with his reason, his free passions cloud and distort his judgment and fracture his agency. They pull him in this way and that, while his reason disposes him in other directions still (*ST*

---

[37] Yearley (1990, 82).   [38] *Ibid.*, 83.

I–II.10.3.2). In short, passions with political freedom are contingent and will require training in the ways of reason before they can be the source of good and praiseworthy action.

But what about the worry that generated this confusion? Does the loss of political freedom in the passions of the virtuous restrict every liberty in the sensitive appetite?[39] Aquinas denies that it does, and on two counts. First, when Aquinas praises reason's control over the sensitive appetite he simply hails the inability of the passions to act independently of cognitive contexts shaped by the judgments of right reason. This does not imply that a passionate response under the influence of right reason must follow every considered judgment. Indeed, the passions might come first, and if they arise in a cognitive context constituted by right reason, nothing prevents them from conflicting with the mistaken *judgments* that arise from some other, irrationally constituted, cognitive context. The human soul, for Aquinas, like language for Wittgenstein, is a motley, and until all its cognitive contexts are rationalized by right reason and perfected by grace there will be opportunity aplenty for passions shaped by right reason to oppose judgments that are not.

Second, although the passions of those with virtues perfected by grace lack political freedom, they do nevertheless move freely toward their objects. Even Adam's passions, although "wholly subject to reason," and therefore perpetually "consequent upon . . . judgment" (*ST* 1.95.2) suffered no loss of freedom in this sense. For Aquinas freedom can only be lost by coercion or by the corruption of the ability to act with knowledge (*ST* I–II.6.2, 5, 8), and neither condition obtains when the virtuous respond to the world with passion. The sensitive appetite of the virtuous is not coerced. It does not respond to the world in ways it would rather not. Instead, its rationalized responses become irresistible, not by force, but because it is moved by the world out of cognitive contexts that are shaped by knowledge of the good. And of course an agent that pursues the good, or responds to it in a particular sort of way, because it is known to be good, and can do no other precisely because of this knowledge, can hardly be considered coerced.[40] In short, it is because Aquinas finds the source of freedom in knowledge of an end judged good – not in the ability to pursue opposite courses of action – that reason's dominion brings liberty, not bondage, to the passions of the

---

[39] *Ibid.*, 82–83, 95–98.
[40] For a contemporary defense of a similar view see Wolf (1980, 67–147). From this view Wolf draws conclusions about the asymmetrical character of both freedom and merit that Aquinas does not. See chapter five below.

virtuous.[41] Thus Aquinas concludes that if the movements of the sensitive appetite "be considered as subject to the command of reason and will, then . . . they are said to be voluntary" (*ST* I–II.24.1).

Of course, some might argue that our own view of freedom is more complex, with rationalist and voluntarist sentiments pulling us in different directions. As such, Aquinas's language of freedom and bondage may not offer *us* the clearest image of virtue's effects upon the passions. Perhaps his language of contingency and difficulty does. At the very least, it allows us to distinguish virtue's effects from the effects of constancy in the continent and persevering. Praiseworthy external action follows from each, but for the constant it comes only with difficulty. Contingent passions "abound in the continent and persevering man, which would not be the case if his sensitive appetite were perfected by a habit making it conformable to reason" (*ST* I–II.58.3.2). As such, his struggle to act as the virtuous do is unceasing. By contrast, the contingent passions have been eliminated in the virtuous, and thus in most instances so has the difficulty of acting in a truly praiseworthy manner. Passion, of course, remains in the virtuous, but it has been transformed by right reason and thus cannot hinder them from acting in accord with their better judgments.

Oddly enough, this comparison may seem to undermine my primary thesis – that Aquinas considers the virtues the means we employ to cope with those difficulties that disrupt our pursuit of the good, for now it appears that what distinguishes virtuous action for Aquinas is the ease with which it is done apart from the hindrance of contingent passions. But this appearance deceives. Granted, perfect virtue expends no effort as it accomplishes its work, but the human virtue we know *in via* falls far short of perfection and thus provides a window upon its hidden labors. Three kinds of circumstances create three counter-factuals that make the case: (1) when we face circumstances that we know would have made virtuous action difficult for us in times past but do not now since we have progressed in virtue and seek the good with ease; (2) when we face circumstances where virtuous actions do not come with ease, thereby permitting us to see what difficulties we would overcome had we greater virtue; (3) when we observe others struggling to act virtuously in circumstances where we act with ease.

---

[41] "But those things which have a knowledge of the end are said to move themselves because there is in them a principle by which they not only act but also act for an end" (*ST* I–II.6.1). For a fuller treatment of Aquinas's intellectualist account of voluntary agency see Bowlin (1998).

3.

By now it should be clear that when we attend to courage we view Aquinas's general account of the moral life through a specific set of notions: that we achieve our proper good only with difficulty, that this difficulty follows directly from the contingency of the passions, that our need for the virtues and their work follows from our need to cope with this contingency, and that in a life of virtue the contingency of our passions is not merely controlled but actually abates. Moreover, I hope my discussion of these notions, and Aquinas's use of them in his account of courage and the irascible passions, has made sufficient reference to his remarks about temperance and concupiscence. It should be apparent how the concupiscible passions can be contingent and why this presents a difficulty that requires the work of temperance.

What remains unclear, however, is just how these notions apply to the other moral virtues. How is it that virtue as strength, work, and steadfastness, the good as difficult, and the difficult as contingency play themselves out in Aquinas's treatment of prudence and justice? Or, as Aquinas reasons, if virtue is about the difficult and the good, then different virtues must be distinguished not only by the different goods they seek but also by the different difficulties that their efforts address (*ST* II–II.137.1). What difficulty then, what contingency, do prudence and justice regard?

CHAPTER 2

The contingency of the human good

The answer I wish to defend is this: Aquinas considers the human good contingent, and it is this contingency, this difficulty, that the prudent and the just must address if they are to avoid moral failure and will true goods with constancy. By the contingency of the good I mean the contingent goodness of the will's objects, both the end of the interior act of the will and the object of the exterior act, or the means (*ST* 1–11.18.6). Moreover, I mean to imply that they are contingent as passions can be: their goodness for us can change as fortune does, haphazardly, unexpectedly, and independent of our bidding.

Putting it this way, emphasizing the will's objects, may lead some to think that my reply bears on justice alone, which Aquinas explicitly locates in the will (*ST* 1–11.56.6). Yet Aquinas insists that the practical intellect and the will share a common object in what is (*ens*), and differ only in how they consider it, either knowable or desirable (*ST* 1.79.11.2; 1–11.8.1; 19.3.1). Moreover, "every act of the will is preceded by an act of the intellect" (*ST* 1–11.4.4.2). Before an end can be willed or a means chosen the intellect must present the will with an object known under the aspect of good (*ST* 1–11.8.1; 9.1 and ad 3; 9.2; 13.5; 19.3 and ad 1–2; 19.10). It follows that the will not only depends on reason but resides there (*ST* 1–11.9.2.3), and this should compel us to treat these powers and their virtues together.

Still, some might object that this approach ignores what Aquinas actually says. He takes great care to argue that the will extends to both ends and means, that these movements must be treated differently, and that rational deliberation concerns means and never ends (*ST* 1–11.8.2; 13.3; 14.2). How then can the will and the practical intellect share the contingent good as an object when one of the will's objects, the end, cannot be an object of the intellect's deliberation?

Aquinas answers simply. Deliberation (*consilium*) is only one act of the practical intellect, apprehension (*apprehensio*) is another, and an end must be apprehended before it can be willed as the intended end that guides deliberation (*ST* I–II.15.3). Whether an object is intended as an end or deliberated over as a potential means depends on context. Ends, considered as such, cannot be the objects of deliberation and choice. Since they are the principles that govern these acts, their goodness must be assumed. Nevertheless, "it may happen that what is the end in regard to some things is ordained to something else . . . and consequently that which is looked upon as the end in one inquiry, may be looked upon as the means in another" (*ST* I–II.14.2). It follows that the distinction between deliberation over means and simple apprehension of the end is merely conditional. Both are at least potentially present in most of our rational perceptions of the good, and thus in nearly every instance the will's movement toward the good presupposes a judgment about the good by the practical intellect, and this in turn justifies common treatment of their different virtues.

The caveat is necessary because the will tends to its last end naturally. Of course, the last end must be apprehended as good before it can be willed as such, and yet the intellect apprehends it as good precisely because the will is naturally disposed to desire it. In this respect the will precedes the practical intellect and moves it to its act (*ST* I–II.9.1.3). In fact, the intellect is oriented toward truth first and is able to apprehend some object as good only because the will is already disposed toward the basic features of the human good that fall under the last end, simply and absolutely. Accordingly, when the will follows the intellect and consents to its judgments it is motivated by what it already wills naturally. Nevertheless, those objects of the will that "come under consideration after the last end, insofar as they are directed to the end" have contingent measures of goodness and thus are not willed with natural necessity (*ST* I–II.15.3).

But how can the will's objects have contingent measures of goodness? How does this contingency make it difficult for us to will the true good with the constancy characteristic of true virtue? And how can we describe the work of prudence and justice as acts of steadfastness in the face of contingent and therefore difficult goods?

I .

Aquinas's reply begins with an assumption: human action is largely indeterminate. In a given circumstance, we are not determined to one course of action but indeterminately disposed to many and various things, precisely "because of the nobility of (our) active principle, namely, the soul, whose power extends in a certain way to an infinite number of things" (*De virt. card.* 6). This nobility follows from our ability to know the end in such a way that permits the choice of means. For it is the deliberation that precedes choice (*electio*), that is both the principal mark of rational human action (*ST* I–II.1.1) and the telling sign of its formal indeterminacy (*In Perih.*1.14.24). Deliberation is needed and choice possible only when the end in question is not gained by certain and determinate means. Choice is thus the "taking of one thing in preference to another" and therefore "in those things which are altogether determinate to one there is no place for choice" (*ST* I–II.13.2; cf. *ST* I.82.2.3).

Of course, some human actions require neither deliberation nor choice, and they are of two varieties. In some instances determinate ends are gained by equally determinate means, "as happens in the arts which are governed by certain fixed rules of action; thus a writer does not take counsel how to form his letters, for this is determined by art." In others, it matters little whether an action is done in this or that way (*ST* I–II.14.4). Similarly, many human actions are habitual and thus appear to be almost thoughtless in origin. For instance, while driving I shift between gears without giving much thought to my actions, certainly without deliberating. Nevertheless, appearances deceive, and actions of this sort certainly do assume a prehistory of deliberation, even if it is now set in habit. It is to this prehistory that I appeal if some doubt is raised as to why I act habitually in one way and not another. In that event, the reasons I provide will trace the process of deliberation and choice had it occurred.[1] Normally this is just a matter of recounting the deliberations that went on when the action was first learned. As a novice driver I asked, "How can I move the car from a dead stop without stalling?" Surely this goal motivated both my deliberations and my reply: "I release the clutch and depress the accelerator *at the same time.*" If an explanatory tale of this sort cannot be given, as is the case when I thoughtlessly and habitually scratch my chin, then Aquinas insists that although the action is surely human, an *actus hominis*, it is neither rational nor voluntary (*ST* I–II.1.1; 18.9).

Still, while deliberation and choice distinguish our agency and indicate the relative indeterminacy of our rational powers, they do not by

---

[1] For an excellent contemporary discussion of this point see Mates (1981, 63–64). For a quite different interpretation of *ST* I–II.14.4 and of the place of deliberation in action see Westberg (1994, 165–174).

themselves tell us how far this indeterminacy extends. Perhaps our powers are indeterminate in relation to some of their potential actions but not others. Here Aquinas is explicit. The practical intellect and will, the rational powers that together cause human action, are almost entirely indeterminate with respect to each of their acts. The object of the intellect is truth considered absolutely (*De verit.* 24.7), and thus the intellect is in potentiality to all things knowable (*ST* I–II.50.4.1 and 2). Moreover, before it acquires particular habits of knowing, the intellect "is at first like a clean tablet on which nothing is written" (*ST* I.79.2; cf. *ST* I–II.50.6), and since the character of the rational appetite is largely derived from the practical intellect (*De verit.* 24.2; *ST* I–II.9.1; II–II.4.7), the will is in potentiality to all things desirable (*ST* I–II.9.1) and is just as indeterminate (*ST* I–II.10.4), or nearly so. That is, the will is indeterminate before it acquires particular habits of affection that simply and absolutely dispose it to some particular goods and not others (*ST* I–II.50.5 and ad 3).[2]

Once again the caveat is important. Aquinas admits that the will is determined with nature's necessity to some ends, principally happiness, which is our last end, and to whatever general goods it includes – physical existence, knowledge of the truth, and so on (*De verit.* 22.5; cf. *ST* I–II.10.1; 10.2.3; 94.2). Nevertheless, despite this necessary response of the will to happiness and its general parts, Aquinas insists that it remains indeterminate with respect to particular goods and courses of action. We need not tend to particular instances of the general goods to which we are naturally disposed. "Under good in general," which is happiness, "are included many particular goods, to none of which is the will determined" (*ST* I–II.10.1.3; cf. 13.2), and notice, here indeterminacy bears on intention, not simple volition. The will is not disposed by natural necessity to intend and pursue certain goods as ends, and this is true despite its simple and absolute determination to the general features of the human good. Volitionally determinate with respect to some goods, the will remains intentionally indeterminate. Health, for example, is a good that I will simply and absolutely, and yet this does not mean that I am bound by natural necessity to intend to have health in any particular instance (*ST* I–II.12.1.4; cf. *In Perih.*1.14.24). It follows that human agency is indeterminate with respect to every particular action, since it is intention that directs us to particular ends and elicits choice of particular means (*ST* I–II.12.1.4).

[2] For an excellent treatment of Aquinas's account of indeterminacy in the will see Gallagher (1991).

From this first kind of indeterminacy in human action a second follows: we need not intend a narrow collection of ends and pursue a fixed repertoire of actions in order to flourish according to our kind. The happiness to which the will is naturally inclined in every human action does not bind the will of necessity to any specific ends that would move it to singular action (*ST* I–II.1.6). The claim can be broken into two parts. First, what happiness actually consists in, "whether in virtues, or knowledge or pleasure or anything else of the sort, has not been determined . . . by nature" (*De verit.* 22.7). As a result, the will remains indeterminate with respect to the specific goods and activities that may in fact constitute happiness in a specific human life. Second, none of these more specific goods and activities are necessarily ordered to our last end, since we are always able, at least in principle, to achieve some measure of happiness without first securing any one of them in particular. Aquinas writes,

there is also a good which is necessarily desired by the will because of its freedom from any admixture of evil, namely, happiness itself . . . From the necessity of that good, moreover, there is not introduced into the will any necessity in regard to other objects, as from the necessity of the first principles there is introduced into the intellect a necessity of assenting to conclusions. This is because to that first object of will other objects do not either really or apparently have a necessary relationship which would make it impossible to have the first object of the will without the others; whereas demonstrative conclusions have a necessary relationship to the principles from which they are demonstrated such that, if the conclusions did not turn out to be true, the principles would necessarily not be true. (*De verit.* 24.1.18)

Aquinas, in short, finds no necessary connection between the possible range of human actions and the actions that constitute human flourishing.

The contrast with animal agency sharpens the point. Consider the humble swallow. Swallows build mud nests, chase after insects, mate with other swallows, fly south in winter, and perhaps a few other things. This is all they do, and they must succeed in each of these activities over the course of a lifetime if they are to flourish as swallows should. By contrast, an almost infinite variety of ends and actions are available to us, and human flourishing does not depend upon securing any particular end or participating in any particular activity. No doubt, Aquinas does say that we are naturally disposed to will a small number of general goods simply and absolutely – pleasure, knowledge, self-preservation, and the like – and that we will intend concrete instances of at least some of them in particular circumstances no matter what kind of life we pursue. Nevertheless, happiness remains variously related to these goods, and may well include the intention to have all of them, only some, or some more than others. Which combination and ordering of these natural goods and activities actually brings human happiness will depend upon all the relevant details that make up a particular human life, its circumstances, and its choices.

Of course, Aquinas does say that the consistent exercise of the virtues offers the only hope for the imperfect happiness available to us in this life (*ST* I–II.4.6). But again, this requirement is so general that it designates no specific actions and activities. To say that we must be just and courageous, temperate and wise in order to flourish according to our kind tells us nothing about the specific activities we ought to pursue, and thus it tells us nothing in particular about the actions that characterize just and courageous, temperate and wise participation in this or that activity. Similarly, he does say that periodic contemplation of truth is the one activity in this life that brings us an approximation of the continuous happiness we will share with the blessed (*ST* I–II.3.2.4; *SCG* III.27.10). He also contends that the contemplative life depends on success in a number of practical matters: relative perfection of the body, peace in the passions, and concord in politics (*SCG* III.37.7). Nevertheless, these are merely general requirements for a life of contemplation, general spheres of activity that permit an almost infinite variety of specific action and enterprise.

So Aquinas considers human agency indeterminate, both with respect to act and to happiness, and it is this dual indeterminacy that enables the contingency of the will's objects to make praiseworthy agency difficult.

2.

Of the potential objects of the will, vast in number and kind, only God is "good universally and from every point of view," only God's goodness is perfect and necessary, and consequently the will, whose natural object is the universal good, "tends to it of necessity, if it wills anything at all" (*ST* I–II.10.2). By contrast, all other potential objects of the will are good contingently, for the most part, from some points of view but not all, even those goods willed simply and absolutely. Besides God who is necessarily good, "any other particular goods, in so far as they are lacking in some good, can be regarded as non-goods: and from this point of view, they can be set aside or approved by the will, which can

tend to one and the same thing from various points of view" (*ST*
I–II.10.2). Thus, for instance, although I necessarily love my life with
nature's necessity, and always wish to have it (*ST* I–II.10.1; 94.2), it is not,
despite all that, necessarily good. Like every other potential object of my
will besides God its goodness is contingent, and therefore intending it as
an end and pursuing it in a particular circumstance will contribute to my
proper flourishing in some contexts and hinder it in others.

When the contingent goodness of the will's objects is united with the
indeterminacy of the rational powers that cause human action, the
distinctive character of choice is revealed. For "the will can tend freely
towards various objects, precisely because the reason can have various
conceptions of good" (*Ex hoc enim voluntas libere potest ad diversa ferri, quia
ratio potest habere diversas conceptiones boni*) (*ST* I–II.13.6). Choice, therefore,
is largely a matter of determining whether some contingently good
means is in fact good in a particular instance for the purpose of
achieving some intended end. In choice,

the will can tend to whatever the reason can apprehend as good . . . [and] in all
particular goods, the reason can consider an aspect of some good, and the lack
of some good, which has the aspect of evil: and in this respect, it can apprehend
any single one of such goods as to be chosen or to be avoided. (*ST* I–II.13.6)

In fact, a means is contingently good even when it alone achieves the
desired end. For although it must be willed without fail in order to
achieve that end, this is necessity conditioned on an intention that is
itself contingent. If I am to finish this chapter, then of necessity I must
choose to work diligently. But since the end in question is good contingently, I need not desire it, in which case the means would lose its
goodness for me (*ST* I–II.13.6.2; 14.6).

The contingency of the good holds most obviously for those means
that are indifferent with respect to their moral species. Most means are
of this sort, by themselves neither good nor evil – reading a book,
walking across a field, eating breakfast, telling a joke, waging a war, and
the like. Each requires a context to fix the measure and character of
their goodness (*ST* I–II.18.8). A context is made up of an end and those
circumstances of the action that specify its object by regarding a special
order of reason (*ST* I–II.18.5, 9, 11; 20.1, 2). And because contexts can
vary, "acts considered the same in their natural species . . . (are) diverse
considered in their moral species" (*ST* I–II.1.3).[3]

---

[3] Those circumstances that do not regard a special order of reason do not become a condition of
the object that specifies the action. They remain circumstances *per se*, mere accidents upon the
action (*ST* I–II.18.10.1–2; 18.11; 19.2).

Consider the objective, "to kill another." Aquinas notes that this action is contingently good since it can be ordained to a good end, such as safeguarding justice, or to a vicious end, such as satisfying anger or fulfilling an inordinate desire for sensible goods (*ST* I–II.I.3). When it is ordained to an evil end, its moral species is fixed. No circumstance can make it a good. But when it is ordained to a good end it remains contingently good until it settles into those circumstances that have a special relation to reason and that can be considered a "principal condition of the object that determines the action's species" (*ST* I–II.18.10). For Aquinas it is the circumstance "who" that has the special relation to reason in this instance. Just authority is at issue, vigilantism the fear. The action is good if it is the civil magistrate who kills and if he does so in order to safeguard justice and secure the welfare of the whole community. If, however, it is a private individual who kills for the sake of this end, the action is evil, precisely because individuals have not been vested with this authority over life and death for the sake of the common weal (*ST* II–II.64.3).

Or, consider the objective, "to defend one's self." If, as a result of defending myself, I kill another, the moral species of the act will depend upon how the deed is done. If I kill him with violence beyond what is necessary to protect myself, or with the intention to take his life directly and not merely to repel his attack, then the object of my action is evil. If, on the other hand, I intend only to protect myself and resort to force that is proportionate to this end and his threat, and if, as a result, death comes accidentally, then my objective is good (*ST* II–II.64.7). But the context could change and what was once an accidental circumstance, one merely "added to the object that specifies the action" and thus unable to attach to the object of the action and determine its moral species, can become "a principal condition of the object" that specifies the action (*ST* I–II.18.10 and ad 2). For instance, in some contexts the consequences of an action bear on its object in precisely this way (*ST* I–II.7.3). If my attacker is much fiercer and stronger than I, then it is unlikely that I can defend myself with force sufficient to repel him. If I should try, it is likely that my own death and my family's sorrow would result. In this circumstance, defending myself by violent means would be an evil course of action on account of the foreseeable, unnecessary, and excessively harmful consequences, consequences that are added to the object that fixes the action in its moral species (*ST* I–II.20.5; 73.8).

Surprisingly, Aquinas also regards an action *bonus secundum suam speciem*, such as giving alms or restoring what belongs to another (*ST*

1–11.18.8), as an object of the will with contingent goodness. Again, the changeable context fixes the moral species. In itself, giving alms is good, but when done for the sake of vainglory it becomes evil because it is ordained to an evil end (*ST* 1–11.19.7.2; 20.1). Circumstances can work a similar effect, but again only on actions already good with respect to their ends. Returning a weapon kept safe for a friend, an action whose generic goodness is equivalent to promise keeping, can be vitiated if, in the meantime, the friend becomes insane with rage or overcome with evil intentions. Returning the weapon in these circumstances would not be proportionate to the distant end of promise-keeping: to give him and others their just due.[4] Indeed, injury would be the most likely result (*ST* 11–11.57.2.1; cf. *ST* 11–11.110.3.5). Because the circumstances effect this loss of utility with respect to the end they change the moral species of the generically good means in this instance. Thus Aquinas writes, "since the goodness of acts consists in their utility to the end, nothing hinders their being called good or bad according to their proportion to extrinsic things that are adjacent to them" (*ST* 1–11.7.2.1). In short, because of the contingent circumstances of action, it is possible to will that which "is good in itself, under a species of evil" (*ST* 1–11.19.7.2) and to find "one action . . . in several, even disparate moral species" (*ST* 1–11.18.10.3; cf. *ST* 1–11.20.6).[5]

It is important to note that the contingent goodness of the will's objects is apparent, above all, to the virtuous. They will regard a potential object of the will as a good reason for action in relation to some ends and circumstances but not in relation to others, while more often than not those without virtue resist this kind of flexibility. The temperate, for instance, can say that a particular pleasure, a cool glass of beer, is

---

[4] Aquinas writes: "Now, everything that is directed to an end should be proportionate to that end. But acts are made proportionate to an end by means of a certain commensurateness, which results from the due circumstances" (*ST* 1–11.7.2).

[5] This, of course, does not apply to an action necessarily at odds with right reason and therefore evil *secundum suam speciem*. Thus, for example, while "to kill another" may be rendered good by intention and circumstance, no equivalent transformation is possible for "to murder another." Lying is the odd exception. One expects Aquinas to regard deception and truth-telling as indifferent in moral species and good – unjust deception or unjust withholding of the truth – as evil by definition. Instead he dissolves the distinction between natural and moral species, *defines* lying as the will to tell an untruth with the intent to deceive (*ST* 11–11.110.1), and insists that lying remains evil in its species (*ST* 11–11.110.3). Moral contortions follow. On this account, deceiving the wicked in order to protect the weak is a sin and cannot be praised or encouraged. Aquinas states this conclusion plainly, and yet throughout, one gets the impression that he resists (*ibid.*). Thus he is forced to insist that when the deception is officious and the good of the neighbor intended, the sin is venial, not mortal (*ST* 11–11.110.4). What explains this anomaly? A guess: Aquinas finds he cannot get around Augustine's authoritative treatments in *De Mendacio* and *Contra Mendacium*, which he refers to repeatedly.

a good that can be chosen as a means to a particular end, such as slaking one's thirst, in some circumstances (in the solitary quiet of one's home at the end of a long hot day), while altogether failing as a good object of choice in others (just before driving a car full of children to the zoo). The continent, on the other hand, consider a cool glass of beer a good object of choice in *both* circumstances but nevertheless act as the virtuous do, pursuing this good in the first circumstance but not in the second, and only because the second circumstance presents some other good (safety for the children) that, in this instance, trumps the goodness of slaking thirst with cool beer. Here there is no real contingency of goodness. For the continent, the world contains a multiplicity of objects each of which remain good and desirable even as they are chosen against. By contrast, regarding this or that sensible pleasure as a contingent good is central to what it means to be temperate. As John McDowell puts it, the principle mark of the virtuous is their ability to consider an object good in one setting while silencing its goodness in another.[6]

Michael Slote objects to this treatment of the contingency of the good shared by Aquinas and McDowell on the grounds that it cannot account for the response of the virtuous when it happens that they act against their virtue and achieve some ill-gotten advantage such as wealth or power. In a cool hour of remorse, they will refuse to profit from their unjust gain, choosing instead to return the money or transfer the power to others more deserving. Since they would act so as not to benefit from the good achieved in their wrong doing, what reason do we have for thinking that the virtuous believe they have lost no good, sacrificed no benefit or advantage, when they *do* act according to their virtue?[7] None, says Slote, and consequently we have no grounds for thinking that the good is contingent or that the virtuous silence the goodness of certain objects in certain settings. Rather, the will's objects possess a determinate goodness, and the virtuous are those who see the goodness of a particular object as a reason for action in one setting, while denying that this same goodness is a sufficient reason for action in another setting. "It is one thing," Slote concludes, "not to be thinking of something as good, another to be prepared to *deny* [his emphasis] that it is good, and we need not regard the virtuous as having the latter tendency."[8]

The trouble with this view, as Aquinas would surely point out, is that Slote has described the actions of the virtuous in a way that makes them

[6] McDowell (1979). For similar views see McDowell (1978). Like Aquinas, McDowell is indebted to Aristotle in these matters.   [7] Slote (1983, 109–117).   [8] *Ibid.*, 116.

indistinguishable from the continent. The confusion is telling, for Aquinas is able to distinguish virtuous and continent action only insofar as he distinguishes general and particular judgments about the good and general and particular states of the will, and it is precisely these distinctions that address Slote's worries about the contingency of the good.

The argument runs this way. Both the temperate and the merely continent discern (*intellectus*) the general goodness of a cool glass of beer. Both will this good simply and absolutely (*voluntas*). However, they differ in the conclusions of counsel (*concilium*), in their judgments about this good as a particular object of choice (*electio*) across a range of particular circumstances. The continent consider a cool glass of beer a good object of choice in circumstances that the virtuous do not. Distinguishing them in this way enables Aquinas to incorporate Slote's insight without collapsing the distinction between the continent and the temperate. The temperate neither deny the general goodness of a cool glass of beer, nor doubt its ability to slake thirst. Moreover, its general goodness and specific utility remain even when the circumstances rule against its goodness in a particular instance. Without fear of inconsistency they can admit that, all things considered, a cool glass of beer on a hot day is a good to which the intellect can assent and the will desire simply, while at the same time denying that it is a good object of choice in every instance. Similarly, if it happens that the temperate act against their virtue, open a bottle of beer, take a few sips, and then realize the circumstances strike against its goodness in this instance, we do not have to conclude that they will then empty the bottle in a sink. Reestablished in virtue, their new judgment that drinking beer would not be good in *this* instance does nothing to diminish their judgment about the general goodness of cold beer or alter their simple and general desire for it as the day warms. Their *velleity* – the general disposition of their will – toward it remains positive, such that if circumstances were different they would will to have it in both general and particular (*ST* I–II.13.5). And their positive velleity should be sufficient to account for their subsequent actions, where they seek out particular circumstances that will make the cold beer a particular good – arrange for another driver, give the beer to a friend, save it for later, and so on.

Of course, some might object that nothing of importance turns on the ability to distinguish virtue and continence. To this objection the reply is at least two-fold. First, the distinction is an ordinary feature of our moral world, and thus we can expect moral inquiries to acknowledge and explain it. If zoologists can be faulted for failing to distinguish reptiles from amphibians, so too moralists should be called to account for their inability to note that the moral world bears this distinction. Second, if the virtuous are collapsed into the continent, then we will not be able to account for what we most admire in the morally mature: their ability to move from perception to action without threats or coercion, legal or otherwise. For of course, in those instances when the praiseworthy course yields disappointment or tragedy, continence is mustered only as external force bears down.

Despite these differences that divide Slote from Aquinas, the insight that an object's goodness has a certain permanence helps us describe Aquinas's account of its contingency more precisely. Indeed, there is a sense in which an object's goodness is permanent and it is for this reason that the will desires it simply and absolutely. On the other hand, insofar as an object's goodness falls short of perfection it can be silenced by the virtuous in particular instances, and in this sense its goodness *is* contingent. In instances of this sort the object remains good in general but not in particular, and failure to silence its particular goodness – either because it is intended as an end or willed as a means – entails willing an object that is good generally under a species of evil.

3.

But how is this variable goodness of the will's objects chance-like and thus out of our control? How is it not simply conditional, but fully contingent? Two contemporary suggestions should be dismissed straight away. Bernard Williams argues that in some instances an action we might consider evil on account of its unjust means can be justified retrospectively by its success, by its ability to achieve an exceedingly good end. And, of course, whether an action succeeds or fails is, at least in part, determined by the twists and turns of fortune.[9]

Consider his now famous example. A struggling painter, call him Gauguin, abandons his wife and children for a life in Tahiti and the chance to realize his artistic genius. Most would concede that the end is noble and good, the means callous and corrupt. Williams, by contrast, insists that this judgment about the means must be provisional and that in fact we don't know how to judge Gauguin's actions until we learn of his success or failure as an artist. If he succeeds magnificently and produces many works of great genius, then according to Williams it

---

[9] Williams (1981b).

makes little sense for Gauguin (and perhaps for us) to admit that abandoning his family for the sake of his art was unjust.[10]

Why? Well, not for the standard utilitarian reasons we might expect. Williams admits that the well-known problems with utilitarian arguments cannot be resolved. Utilitarians must be able to say how one outcome is better than another by appealing to a common currency between them, and this demand, Williams concedes, cannot be fulfilled given the fundamental diversity of goods we recognize.[11] So he tries another tack. Gauguin's actions should be judged by the relative influence of success or failure upon his life and character. If he succeeds, he will have transformed himself into an artistic genius, and "his standpoint of assessment will be from a life which then derives an important part of its significance for him from that very fact."[12] From this standpoint, how could he fail to judge his actions good? If, on the other hand, he does not succeed, this stand-point will be unavailable. His sense of what is significant about his life will not have changed, and thus remorse will attach to his decision, not warrants. In both cases, the outcome determines what he has done and settles his judgment about the good or evil of the action as a whole. An overwhelmingly good outcome retrospectively transforms an evil means into good. Of course, he might fail, and success and failure here have much to do with matters beyond his control. His ship might wreck, the islanders might refuse to pose, he might catch a tropical fever and perish, and so on. Or it may turn out that his paintings are common, not ground-breaking. In short, misfortune might defeat his effort to transform himself. In that event he must say that what he did was insupportable, if only because he could have been justified only by the great art he had hoped to produce, the great artist he had hoped to become, and those hopes are not just negated, but refuted, by what happened.[13]

The argument draws upon the ambiguity within our own moral sentiments about Gauguin, his life, and his work. On the one hand we praise his paintings and find it difficult to say that it would have been better if he had remained in France and failed to realize his genius. On the other, we know that if his artistic exile in the South Seas had ended in failure we would not have his paintings to quiet our contempt for his actions. For us, only his success blunts our willingness to blame, and this

---

[10] Although Williams admits that Gauguin may not be able to justify his actions to everyone, particularly to his family. *Ibid.*, 23.

[11] *Ibid.*, 24. For the best account of this inability see Taylor (1982, 129–144).

[12] Williams (1981b, 35–36).   [13] *Ibid.*, 27.

seems to warrant Williams's view. Still, we might wonder whether we need to resort to a view that makes moral goodness dependent upon luck in order to account for this ambiguity.

Aquinas insists that we need not. The goodness of a particular means that is already fixed in its moral species cannot have its moral status transformed retrospectively by the success or failure of the action. If we have determined that a particular means is vicious, then its success in achieving some praiseworthy end has no effect upon its moral status or upon the moral status of the action as a whole. If I thieve in order to give alms, the success of my beneficence can do nothing to make the means good. Theft is an action that is "evil in its species . . . because it has an object in discord with reason . . . to appropriate another's property" (*ST* I–II.18.5.2). Nevertheless, we will undoubtedly praise my desire to help the poor, and if my efforts end the destitution of some, nothing prevents us from saying that good was accomplished despite the viciousness of the means. And this moral difference between ends and means seems to be sufficient to account for our conflicting moral sentiments.

If the actual success or failure of an action cannot create an avenue for the influence of fortune upon the moral status of the means and thereby account for its contingent goodness, then perhaps its accidental consequences can. This is Thomas Nagel's view. Nagel argues that if I drive recklessly, the substance of the action, and thus its moral species, changes if I accidentally run down a pedestrian instead of getting home without incident. The accidental consequences of my negligence work themselves into the action itself and specify its character. Now it is manslaughter, which we condemn with greater force than we do negligence and yet only misfortune divides them.[14] Yet by Aquinas's lights accidental consequences of this sort cannot work themselves into the substance of the action. Misfortune of this kind cannot specify what is done, as Nagel would have it, precisely because an accidental consequence does not "regard a special order of reason" (*ST* I–II.18.11), and therefore the harm that results "is connected with the sin accidentally" (*ST* I–II.73.8). That is, we can reasonably characterize what I did without referring to the accident. I drove negligently, and nothing about my driving in this manner directly bears on my chance meeting with the pedestrian. In fact, nothing that I can possibly do bears on my chance meeting, for insofar as it is a chance occurrence it can be neither predicted nor controlled.

---

[14] Nagel (1979, 25).

Of course, Aquinas insists that when accidental consequences of a sinful action are harmful, the agent is responsible for them "on account of his neglecting to consider the harm that might ensue" (*ST* i–ii.73.8). I am responsible for this death, because it is always possible for pedestrians to cross my path, and I am obliged to know that when I drive recklessly I cannot easily avoid them. But the fact that I am responsible for the accidental consequences of my action does not mean that they determine the moral status of what I have done. It simply means that my negligence expands the range of my responsibility.

Nor does Aquinas believe that the moral status of indifferent means can be fixed by the good or evil consequences of an action; nor can they "make an action that was evil, to be good," or "one that was good to be evil" (*ST* i–ii.20.5, *sed contra* not denied). The reason is simple. Strictly speaking, consequences are always accidents of the action itself, outside of what the agent intends as an end and wills as a means, and as such they cannot be included in our description of what the agent has done. Nevertheless, Aquinas admits that there are some consequences that "follow from the nature of the action, and in the majority of cases," (*per se sequitur ex tali actu, et ut in pluribus*) and these can increase the goodness or malice of the action. Why? Because "an action is specifically better, if better results can follow from it; and specifically worse, if it is of a nature to produce worse results" (*ST* i–ii.20.5). Consider scandal.

Scandal occurs when something said or done causes another to sin and can arise either directly or accidentally (*ST* ii–ii.43.1 and ad 4): directly, when one intends to lead another to sin, accidentally when one does not. Here we might expect Aquinas to conclude that accidental scandal leaves the goodness of the precipitating action unaffected, but he does not. Instead he insists that some actions are of "such a nature as to lead another into sin." He has in mind vicious deeds executed in public, or at the very least, public deeds that give the appearance of viciousness. In either case, the action "affords an occasion of another's spiritual downfall," not by intention, but rather by its public nature (*ST* ii–ii.43.1.4). The occasion for scandal is a *per se* consequence of public sin, not an accident, at least not strictly speaking, but rather an outcome that follows from the nature of the action itself.

It follows that, as Aquinas characterizes them, neither simple accidental consequences, nor *per se* consequences can act as an avenue for the influence of fortune upon the moral status of human acts. If a consequence is a simple accident, then it is not a part of the substance of the act and as such cannot affect its goodness. If it is a *per se* consequence, then it affects the moral goodness of the act in every instance; thereby excluding the influence of fortune by the necessity of its connection to the act itself.

Where then should we look for fortune's influence upon the goodness of the will's objects? And note, this influence *must* be found if I am to defend my two-part thesis: that Aquinas considers the good contingent, and that he regards coping with contingency to be the proper work of the virtues.

I suggest we look to the circumstances of an action. We have already noted that the circumstances create the field in which actions reside, choice works, and goodness is determined. If we assume the ends are good, then both generically good and naturally indifferent means have their moral species fixed by the circumstances in which they reside. This happens in two ways. First, since the means are good only insofar as they achieve a given end, what Aquinas calls their "utility to the end" (*utiles ad finem*), they are judged "good or bad according to their proportion to extrinsic things that are adjacent to them" (*ST* I–II.7.2.1). That is, the due circumstances of the act determine whether the means are usefully proportionate to the end (*ST* I–II.7.2). Jogging is a good means to improve my health, at least in part, only if it can, all things being equal, in fact improve my health, and success is possible only if the circumstances are of a certain sort – if the air pollution is not at harmful levels, if packs of ferocious dogs do not roam the park where I run, if the weather conditions are not too extreme, and so on.[15]

But, of course, success does not exhaust the goodness of the means. An effective means can be evil, and here again circumstances are the determining factors. Pawning an antique vase is an effective means to get some cash, but if the vase belongs to another, then the circumstance "what" can be considered "a principal condition of the object that determines the action's species" (*ST* I–II.18.10). ("In what did the act consist" [*ST* I–II.7.4]? Taking what belongs to another, of course.) Because of this circumstance, which now is no longer a proper circumstance because it is no longer an accident added to the object that specifies the action but a condition of the object itself, the goodness of the action, or its lack, is determined (*ST* I–II.18.10.2). The action is theft: taking what rightly belongs to another.

---

[15] The caveat is necessary because, of course, it may happen that jogging is in fact, all things being equal, an effective means for me to achieve health, but ineffective today when I am flattened to the sidewalk by a falling baby grand that slips from the hands of movers above. Chance accidents of this sort are not circumstances which affect the goodness of the chosen means because "their uncertainty and infinity" make it impossible for an agent to consider them in her deliberations (*ST* I–II.7.2.1).

These relations between the goodness of the means and its circumstances make deliberation a matter of determining how a means and its circumstances fit together. A good fit makes the means good, and thus deliberation seeks to determine what means in fact fit the circumstances or how the circumstances can be adapted to fit the favored means. The act of choice, then, is a matter of bringing a specific action, both means and end, across the path of a certain set of circumstances. If deliberation provides sound judgments about the fit between means and circumstances, then the goodness of the means that results from their coincidence is determined by choice and not fortune. The example Aristotle uses to distinguish fortune and choice portrays the point well.[16] The agent who determines the goodness of the means by choosing to act in some circumstances and not others is like the master who sends a young servant to market, knowing that the lad will meet his debtor there. Their encounter, and the good that follows from it (the return of his property), like the encounter of means and circumstances, is not governed by fortune, but by providential choice.

But fortune changes circumstances. Imagine you decide to fulfill the love commandment by giving alms, ten dollars a week to the blind man who sits at the corner. The circumstances are right. They make the means effective and they do nothing to place the action in an evil moral species. But then one evening a comet traverses the sky, and a friend, who is just then crossing the street, glances up to watch its progress. Transfixed, she misses the open manhole in front of her and drops thirty feet into the ooze. With both legs broken, hospitalized and in traction, she needs you at her bedside. Is now the right time to dash across town and give alms? The blind man counts on your donation on this day at a regular time, but how can you abandon your friend in her hour of need? And what amount should you give now that your friend's financial needs are rapidly depleting your resources? Would ten dollars be too liberal? Later that day a letter arrives, an anonymous note with word that the blind man has ties to a local street gang that has been terrorizing the neighborhood. Assuming the truth of this report, does the love commandment require giving alms to *this* man?

If your friend's injury grieves you so that you cannot attend to these

---

[16] The example is Aristotle's (*Ph.*196b33–197a5), although we have already seen that Aquinas puts it to his own use in order to argue that creation viewed from the heights of Providence excludes chance (*ST* 1.116.1). Aquinas considers prudence and Providence analogically related notions. Both cause occurrences in the world by choice, and thus both can be opposed to accidental coincidence.

changes and you continue to act as before, then your action meets a set of circumstances that you neither consider nor control and that change as fortune does. The goodness of the means is now conditioned, at least in part, by fortune and not by choice.[17] Of course, caution is required here. Fortune cannot determine the goodness of the chosen means independently and exhaustively, for this would indicate that the means were not chosen at all. Recall that the goodness of the means is not only conditioned by the circumstances that fortune commands, but also by the end that precipitates choice. It follows that a means whose goodness is entirely determined by fortune is impossible, for this would imply that it had not been chosen for the sake of some intended end. Nevertheless, when the means is chosen without due attention to its circumstances, either because of sorrow or some other disturbance, a significant measure of its goodness is conditioned by fortune and not choice. In this instance, it is as if the servant and the debtor meet at the market on separate errands quite apart from the direction of the master's choice, and where the good or evil that results is caused, at least in part, by fortune.[18]

If, on the other hand, your sorrow is moderate and you are able to consider whether it remains appropriate to give alms in these new circumstances, then you face a task that Aquinas considers difficult. It is difficult because the circumstances are many, and they change frequently on account of numerous causes that you neither control nor know with ease (*ST* I–II.14.6). When circumstances change in this fluid and chance-like manner our knowledge of them is uncertain, and when this uncertainty is united with the fact that in most instances there are many potential means to a given end, a situation is created where the context of choice is diverse and complex and the goodness of any potential means doubtful and uncertain (*ST* I–II.14.4). In Aquinas's language of virtue and difficulty, choosing a good course of action is arduous because its goodness is contingent, and it is contingent precisely because "actions are about things singular and contingent" (*actiones sunt circa contingentia singularia*) (*ST* I–II.14.3).

---

[17] Notice the unity of virtue and agency in this example. The goodness of the means is determined by fortune and not by choice because sorrow makes it difficult to give due attention to the circumstances of choice. Sorrow is able to work this distraction because it too is contingent. Its contingency follows from the union of imperfect temperance with the chance meeting of a loved one and an open manhole.

[18] Of course, the moral character of the means is one thing, responsibility for that character another. The person who ignores the influence of fortune on the moral status of what is chosen can, in some instances, be charged with negligence.

Since the good is contingent and therefore difficult to know and choose with constancy, choosing merely apparent goods is always a possibility and thus moral failure haunts choice (*ST* I–II.18.4.1; 19.1.1). Giving alms does have some measure of goodness, insofar as it is a means of loving one's neighbor, but not a full measure, and thus its moral status depends upon a proper fit with its circumstances. But circumstances are complex and variable, and thus difficult to know well. This in turn can bring us to choose to give alms in circumstances that work against its goodness. Notice, there are two different levels of difficulty here. Some agents know that giving alms with the right intention in the standard circumstances will in fact fulfill the love commandment. For them the difficulty is in determining whether the circumstances are standard or not. Others, call them the inexperienced, do not know what means will normally achieve this end. For them, there is the added difficulty of determining what means are effective in the standard circumstances, a task made more difficult by the contingency of those circumstances.

Difficulty is added to difficulty by the fact that the contingent circumstances of choice can be described in various ways. This creates diverse perspectives from which to judge the goodness of a particular course of action. And since the point of view created by a particular description of the circumstances of choice is dependent upon regarding some goods as ends worth pursuing and not others, the difficulty in choice is not simply a matter of determining the best description of the circumstances and matching it with potential means, but also a matter of determining which ends are best to pursue in this or that context. This not only makes the work of choice a holistic effort, where the means chosen, the ends desired, and the description of the circumstances are all revised in relation to each other, but it also increases the difficulty of the labor. For ends are diverse and often conflict and consequently an action that is a good means when judged from the point of view established by one end may be evil when viewed from the perspective established by another. For Aquinas, this is perfectly ordinary, for "a thing may be considered in various ways by the reason, so as to appear good from one point of view, and not good from another point of view" (*Contingit autem aliquid a ratione considerari diversimode, ita quod sub una ratione est bonum, et secundum aliam rationem non bonum*) (*ST* I–II.19.10). Thus, for example, while a magistrate may consider it good to execute a thief because this punishment in this instance serves the ends of civic justice, the thief's wife and son will not, precisely because death (quite obviously) prevents them from achieving some significant goods of the family (*ST* i–ii.19.10).

Aquinas does not believe, however, that moral conflicts of this sort are intractable. Nor does he consider them unavoidable consequences of the diversity of human ends. If different ends generate conflicting judgments about the goodness of a particular action, the judgment that follows from the end with the greatest connection to the common good tracks the truth. For "a man's will is not right in willing a particular good, unless he refer it to the common good as an end" (*ST* i–ii.19.10). For this reason we should prefer the judgments of the magistrate who is, we assume, attentive to the common good. By the same token, we should be able to say what the wife and son can desire justly. On the one hand, they should desire, simply and absolutely, that justice be done within their political community. They should, therefore, consent to the judge's intention to serve justice in this instance by putting the thief to death. On the other, they should desire, simply and absolutely, the thief's life and their friendship with him. They should, therefore, wish to avoid the impending natural evil, the death of a loved one. Moreover, since willing a good simply and absolutely is a different matter from intending a good as an end in a particular instance, their general desire for these goods of the family should not abate simply because they consent to the judge's intention.

But note, this solution leaves untouched the potential for moral conflict in particular circumstances of choice, and I suspect Aquinas understands this. He gives us no reason to assume that the potential for conflict among diverse goods dissolves once we recognize the moral significance of the common good. Difficult deliberations remain, largely because the complex list of ends that we judge good and will simply remains unmodified. He does not simplify, he does not reject altogether the private good of the family, or any other human good for that matter, and thus he retains the possibility that "various wills of various men can be good in respect of opposite things" on account of the various ends they are generally justified in considering good (*ST* i–ii.19.10).[19] What he does reject is the belief that there is no way, in principle, to resolve the conflicting evaluations of an action that arise from different points of view established by willing different goods as ends. Ends that serve the common good and means that achieve them always trump those that do not. Still, this does little to ease the difficulty associated with the diversity

19 On simplification as a strategy for reducing the potential for conflict among ends see Nussbaum (1986, 51–82).

of ends, since most have contingent and complex relations to the common good. Ends that appear to serve strictly private purposes may also serve the common weal in various ways, and in fact, for Aquinas, they must, since he believes that every good as such must contribute to the common good in some way. Consequently, we should not think that Aquinas's emphasis upon the common good provides easy solutions to moral conflicts of this kind. Rather, we should regard his remarks about the common good as an attempt to note that the contingency of goodness generates a distinctive kind of difficulty at the juncture of public and private aims.[20] Consider again the thief's family.

Their happiness is diminished even if they consent to the end intended by the magistrate. Why? Because they are able to perceive good in both public justice and private friendship. As such, they are able to judge the punishment of their beloved as both a particular good, insofar as it serves the common weal, and as a natural evil, insofar as it undermines the goods of the family. Misery follows precisely because their just intention prevents them from achieving the private good that they continue to will simply. No doubt, this outcome may lead them to believe that they are tragic figures, victims of circumstances where no course of action can be chosen without leaving some binding obligation unfulfilled. Aquinas, however, considers this conclusion mistaken, and for two related reasons. On the one hand, his insistence that moral goodness increases with proximity to the common good indicates that he considers strong moral conflicts of this sort impossible. On the other hand, his insistence that the good is contingent implies that, at least in this instance, intending a course of action that serves the good of the family is to will something that is good simply and absolutely under a species of evil. That is, Aquinas rejects the notion of strong moral conflict because every moral dilemma has a solution, and solutions are available – even in instances where every choice leaves some good sabotaged – precisely because the good is contingent and can be silenced.[21]

If this is correct, then it indicates that Aquinas does not consider the difficulty created by the contingent nature of the good a cognitive matter alone. It is also an appetitive difficulty. Determining what good ought to be intended or chosen in this or that instance is one matter. Silencing the good that is not intended or chosen by willing in a manner that recognizes its diminished desirability in some particular instance is another matter

---

[20] On this point Aquinas and Williams agree. See Williams (1981a, 81–82).
[21] My understanding of Aquinas on moral tragedy is indebted to MacIntyre's discussion (1988b, 185–188).

still. Moral conflicts are resolved only when the will responds with this kind of recognition, and only those with rational appetites of sufficient complexity succeed here. They must be able to will a good simply and absolutely at all times while refusing to intend it in some instances. At the same time they must be able to intend some other end that is strictly at odds with goods they will simply and absolutely. Consequently, if the wife and son of the thief think that they face a strong moral conflict it is precisely because their desires lack this subtlety. It is because they continue to consider the thief's life a good that ought to be intended and pursued even as they consent to the judge's desire to intend and pursue the public good. If their mistake has a moral, it is this: although the good is contingent, acknowledging that fact in particular instances with particular acts of the will – by silencing its goodness in some instances and not others – is difficult. Indeed, for Aquinas, it is the kind of difficulty that cannot be overcome without the assistance of moral virtues.

4.

If the contingency of the good and the uncertainty in choice that contingency creates are the difficulties that prudence and justice must solve, then we should not be surprised to find Aquinas describing these virtues by referring to these difficulties. Moreover, we should not be surprised to find him speaking of prudence and justice by referring to their work, describing their work in terms of steadfastness in the face of change, and casting the vices opposed to these virtues in terms of withdrawal from the contingent and therefore difficult good.

"Prudence is right reason applied to action," and has three acts: taking counsel about the means, making judgments about the conclusions of counsel's inquiry, and command, which "consists in applying to action the things counseled and judged" (*ST* II–II.47.8; cf. 47.10). Aquinas argues that command (*imperare*) is the principal act of prudence, since it brings the first two acts to their proper conclusion in a completed human action (*ST* II–II 47.8). Nonetheless, the chief work of prudence, its function, is counsel. Citing Aristotle (*EN* 1141b8–10) Aquinas says, "the work of prudence is to take good counsel" (*opus prudentis est esse bene consiliativum*) (*ST* II–II.49.5). Taking counsel is the "work of reason" (*opus rationis*), "a research proceeding from certain things to others" (*ST* II–II.49.5), from generals that are known (that it is good to give alms) to particulars that are not (whether giving alms in *this* particular context is good) (*ST* II–II.47.3; 49.5.2). An inquiry of this sort is needed when uncertainty arises about the goodness of a course of action that could serve as a means to an end in a particular circumstance (*ST* i–ii.14.4). And we have seen that uncertainty about the goodness of an action follows from the fact that "the means to the end, in human concerns, far from being fixed, are of manifold variety" (*ST* ii–ii.47.15), and because the circumstances in which choice occurs have an "infinite number of singulars" that affect the goodness of these manifold means (*ST* ii–ii.47.3.2). In Aquinas's shorthand, counsel, the work of prudence, is needed because human "actions are concerned with contingent singulars, which by reason of their vicissitude, are uncertain" (*ST* i–ii.14.1; cf. ii–ii.51.1.obj.2, not denied).

This uncertainty means that reason cannot pronounce judgment without an inquiry that is at times arduous. Indeed, taking "several conditions or circumstances into consideration . . . is not easy" precisely because "counsel is concerned properly speaking, with contingent singulars" (*ST* i–ii.14.3). In fact, Aquinas contends that the prudent, like the courageous, pursue the work of virtue fearfully; not because they always labor under external threats (although at times they do), but rather because they fear choosing a merely apparent good when "human reason is unable to grasp the singular and contingent things which may occur" (*ST* ii–ii.52.1.1). If excessive, this fear can make those who take counsel to withdraw from their labors. If moderate, it can sharpen their attention and make them deliberate with greater care (*ST* i–ii.44.2).

When we consider the integral parts of prudence we find that those belonging to counsel, the principal *opus prudentis*, help keep it steadfast in the good in various ways. Reason (*ratio*) determines whether a given end can be achieved by this or that means given the many contingent singulars in the circumstance of choice that make the relation between ends and means, universals and particulars, difficult to determine. Making the right determination normally requires slow and careful research, and reason acts accordingly (*ST* ii–ii.49.5). But of course, it is often the case that "something has to be done without warning," and then slow and careful deliberation is impossible. Thus another part of counsel is needed, shrewdness (*solertia*), which is the ability to revise one's judgments about the appropriate means to a given end, quickly and with ease, when faced with sudden changes in the circumstances of choice (*ST* ii–ii.49.4). Aquinas refers to it as *bona coniecturatio*, which Josef Pieper aptly interprets as "nimbleness in response to new situations."[22] How-

---

[22] Pieper (1959, 34–35).

ever it is named, nimbleness of this sort is needed only because the effectiveness of a means, and thus its specific goodness, can change as quickly as the circumstances in which it is embedded.

Shrewdness, however, is similar to precipitation (*praecipitatio*), a vice opposed to prudence (*ST* II–II.53.3), and they are not easily distinguished. Precipitation is rash and impulsive deliberation that ignores the fact that "many things have to be considered in the research of reason" (*ST* II–II.53.3.3). Precipitous counsel fails to be steadfast in the difficult work of sorting through the many contingent singulars that make up the circumstances of choice. Instead, it rushes quickly to a conclusion without knowing that "one should be slow in taking counsel" when the circumstances demand it (*ST* II–II.53.3.3). What then distinguishes the vice from the virtue? The answer comes when we notice that shrewdness works well, and counsel perseveres in mapping the details of the circumstances of choice, only when accompanied by sufficient experience with similar circumstances. Experience helps us recognize resemblances between circumstances and perceive patterns among the infinite number of contingent singulars that constitute them, and this in turn helps reduce the uncertainty and difficulty of our deliberations (*ST* II–II.47.3.2).[23] The experienced do not see new circumstances as entirely new, and this helps them know which contingent singulars to observe and which to ignore. Thus it is experience that makes the shrewd tarry over those contingent singulars that the precipitous hurry past. And since experience becomes useful only when it is remembered, Aquinas maintains that memory is the part of prudence that makes it possible for all the other parts to work well (*ST* II–II.49.1).

Unfortunately, our experience of the contingent matters of action that counsel must consider is by definition incomplete, for

such matters are of infinite variety, [and] no one man can consider them all sufficiently; nor can this be done quickly, for it requires a length of time. Hence in matters of prudence man stands in very great need of being taught by others, especially old folk who have acquired a sane understanding of the ends in practical matters. (*ST* II–II.49.3)

That is, self-sufficiency in counsel is neither desirable nor possible for it diminishes the experience we need and as a result undermines good inquiry. Since "it is a mark of docility [*docilitas*] to be ready to be

---

[23] Thus Aquinas writes, "though the number of possible circumstances be infinite, the number of actual circumstances is not; and the judgment of reason in matters of action is influenced by things which are few in number" (*ST* II–II.49.7.1). Experience divides the actual from the possible.

taught," to seek and accept good advice, Aquinas regards it a part of prudence as well (*ST* II–II.49.3). He praises friendship for similar reasons: "in contingent particular cases, in order that anything be known for certain, it is necessary to take several conditions or circumstances into consideration, which is not easy for one to consider, but are considered by several with greater certainty, since what one takes note of, escapes the notice of another" (*ST* I–II.14.3).

Notice how these last three parts of prudence provide functional justification for two assertions that have troubled exegetes, both friend and foe: that common goods trump private goods, and that the judgments of the wise provide the principle measure of virtuous action *quoad nos*. If the prudent cannot do the difficult work of coping with the contingent singulars that make up the circumstances of choice without drawing on the experience of prudent friends, then life in the company of others who share common ends and confront similar contingencies is a prerequisite for prudence. From this it follows that the welfare of this common life, this company of friends, must be a greater good than the good of any one member; for the good of any one member depends upon the excellent exercise of his or her practical reason, and such excellence cannot be had apart from this company of friends. In short, the difficulty of practical deliberation given the contingency of the human good binds us together in a common need, which in turn warrants the priority of the common good (*ST* I–II.19.10; 100.8).

Similarly, because it is singular and contingent, the good cannot be captured in a simple set of rules that could serve as the standard of virtuous action, and even if there were such rules there would be no rules for applying them in contingent and singular circumstances. Consequently, there is no substitute for prudential judgment, no procedure for discovering the good apart from its labors, no standard of concrete goodness in human action that we know apart from the judgments of right reason (*ST* I–II.18.5). And, since a rich reservoir of experience is needed to judge well, and since it is the wise who possess such experience and use it well, their judgments quite naturally become the standard of good and praiseworthy human action for us in this life (*ST* I–II.2.1.1; 100.1,3; II–II.47.5.obj.1, not denied; 49.3 and ad 3; 52.1.1).[24]

When we turn to Aquinas's treatment of the parts of prudence that belong to its other acts we find that each assists the principal *opus prudentis*.

---

[24] The caveat is important. The conclusion bears only on our access to justified beliefs about the good. It does not imply that reason is autonomous, its own measure with respect to the truth of moral judgments. This distinction Aquinas reserves for God's eternal law.

Each provides counsel with some necessary and unique ability to cope with the contingent and singular circumstances of choice and the contingent and uncertain goodness of the means. For example, command, the third act of prudence, has three parts, and each encourage the prudent to cast a skeptical eye upon counsel's uncertain conclusions. This in turn helps the prudent avoid those contingent circumstances that may ambush the means, undermine its goodness, and make it unsuitable to command.[25]

First is foresight (*providentia*), which bears on "the contingent matters of actions which can be done by man for an end." It ranks first because its "proper work is to set [the means] in due order to the end," which is the work of prudence generally and the task that calls for the distinct work of its parts (*ST* II–II.49.6). It is distinguished from the other parts by the attention it gives to the foreseeable uncertainties that can disrupt action, prevent the successful achievement of the end, and thus diminish the goodness of the means (*ST* II–II.47.1; 49.6). If foresight determines that the means that counsel has discovered is not suitable to the end, given this or that collection of foreseeable future contingents, then it will refuse to command the action and return counsel to its work.

Close behind foresight in importance is circumspection (*circumspectio*), which considers whether a means judged good by foresight because it is suitable to the end remains good insofar as it sits in a particular set of circumstances. Circumspection is needed to prevent foresight from commanding a means that is "good in itself and suitable to the end, and nevertheless . . . evil or unsuitable given the contingent circumstances" (*ST* II–II.49.7). Recall that the circumstances of an action can diminish or destroy the goodness of the means in two ways. They can prevent a means from effectively achieving the end, and they can prevent a means from being good despite its effectiveness. Foresight's efforts are needed to cope with the difficulty associated with the first sort of circumstances, while circumspection works upon the second. A judgment about the goodness of the means that has foresight but lacks circumspection has not attended to the totality of the circumstances. Thus, for example, "to show signs of love to someone seems, considered in itself, to be a fitting way to arouse love in his heart, yet if pride or suspicion of flattery arise in his heart, it will no longer be a means suitable to the end. Hence the need of circumspection in prudence: to compare the means with the circumstances" (*ST* II–II.49.7). Showing signs of love will arouse love in

---

[25] The language here is Augustine's (*De trin.* xiv.9), who describes the work of prudence as "the avoidance of ambushes" (*ST* II–II.47.8).

the heart of the beloved, but in some circumstances it also triggers unwelcome passions and beliefs, which in turn diminish the goodness of this otherwise effective means.

Just as foresight is blind without circumspection, circumspection will make mistaken judgments about the relation between a potential means and its circumstances without another part of prudence, caution (*cautio*). Caution is what makes circumspection succeed, if it succeeds at all, for it is concerned with

> contingent matters of action, wherein, even as false is found with true, so is evil mingled with the good, on account of the great variety of these matters of action, wherein good is often hindered by evil, and evil has the appearance of good. Wherefore prudence needs caution, so that we may have such a grasp of good as to avoid evil. (*ST* II–II.49.8)

Caution makes circumspection circumspect in its work. Circumspection moved by caution gives careful and due attention to the contingent circumstances, the "outward hindrances" (*impedimenta extrinseca*), that can undermine the goodness of a means already judged suitable to the end by foresight (*ST* II–II.49.8.2).

Solicitude (*sollicitudo*) is an additional part of the third act of prudence, which Aquinas includes under foresight (*ST* II–II.48.obj.5, not denied). Like foresight, it is concerned with the goodness of the means that follows from success, when various contingencies make judgments about success difficult and uncertain. It "denotes an earnest endeavor to obtain something," and our endeavors must be particularly earnest "when there is fear of failure" on account of some difficulty (*ST* II–II.55.6). Earnest desire and fear of failure combine to make us slow in accepting the judgments of counsel (*ST* II–II.47.9), and thus solicitude provides assistance to foresight that is analogous to the assistance caution provides circumspection. Just as caution causes circumspection to give slow and careful attention to the circumstances that may affect the goodness of means already determined to be effective, solicitude causes foresight to give slow and careful attention to the circumstances that may affect the effectiveness of the means. Solicitude, then, is a kind of diligence.[26] It provides the earnest effort, the steady attention, required to command a means that will successfully achieve the end when various contingencies make success uncertain and difficult. Its opposite, negligence, succumbs to this difficulty, proceeds without this diligence, and

---

[26] "Diligence seems to be the same as solicitude, because the more we love [*diligimus*] a thing the more solicitous we are about it" (*ST* II–II.54.1.1).

thus fails to command a successful means, either by failing to command altogether, or by failing to command a means that will be successful in the given circumstances (*ST* II–II.54.1.3).

If any one picture follows from Aquinas's account of prudence and its parts it is that of a flexible tool for coping with the difficulty presented by the contingency of the human good. Excellence in practical rationality does not make the prudent free of this difficulty, but it does allow them to choose the good with some constancy by making them attend to the relation between a contingently good means and its contingent circumstances. It enables them to "adjust contingencies to other contingencies" in order to seek out the good and remain steadfast in it in spite of its vicissitudes.[27] And this is largely a descriptive skill, a talent for describing and redescribing means, their place in a set of circumstances, and their relation to a given end, all in the hope of finding and preserving their goodness.

Prudence, however, cannot cope with the difficulty posed by the contingency of goodness without justice. The reason is simple. The goodness of the end is as contingent as the means that cause the prudent to take counsel, and for similar reasons. With God as the one exception, every end sits in a set of contingent circumstances and can be ordered to other ends as a means. Consequently nearly every object of the will besides God, both means and ends, can be described as either good or evil, not absolutely of course, but in this or that circumstance and in relation to this or that end. It follows that the goodness of every potential object besides God is potentially open for rational consideration in every circumstance of choice. If prudence is the virtue that describes a means, its circumstances, and the intended end all in order to find and preserve its goodness, and if the goodness of every end besides God is contingent, changing with its circumstances and with its status as a potential means to some other end, then prudence could, in principle, work on every end that comes before it. It could play descriptions off of descriptions and thereby call into question the goodness of every potential end. Obviously, this would make action impossible, for no ends could be assumed and intended and thus there would be no stable principles to guide our deliberation over particular means.

Accordingly, when Aquinas says that deliberation and choice are never about ends but only about means, and that the end is the principle "presupposed in every inquiry," he is simply making a procedural

[27] R. Rorty (1989, 33).

remark about action given the contingent goodness of ends (*ST* I–II.14.2; 13.3). Some ends must be held in place, their goodness assumed and intended, at least for now, before prudent deliberation over the means can proceed. And this must occur not only in individual instances of choice, but also over the course of many such instances. That is, some ends must be judged good, steadfastly willed, and consistently tended to over time if there is to be action at all. This does not mean that the goodness of these ends can never be reconsidered in light of other ends and circumstances, but rather that action is practically feasible only when the nearly infinite list of potential ends is reduced to a standard repertoire. Thus Aquinas writes, "the will from the very nature of the power is inclined to the good of the reason. But because this good is varied in many ways, the will needs to be inclined, by means of a habit, to some fixed good of the reason, in order that action may follow more promptly" (*ST* I–II.50.5.3; cf. *ST* I–II.49.4).

But note, this doesn't get us to justice. If the difficulty is the contingent goodness and the obvious diversity of potential ends, and if the solution is a habit that disposes the will to intend some ends and not others, then any habit will do, even one that disposes the will to vicious ends. Consider the clever rogue, the scheming tyrant, the resourceful swindler. Each appear to possess practical wisdom. They complete the difficult task of discovering the means that will achieve a given end within a particular set of contingent circumstances, and yet their *prudentia carnis* falls short of true prudence insofar as their efforts are directed to ends that are "good not in truth but in appearance" (*ST* II–II.55.3). It follows that our need for justice and its work cannot be a simple matter of fixing the rational appetite on some ends so that deliberation might proceed. For when the will fixes upon a merely apparent good, this procedural problem is solved, and yet Aquinas considers the successful act of deliberation that follows a merely apparent act of prudence.

Some additional difficulty must create the need for justice, and Aquinas's account of *prudentia carnis* points to an answer: if prudence is to function at all, and if it is to assist in the choice of means that are in fact good, then the will must be constantly inclined to true and not apparent goods. In most instances this poses no difficulty. We have already noted that Aquinas finds the rational appetite naturally inclined to will the universal good, and when the practical intellect apprehends some particular good the rational appetite normally wills it with ease. The nature of the rational appetite suffices for its movement, just as the nature of the senses suffice for theirs (*ST* I–II.56.6.1). When confronted with their objects they move to their proper acts with ease. What difficulty do healthy eyes encounter? When an object is before them they see it. Similarly, when a good of reason is presented to the rational appetite it normally desires that good without difficulty. There is, however, one exception, one good that the rational appetite cannot will without difficulty. When presented with our neighbor's good, with the chance of offering him his due with a perpetual will, we often find that we cannot. We often find that we tend to withdraw and will an apparent good instead (*ST* I–II.56.6).[28]

Caution is required here. Some ends we will with difficulty because we have difficulty knowing them as such, and this can happen for two reasons. Some ends can be achieved only by means that are contingent, multiple, and complex, means that are difficult to know with ease. And of course when the means are difficult to know and master, the goodness of the end they achieve may diminish in our eyes. Consider, for example, the difficulty young children have seeing the good in the ends of baseball and chess when compared to the ends of hop-scotch and checkers. Alternatively, we may find it difficult to intend a particular end because we cannot see how it fits together with the other ends we consider good and intend with a constant will. It may conflict with these other ends directly, or it may be so new and strange that wholesale revision of belief and sentiment – a great and difficult effort – is required before its place can be found in the rest of what we know and desire.

Now, it may happen that our neighbor's good is difficult to know confidently and will habitually for either of these reasons, and in this respect it is no different than any other potential end. That is, it may happen that understanding our neighbor well enough to know what good is due him proves so intolerably difficult that we withdraw our will from his welfare altogether. Or we may not know the good that is due him because the activity that we must master in order to secure it is so complex and convoluted that we come to doubt whether any good can come from it. This is James Thurber's view of marriage. On the one hand it is an activity that each of the partners must do well if the good of the other is to be secured, and on the other it is so difficult to master that one comes to doubt whether the good of the other can be secured in it.[29] Or it may happen that we have difficulty knowing and

---

[28] Aquinas also insists that our Divine good "transcends the limits of human nature," and for this reason charity is needed to perfect the will and direct its acts to God (*ST* I–II.56.6).

[29] Thurber (1945).

willing our neighbor's good because it conflicts with everything else we know and will habitually. This is the lesson that every moral reformer knows.

But Aquinas insists that even when we know the content of our neighbor's good and find a place for it within the other ends that we intend (which of course we normally do), we nevertheless will it only with difficulty, and therefore some other explanation is needed. I suggest we return to Aquinas's remarks about courage, to the language of difficulty, contingency, constancy, and withdrawal, for it is in these terms that Aquinas speaks of our relations to our neighbor's good. This should not be surprising. Recall that courage strengthens us to will goods that are difficult precisely because their pursuit endangers other goods that we love. Danger incites fear, and fear makes it difficult for us to intend and pursue the good that we ought with a perpetual will. Fear distorts our judgments about the good, making true and difficult goods appear apparent and apparent goods true. The fallout is that we withdraw from the good that is true and difficult and turn to one that is apparent and easy. All of this is familiar terrain. Recall as well that the *bonum arduum* is normally a requirement of justice (*ST* II–II.123.11.3). The good that elicits fear is the good that is due the neighbor, and it elicits this response because pursuing it normally threatens some other good that we tend to love inordinately: life, wealth, power, pleasure, and so on. This, in turn, explains both our inability to will this good with constancy and our need for the distinctive work of justice.

For Aquinas, then, justice is needed to address two difficulties. First, it is needed because the goodness of the ends that guide deliberation can be doubted if placed in relation to certain other ends and circumstances. Justice copes with this difficulty insofar as it creates a habit in the will that causes us to tend to some ends and not others, which in turn makes "action follow more promptly" (*ST* I–II.50.5.3). And second, it is needed so that our wills might tend to a specific end, the good of our neighbor, which we will with great difficulty and little constancy. Borrowing from Aristotle's definition, he refers to both functions. Aristotle, he notes, refers to justice as a habit in the will that moves us to act knowingly to some ends and not others, and then "mention is made afterwards of its constancy and perpetuity in order to indicate the firmness of the act . . . whereby a man renders to each one his due by a constant and perpetual will" (*ST* II–II.58.1). And of course, constancy is emphasized in the definition precisely because we find the good of another – the end to which justice habitually inclines us – difficult to will.

With these connections between prudence, justice, and difficulty in view, four related observations are worth noting. First, Aquinas's account of our need for justice helps distinguish prudence and its semblances. It helps us see, for example, that *prudentia carnis* is a failure in practical reasonableness, despite appearances to the contrary, precisely because it presupposes a failure to seek the difficult good that justice demands. Indeed, it is practical deliberation that habitually copes with one sort of difficulty – contingency in the circumstances of choice – while bypassing another. Aquinas's discussion of craftiness (*astutia*), another variety of false prudence, falls into place in a similar fashion. The *astutus* deliberate with care and normally achieve the ends they desire, yet the means they employ "are not true but fictitious and counterfeit" (*ST* ii–ii.55.3 and ad 2). They do not necessarily know that their choices are unjust, but they should, and thus even if they act without full knowledge of their failure, they act unjustly (*ST* i–i.6.8; 19.6). And, as Josef Pieper points out, since the just seek the difficult good, the unjust means that the crafty choose will be those that are easy to will.[30] In fact, the crafty fail in practical reasonableness precisely because they seek the path of least resistance when justice calls for a more difficult course. It follows that prudence is not merely the ability to adjust contingencies to other contingencies in the circumstances of choice, it is also the ability to do this difficult work in pursuit of ends that are just, and thus often difficult. For deliberation to be prudent it must cope with difficult contingency, but it must do this while pursuing the difficult good.

Second, when interpreters ignore these connections between virtue and difficulty, they distort Aquinas's treatment of the false virtues. Jean Porter, for instance, insists that Aquinas encourages us to "admire and commend" those with the "seeming virtues" and for two reasons. They have "something of the character of true virtue" and this is better than nothing at all; and their false virtue allows them "to sustain a course of activity," a consistent path to the good, which is better, all things considered, than no course at all. These reasons lead her to conclude that we should consider Nazis with false virtue more admirable, more desirable, than those with no semblances of virtue at all.[31]

This is odd. Most, I suspect, are terrified by the thought of crafty Nazis with solid command of their fears. Most, I suspect, prefer them less capable of harm; real bumblers, genuinely inept, and thoroughly stupefied by fear. This misstep points to two others. Porter's first reason,

---

[30] Pieper (1959, 33).   [31] Porter (1990, 120–122).

the remarks that precede it, and the article she cites (*ST* I–II.65.1) together indicate that she has mistaken false for imperfect virtue. The latter is desirable in the absence of perfect virtue, the former is not. When Aquinas discusses imperfect virtue he refers to the inconsistency and corruptibility of the virtues in this life (*ST* I–II.5.4; 58.4.3; 63.1). Those with imperfect virtues do not always act virtuously. At times they slip into continence, or worse, moral weakness. By contrast, when he discusses the false virtues he refers to those habits that give the appearance of true virtue but are in fact vices in disguise (e.g., ST II–II.55). Her second reason, her defense of consistent human activity of any sort, follows from her interpretation of Aquinas's treatment of the natural law and the basic human good, which we will consider in chapter three. But even before we settle these exegetical differences we can see the trouble with her conclusion. The human good is achieved by consistent human activity, no doubt, but it is activity that acquires its consistency from virtue (*ST* I–II.5.4). And as we have seen the moral virtues are directed to goods that are, for one reason or another, difficult to achieve. This means that in most instances those who possess only semblances of virtue will not only fail to pursue true goods, they will also fail to address the most arduous difficulties. Thus, the Nazi who cleverly manipulates all sorts of contingencies in order to achieve vicious ends not only fails to achieve the good, he also fails to use his practical wisdom to address the truly difficult. Indeed, the pursuit of just and dangerous courses of action (opposing genocidal tyrants, harboring neighbors, eluding the police, etc.) presents difficulties, both affective and cognitive, that far exceed the technical difficulties associated with the pursuit of Nazi terror.

Third, these connections between prudence and justice that Aquinas assumes throughout allow him to answer one of the standard objections lodged against a functional account of the virtues. According to Amelie Rorty, once we highlight the connection between virtue and the strength, between praiseworthy conduct and the need to cope with those difficulties that hinder the achievement of the good, the picture that follows tends to "toxify" the virtues. It tends to equate the virtuous with the "confrontational and combative."[32] Once the virtues are equated with the ability to overcome a contingent and external other, our image of the virtuous naturally drifts from the courageous citizen or the persevering martyr, each of whom face dangers and difficulties in pursuit of the common good, to the Machiavellian prince who exercises

---

[32] A.O. Rorty (1988c, 300).

his *virtu* in order to secure his power against hostile forces from without and within.[33] Soon we confuse the virtuous with the ambitious, the clever, and the strong, those who use their ability to cope with contingency in order to pursue unjust ends or preserve the *status quo* by unjust means. And, as various critics have remarked, once the virtuous are identified with the desire for this sort of power, it is often the case that the powerless – women,[34] racial and ethnic minorities,[35] nature,[36] and so on – are identified with contingency in need of control. A troubling picture indeed.

Even if we can avoid these confusions and detach the images of prince, colonial master, and robber baron from our picture of the virtuous, we are still not out of the woods, for as Rorty points out, we cannot emphasize the functional character of the virtues without assigning them unwelcome "magnetizing and expansionist features."[37] When the virtues are distinguished by strength and labor, then it may happen that the virtuous will be drawn to dangerous and difficult circumstances in order to exercise their powers. They may even create those circumstances, those opportunities![38] Of course, in some instances, these expansionist features may well elicit praiseworthy actions. The liberal, for instance, will be generous not only when the occasion arises, but also in circumstances of their own making. But in others, the result is simply the corruption of the virtues. The courageous, for example, may seek out difficult and dangerous circumstances, not because justice demands it, but because they need an opportunity to exercise their strength. In a similar manner, the prudent may pursue ends that can be attained only after complex and uncertain deliberations, not because they are compelled by justice, but because difficulty and risk excite and attract.

But Aquinas's account of the varieties of false prudence indicates that the work of the virtues is inextricably tied to the pursuit of just aims by just means. False prudence fails to pursue the difficult good that justice demands. The genuinely prudent act with the just among difficulties and dangers. As such, an act of strength and power can be called virtuous only as it seeks justice by coping with the right sorts of contingent events. When the strong and the cunning employ their skill to

---

[33] For a discussion of Machiavellian *virtu* in terms that track the concerns of this work see Pocock (1975, 3–218).   [34] Pitkin (1984, 109–169).   [35] W. Jordan (1977, 3–43).
[36] Merchant (1980).   [37] Rorty (1988c, 301).
[38] Pocock (1975, 167) finds this ambiguity at the heart of Machiavellian *virtu*. On the one hand *virtu* copes with contingencies of various sorts. On the other, it carries human agency into new spheres of life and therefore "lets loose sequences of contingency beyond our prediction or control so that we become prey to *fortuna*."

pursue ends that are difficult and yet unjust, or when they go hero-questing after formidable challenges in alien environments, their actions, by Aquinas's lights, are mere semblances of virtue.

Rorty considers this reply inadequate, a "flick of the wrist solution" that distinguishes putative virtuous actions from bona fide instances of virtue quite arbitrarily, but this complaint is too contemptuous, too hasty.[39] Aquinas distinguishes the right use of virtue's strength from the distorted powers of those with mere semblances of virtue by referring to the prudent judgments of the wise about the good that ought to be pursued in a given instance, and these judgments are hardly arbitrary (*ST* II–II.47.5.obj.1, not denied). Of course, accepting this reply depends upon accepting Aquinas's account of the unity of the virtues and his belief that the difficult work of distinguishing virtuous action from its semblances can be best accomplished by the virtuous themselves, and so far I have done little to defend either of these claims. And yet, until Rorty has convinced us that virtuous action can be identified without referring to the other virtues or without calling upon the judgments of the wise, we have little reason to share her worries about an account of the virtues that highlights their utility and strength.

Notoriously, Aquinas does consider women more subject to passionate impulse and thus less capable of rational thought than men, which in turn enables him to justify their subordination within marriage (*ST* 1.92.1.2). He does associate women with virtue-threatening contingency and men with the rational powers that carve virtuous action out of chaos. This may lead some to believe that Aquinas's functional account of the virtues is in fact noxious and that Rorty is right to complain that his attempt at detoxification is a mere flick of the wrist, but I think they would be mistaken. Aquinas's wrong-headed beliefs about women simply show us that the wise of his day had not yet progressed far enough in their dialectical inquiries into the good and the best to see their mistake.[40] Whether their failure was culpable or not is a different question altogether and cannot be addressed without determining what thirteenth-century intellectuals were capable of knowing about the matter. But even if we judge their ignorance blameworthy we should not regard their failure here as grounds for thinking that we can distinguish the virtuous use of virtue's strength from its semblances without appeal to the corrigible and corruptible judgments of the wise. Indeed, contin-

---

[39] Rorty (1988c, 308).
[40] For more on Aquinas's view of moral justification as dialectical inquiry see MacIntyre (1988b, 171–182).

gency and complexity in the circumstances of choice guarantee that we cannot hope to draw these distinctions well without prudent judgment.

Finally, of the two difficulties that call for the work of justice – the first procedural, the second moral – only the first is derived directly from the contingency of the good. Of course, the second *does* depend upon our tendency to confuse true and apparent goods, which in turn depends upon the imperfect and thus contingent goodness of the ends we consider. But something else is needed to account for this tendency and explain why, for us, true goods are difficult to will, particularly the good of another. For this, Aquinas turns to the contingent passions of the sensitive appetite: excessive fear of the difficulties and dangers that often accompany the pursuit of our neighbor's good, and inordinate desire for those sensible pleasures that too often disrupt the pursuit of every other good. These passions make our neighbor's good difficult to will with any constancy, which in turn generates our need for a virtue in the will that habitually disposes us to that good. But note well, the fact that Aquinas derives our need for justice from the passions that create our need for courage and temperance does not make justice functionally superfluous, its work redundant. For Aquinas also believes that after our fall from grace perfect virtue eludes all and that the passions remain contingent even in those with great and steadfast virtues. Consequently justice is needed as a kind of repository of moral wisdom that disposes us to will the good of our neighbor even when our passions direct us elsewhere (*ST* i–ii.58.5). Justice makes constant action possible, when constancy is often the best we can manage this side of Eden.

This is further evidence of the will's diminished place in Aquinas's treatment of the moral life. In chapter one (note 17) I noted that apart from a single incident in Eden, he does not consider the will an independent cause of moral failure. Here we discover that his treatment of the virtues proceeds with little reference to the will. These are related findings. For of course, it is because the will is not autonomously troublesome, at least not for us, that there is no difficulty that Aquinas can assign exclusively to the will, no *infirmitas* that afflicts it alone and that calls for the work of a unique virtue. In fact, its particular weakness, its inability to will our neighbor's good, is entirely derivative. An agent with perfect virtue in the sensitive appetite would have no difficulty intending the neighbor's good. In that event, a habit would be needed in the will for procedural reasons only.

In many ways these four observations are all of a piece, and each circles us back to the start of this inquiry. The first three show us that

Aquinas can make sense of the difficulty that prudence must address only by referring to the difficulty that justice must. The last shows us that Aquinas can make sense of the two difficulties that justice must address only by referring to the combined contingencies confronted by prudence, courage, and temperance. When we add that Aquinas demonstrates our need for the work of courage and temperance by showing how contingent passions distract and distort the already difficult deliberations of reason, the consequence is a kind of functional unity, a complex web of overlapping difficulties and virtues, where the cardinals ultimately succeed or fail together in their respective attempts to cope with contingency.

5.

In his discussion of magnanimity, Aquinas offers a terse account of our themes. He writes,

> now the difficult and the great (which amount to the same) in an act of virtue may be considered from two points of view. First, from the point of view of reason, in so far as it is difficult to find and establish the rational means in some particular matter: and this difficulty is found only in the act of intellectual virtues, and also of justice. The other difficulty is on the part of the matter, which may involve a certain opposition to the moderation of reason, which moderation has to be applied thereto: and this difficulty regards chiefly the other moral virtues, which are about the passions, because the passions resist reason as Dionysius states in *On the Divine Names*.[41]

The interpretation of Aquinas's account of the virtues that I have been developing over the last two chapters is best described as a lengthy exegesis upon these remarks and others like them (*ST* i–ii.53.5.1; ii–ii.85.3 and ad 5; 129.5). Here, in his discussion of one of the parts of courage, he speaks of the various difficulties that obstruct our ability to know and will the good, difficulties that generate our need for the moral virtues. This leads him to conclude that "it is essential to a virtue to be about the difficult and the good" (*ST* ii–ii.129.2). Virtues are built around goods that we find difficult to achieve with constancy. A good that presented us with no difficulty whatsoever would have no virtue

---

[41] *ST* ii–ii.129.2: *Difficile autem et magnum, quae ad idem pertinent, in actu virtutis potest attendi dupliciter. Uno modo, ex parte rationis: inquantum scilicet difficile est medium rationis adinvenire et in aliqua materia statuere. Et ista difficultas sola invenitur in actu virtutum intellectualium, et etiam in actu iustitiae. Alia autem est difficultas ex parte materiae, quae de se repugnantiam habere potest ad modum rationis qui est circa eam ponendus. Et ista difficultas praecipue attenditur in aliis virtutibus moralibus, quae sunt circa passiones: quia passiones pugnant contra rationem, ut Dionysius dicit, iv De Div. Nom.*

assigned to it, for without difficulty there would be no reason for virtue's labor.

Accordingly, when Aquinas contends that "where there is a special kind of difficulty or goodness, there is a special virtue," he is not implying that some virtues have to do with pursuit of the good, while others have to do with overcoming difficulty (*ST* II–II.137.1). Difficulty needs to be overcome only insofar as some good is desired, and the pursuit of some good requires a virtue for assistance only insofar as it is difficult to know and desire with constancy. The only difference here is that some virtues first become intelligible to us when we locate the good they seek, while others first become intelligible when we locate the difficulty they overcome. This is what divides temperance and courage. Yet the complete intelligibility of any virtue comes only after we locate both the good that it seeks and the difficulty it overcomes. Thus, when Aquinas speaks of temperance he cannot refer to the good it seeks without immediately mentioning the difficulty it must overcome in order to achieve the good: "temperance . . . moderates pleasures of touch (which of itself is a difficult thing)" (*ST* II–II.137.1).

To these conclusions two significant objections come to mind, both at once exegetical and philosophical. First, some might object that Aquinas does not consider the good all that contingent, all that difficult to know. Nor does he consider the conditions of human happiness all that indeterminate. Rather, he regards human beings as a particular sort of creature that Providence has assigned a particular collection of goods, which in turn create a particular profile of human happiness. Indeed, in his remarks about the natural law he insists that these goods can be known by all with relative ease, and together they offer a standard that can, and indeed ought to, guide our deliberations and order our choices. It follows that he has no reason to make the hard work of prudence a precondition for knowledge of the good, no reason to regard the virtues as the heart of the moral life.

Second, if virtue is about the difficult as well as the good, then how can a life of virtue be the principle cause of human happiness? Aquinas, of course insists that it is (*ST* I–II.4.6–7), and yet, if he identifies the life of virtue with overcoming one difficulty after another, he may in fact have painted a picture of dreary, unrelenting toil. It appears that a virtuous life is as undesirable as difficulties are many, as unhappy as the conditions that make the virtues intelligible in the first place.

It is to these objections that I turn in the next two chapters.

CHAPTER 3

Natural law and the limits of contingency

One of the curious features of the contemporary debate over the character and content of Aquinas's remarks about the natural law is that so many of the competing interpretations are alike in so many respects. To be sure, contentions flourish, genuine disagreement abounds, and thus we should not be surprised when some of the contenders – Finnis, Grisez, and Boyle, MacIntyre, Porter, McInerny, and Yearley – complain about the company when lumped together. Nevertheless, their disagreements remain at the level of detail, while their agreement regards fundamental assumptions about the intentions that motivate Aquinas's efforts. What distinguishes their agreement, their shared understanding? All agree that Aquinas treats the first precepts of the natural law as a general outline of the human good that must be pursued in order to perfect human agency and secure human happiness. All agree that rules of conduct can be derived from this outline of the human good, rules that specify the concrete content of morally praiseworthy action. All agree that together this outline and these rules constitute Aquinas's moral theory, a theory that tells us what to do by offering a collection of precepts from which specific obligations can be derived. And all agree that Aquinas's moral theory is a rational choice theory, where the demands of practical reasonableness specify concrete moral obligations.[1]

This abundant agreement about Aquinas's purposes has its origin, one suspects, in the discontents of modern moral philosophy. Unsettled by the interminable character of moral debate in modern societies, dismayed by the uncertainty and diversity of moral judgment, many moral philosophers find solace in rules that guide conduct and theories that quiet doubts about obligation. Interpreters who wish to consider

---

[1] There are notable exceptions. See Bourke (1974; 1983); Hall (1994); Hibbs (1990); Nelson (1992); and Veatch (1990).

Aquinas a useful resource in this enterprise will in fact be obliged to find a moral theory that generates rules of conduct in his remarks about the natural law.[2] The exegetical stakes are high. If those remarks do not yield a moral theory of the right sort, then they offer neither theoretical comfort nor contemporary significance, and in that event, Aquinas's efforts may in fact be reduced to irrelevance, to mere antiquarian appeal.

It is equally certain that this agreement about Aquinas's treatment of the natural law challenges the interpretation of his views that I have been defending. For if the human good in this life has specific content, if happiness *in via* has a particular shape, and if acquaintance with the rules that generate concrete obligations is the first feature of the moral life, then Aquinas can neither insist that the human good is contingent, nor that human happiness in this life is indeterminate, at least not without grave inconsistency. Of course, most contemporary interpreters of Aquinas's remarks on the natural law regard this potential inconsistency as a strike against the contingency of the good and the indeterminacy of happiness *in via*. That is, most agree that the natural law must provide concrete moral guidance, and most assume that Aquinas honors this necessity with a theory that specifies the content of the good and determines the shape of human happiness.[3] As such, most either ignore his remarks about contingency and indeterminacy (*ST* I–II.1–21), or offer interpretations of them that save the consensus.

The considerable power of this exegetical assumption among contemporary interpreters is best seen in the work of those who lament its demands. Lee Yearley, for instance, finds the "sharp divergences among ways of life" undeniable and therefore objects to the inability of Aquinas's treatment of the natural law to account for the ordinary facts of moral diversity. By Yearley's lights, Aquinas's treatment "shows little awareness of how differences in ethos might produce different judgments about the content of injunctions or even of virtues." In short, it restricts contingency and constrains indeterminacy. Given this complaint one might expect Yearley to take a second look at Aquinas's remarks on the natural law in the hope that an alternative interpretation might be found, one more compatible with the facts of moral diversity. Or, alternatively, one can imagine him downplaying the importance of those remarks, while directing our attention elsewhere. Yearley, however, chooses neither course, retaining instead both the standard exe-

[2] This is Jordan's diagnosis (1986, 135).   [3] Grisez makes this condition explicit (1983, 184).

getical assumption and the complaint of insensitivity to ethos that follows from it.[4]

But why accept this assumption, concede these charges? If the inquiries and conclusions in chapters one and two are sound, if Aquinas in fact insists that the good is contingent, that happiness, at least in this life, is indeterminate, then his account of the moral life will have little difficulty accommodating the ordinary and unobjectionable diversity of moral belief and practice that Yearley considers incompatible with his remarks on the natural law. In that event, those remarks deserve a second look, a different interpretation, one more compatible with the contingency of the human good, the indeterminacy of happiness, and the difficulty of the life of virtue.

I .

The principal point of contention among the interpreters considered below turns on whether Aquinas's remarks about the first precepts of the natural law pass muster as they stand. Alasdair MacIntyre, Ralph McInerny, and Jean Porter contend that Aquinas's remarks can, by themselves, yield prescriptions that provide concrete moral guidance. Three others, John Finnis, Germain Grisez, and Joseph Boyle, maintain that they cannot, and that additional work must therefore complete what Aquinas started well enough but left unfinished. Other issues fracture the consensus even further: whether the basic precepts of the natural law are *per se nota* in themselves or only for the wise; whether our knowledge of those precepts is theoretical or practical (put another way, whether the basic goods are pre-moral or not); and whether concrete prescriptions follow from the hierarchical ordering of the first precepts or from something else. Nevertheless, these differences do little to diminish the basic agreement. All agree that a complete account of the first precepts generates a set of rules that guide concrete action by specifying the character of rational choice, which in turn specifies the good and the praiseworthy in human action. All agree that Aquinas believes that the first precepts of that natural law guide human action in precisely this way, and all agree that his remarks are designed to spell out this effect.

---

[4] Yearley (1990, 48–51, 75–78).

(i) Finnis, Grisez, and Boyle, and the subversion of regret

According to Finnis, Aquinas's great achievement is his specification of the first principles of practical reason, all basic human "goods to be done and pursued."[5] By Finnis's lights, this represents a significant advance beyond Aristotle, whose ethical treatises he regards as "decidedly hazy about the starting points of practical reasoning."[6] Nevertheless, Finnis contends that "Aquinas did not carry through and consolidate his advance."[7] He failed to specify the prescriptive content of the natural law. In particular, he failed to provide "intermediate principles" that "guide the transition from judgments about human goods to judgments about the right thing to do here and now."[8] Between the first principles of practical reasonableness and the concrete moral norms such as we find in the decalogue stands a "gap which Aquinas failed to fill."[9]

Finnis, Grisez, and Boyle regard the history of moral philosophy after Aquinas as a series of bungled attempts to uncover the intermediate principles that fill this gap.[10] Not that every attempt was a complete failure, but rather that every attempt was incomplete. Thus, for example, Finnis regards Kant's three formulations of the categorical imperative as an attempt to articulate the significance of consistency in moral judgment.[11] But consistency, as Grisez points out, is only one of the principles that ought to guide the deliberations that carry us from basic goods to concrete norms.[12] Universalizing prescriptivists, existentialists, Stoics, and utilitarians each offer their own, but like Kant they fall victim to the belief that a single principle can move us from the good to the right.[13] Finnis, Grisez, and Boyle hope to avoid this mistake with their more exhaustive list of normative principles, a list that directs us to right choices by specifying the collection of attitudes that one ought to have toward the human good specified by the natural law.[14]

They begin, as Aquinas does, with the first precepts of the natural law, which they refer to as basic goods and, alternatively, as the first principles of practical reason. These precepts are goods because they are the sorts of things that we desire and pursue as the ends of our actions. They are principles of practical reason because we refer to goods regarded as ends when we offer reasoned justification for what we do. Why did I go to the market? In order to purchase some food. This

[5] Finnis (1983, 68).   [6] *Ibid.*, 67.   [7] *Ibid.*, 68.   [8] *Ibid.*, 70.   [9] *Ibid.*, 69.   [10] *Ibid.*, 70.
[11] *Ibid.*, 121.   [12] Grisez (1983, 109); cf. Finnis, Boyle, and Grisez (1987, 276).
[13] Finnis (1983, 70).   [14] Finnis, Boyle, and Grisez (1987, 282).

reply makes my action intelligible, and, in most instances, justifies what I have done, precisely because human beings consider food desirable and good, and thus a reasonable end to pursue, at least for the most part. It follows that basic goods are not simply reasons that justify actions but also the principles that guide practical reflection, the ends that initiate deliberation.

The first precepts of the natural law are *basic* goods and *first* principles of practical reason because they are the "ultimate rational grounds (principles of practical reasoning) for proposing actions to be done."[15] The best way to locate them "is by considering actions and seeking their reasons,"[16] asking, "'why are you doing that?' and 'Why should we do that?' and so on. Persisting with such questions eventually uncovers a small number of basic purposes of diverse kinds."[17] These basic purposes are so unquestionably good that the absurdity of doubting their desirability distinguishes them from less basic goods and purposes. Grisez offers the following example: "'Why do you want to work?' 'To make money' 'Why do you want money?' 'I have to eat.' 'Why bother about eating?' 'Don't be silly. I'll die if I don't.'"[18] And it is precisely this inability to indicate why the preservation of physical existence is a good reason for action that captures what it means for Aquinas to say that its goodness is *per se nota*. Nothing need be said in defense of its desirability.[19] It is a good reason for action that cannot itself be warranted with further reasons.[20] Its goodness is rationally justified, that is, known and intelligible, and yet no reasons need be offered that would justify it.[21] Moreover, its goodness is *per se nota* for all. Not because all can, when

---

[15] Grisez, Boyle, and Finnis (1987, 106).   [16] *Ibid.*, 113.   [17] *Ibid.*, 106–107.
[18] Grisez (1983, 124).
[19] Finnis, Boyle, and Grisez (1987, 278); cf. Grisez, Boyle, and Finnis (1987, 103).
[20] Grisez, Boyle, and Finnis (1987, 110).
[21] At times Finnis, Grisez, and Boyle say that the goodness of the general precepts of the natural law is self-evident, "known just by knowing the meaning of their terms" (Grisez, Boyle, and Finnis [1987, 106]). This is a dangerous way to put the point because it threatens to collapse the *per se nota* character of the basic goods into modern notions of immediacy and analyticity, a confusion they quite rightly wish to avoid (*ibid.*). McInerny is even less cautious. He maintains that the general precepts of the natural law are self-evident propositions because, "no one can fail to know the meanings of their terms and thus fail to see that they are so" (1992, 114). Better to avoid reference to self-evidence altogether. Better to say that our knowledge of the first precepts of the natural law is non-inferential. It does not depend upon inference from something else that we know. This does not mean that it is knowledge that stands by itself, unrelated to everything else that we believe. It is not immediate in this sense. Rather, it is immediate only insofar as it is not mediated by inference. Thus, for example, physical existence can be known as a basic good without inferring that knowledge from something else that is known. That said, this knowledge does presuppose knowing what sort of thing physical existence is and how it differs from other sorts of things.

asked, respond with a list of basic goods that includes physical existence, but rather because all can be prodded with "why" questions to exclaim, "Don't be silly!" when confronted with doubts about its goodness.

Aquinas lists three general precepts of the natural law, three classes of basic goods: physical existence and all those activities ordered to the preservation of human life; sexual relations between husband and wife, the education of offspring, and all those activities ordered to the preservation of the species; and knowledge of the truth, civic friendship, and all those activities that pertain to our rational nature (*ST* I–II.94.2). He also admits that the natural law can be changed "by way of addition" (*ST* I–II.94.5) and Finnis, Grisez, and Boyle take full advantage of this permission, bringing the number of basic goods to eight.[22] At this point a careful study of their list is unnecessary. Arguments for and against the inclusion of this or that good have been developed by others.[23] Instead our purposes are best served by considering how Finnis, Grisez, and Boyle regard the first precepts of the natural law; in particular, by asking how those precepts, as basic goods, can and cannot function as the foundation of morality.[24]

Together the basic goods offer a complete picture of human agency in all of its complexity. Human beings do all sorts of things, and yet every human action is the pursuit of one or more of the basic goods.[25] Indeed, human action is rational action precisely because human beings can, in principle, explain all that they do by offering reasons that refer to one or more of the basic goods. If it turns out that a basic good cannot be located as the ultimate end that explains what was done, then we cannot speak of voluntary human action. Finnis, Grisez, and Boyle draw the proper conclusion: the general precepts of the natural law "do not tell us what is morally good."[26] They do not, that is, prescribe specific actions and prohibit others, at least not by themselves. They do not generate concrete obligations. Rather, they specify those general human goods that create "the field of possibility" where deliberation and choice proceed and where *every action* finds its point in a basic good that "has the nature of an end" (*ST* I–II.94.2).[27] And of course, "even morally bad actions have their point."[28] This is the banal truth discussed in the

[22] Grisez, Boyle, and Finnis (1987, 107–108); Grisez (1993, 567–569).   [23] See Hittinger (1987).
[24] Finnis, Boyle, and Grisez (1987, 282).
[25] Since Aquinas insists that rational desire follows from judgment about the good, the list of basic goods is as much a list of our natural inclinations as it is an account of the ends our wills are naturally inclined to desire (Grisez, Boyle, and Finnis [1987, 108]; *ST* I–II.10.1).
[26] Grisez (1983, 183).   [27] *Ibid.*
[28] Grisez, Boyle, and Finnis (1987, 121).

opening article of the *prima secunda* (*omnes actiones humanae propter finem sint* [*ST* I–II.I.I]), which Aquinas repeats in the first precept of the natural law: "good is to be done, and evil is to be avoided" (*ST* I–II.94.2).

Finnis, Grisez, and Boyle call the first precept of the natural law the first principle of practical reasoning,[29] and they make good use of Aquinas's analogy with the first principle of speculative reason in order to clarify its character.[30] Just as the principle of non-contradiction is presupposed in all that is known, the first principle of practical reasoning is presupposed in all that is done. Just as a knower who violates the principle of non-contradiction cannot be said to know, the human agent who does not act for the sake of some good that is known cannot be said to act. And just as the principle of non-contradiction does not specify what should or should not be known but simply draws the logical bounds within which human knowing takes place, the basic goods and the first principle of practical reasoning do not specify obligatory courses of action but merely create the logical space of reasons where human actions of every kind and character are pursued, justified, and explained.

The fact that the first precepts of the natural law – the basic goods – do not prescribe or prohibit concrete actions leads Finnis, Grisez, and Boyle to call them pre-moral.[31] They reason this way: if the basic goods mark the general outlines of human agency, the conceptual space within which every human action and inclination resides, both good and evil, then our knowledge of them is anthropological not moral, a matter of fact not value. In turn, this conclusion lends indispensable support for their principle suspicion: that Aquinas's account of the natural law is an incomplete moral theory. For if the basic goods (the first precepts of the natural law) are pre-moral, they cannot oblige or prohibit this or that action, since "the moral *ought* cannot be derived from the *is* of theoretical truth."[32]

Unfortunately, this conclusion distorts Aquinas's actual view. Ralph McInerny, for instance, quite rightly points out that the naturalistic fallacy makes sense only to those who think that judgments about matters of fact are different in kind from judgments about moral matters, that the theoretical and practical intellects are altogether different faculties of mind. Aquinas, he notes, avoids both confusions, and for good reason.[33] The human intellect is uniform, human knowledge one sort of thing. When it is put to use it is practical. When it is desired for

[29] *Ibid.*, 119.   [30] *Ibid.*, 119–121.   [31] *Ibid.*, 126.   [32] *Ibid.*, 102.   [33] McInerny (1992, 118).

its own sake it is speculative (*ST* I.79.11).[34] It follows that Aquinas has little reason to exclude normative judgments as the first precepts are specified.

Consider knowledge. It is, all agree, one of the first precepts, one of the basic goods that we refer to in order to make our inquiries intelligible to others, one of the ends that distinguish our agency as human. But does this imply that every sort of inquiry counts as an intelligible human activity, that any kind of knowledge can be pursued rationally? For Finnis, Grisez, and Boyle it does, precisely because they consider knowledge a pre-moral good, one that can be specified without making judgments about the kind of knowledge worth having.

But now imagine your retired neighbor in the flat above reads phone books all day, every day. In his rooms they are stacked pile upon pile, yellow and white. He rarely leaves. Empty take-out boxes litter his hallways. When you ask him about his peculiar devotion he says he is memorizing phone numbers. Pressing further you ask, "But why?" and he answers, "Don't be silly, everyone knows that knowledge is a basic good." Do you then slap a palm upon your forehead and reply, "Of course, silly me?" Probably not. In fact, you would probably ignore his explanation for the behavior and seek an alternative in a mental pathology of one sort or another. Indeed, you would press your inquiry further, bypassing his replies and casting about for a reductive explanation precisely because you cannot interpret his behavior in a way that preserves the basic rationality of what he does. By all appearances, he is not pursuing an activity that can be made intelligible (that is, rational and human) by referring to a basic human good as a reason for acting. Of course, your neighbor *is* seeking knowledge, and this is the point of significance. For if that fact cannot make his actions intelligible, then it cannot be the case that the pursuit of knowledge of just any kind instantiates a basic good. Rather, the knowledge that is a basic good is knowledge that is somehow good for creatures like us, either good for some possible human purpose, or simply good for us to know quite apart from our purposes. Indeed, knowledge can provide good reason for

---

[34] One of the best criticisms of the fact/value distinction comes in Michael Walzer's argument against realist accounts of the morality of war (1977, 3–20). Realists maintain that talk of good and evil has no purchase in the affairs of state, in the power politics of national self-interest. Walzer retorts that a faithful realism, if possible, would only distort the truth about war. It wouldn't get the facts right. He writes: "here are soldiers lining up the inhabitants of a peasant village, men, women, and children, and shooting them down: we call this a massacre." To call this event anything else would misdescribe it. The facts of the matter would be missed. And yet, "massacre" is a morally charged notion, one that brings moral condemnation to bear upon the facts it describes.

action, even in the most minimal sense, only when it meets this normative test. Only then can it make our inquiries intelligible. Thus, when
Aquinas says that knowledge is a first precept of the natural law he does
not refer to knowledge as such, but rather to knowledge that is a *human*
good, knowledge that finds a place in our human form of life. He does
not speak of knowledge simply, but rather of our "natural inclination to
know the truth about God" (*ST* I–II.94.2). This way of putting it not only
restates what he has already said – that God alone captures all that can
be known about the human good (*ST* I–II.2.8) – it also indicates that
inquiries in accord with the first precepts of the natural law must pursue
knowledge that is good for human life in some form or fashion.

But even if Aquinas's account of the first precepts of the natural law is
normative to the ground, even if he considers the naturalistic fallacy a
senseless worry, the complaint that Finnis, Grisez, and Boyle lodge
against him remains. In the basic goods and the first principle of
practical reasonableness Aquinas describes the bare outlines of rationality in human action, the ends that precipitate deliberations, the starting
points of all choices, the resting points of all interpretations and explanations. By themselves they do not provide much moral guidance. By
themselves they do not prescribe or prohibit concrete courses of action.
It is indeed one thing to apprehend knowledge as a good, one thing to
will it simply as a result of that apprehension, quite another to be obliged
to pursue knowledge of this or that kind in this or that instance. Of
course, Aquinas does tell us that morally praiseworthy action tracks
both the natural law and the judgments of right reason, but he does not
tell us what fully rational judgments are like or how they manage to
fulfill our nature.

Taking up where Aquinas left off, Finnis, Grisez, and Boyle identify a
collection of normative principles implied in the first precepts. Since
action derived from these "modes of responsibility" will be morally
praiseworthy it will also be fully rational, and therefore specifying the
demands of practical reason will also articulate the demands of morality.[35] This conclusion clarifies their understanding of Aquinas's failure,
and points the way forward. Aquinas fails to provide a complete moral
theory because he does not offer a complete account of practical
reasonableness. In the first precepts he describes the starting points of all
practical deliberation, the minimal requirements of rational human
agency. He does not, however, specify the rules of practical reasonable-

<hr>

[35] Grisez (1983, 189).

ness that are the source of every morally praiseworthy action. Completing his moral theory is, therefore, largely a matter of completing his account of the demands of practical reason, of specifying the rules that govern fully rational human action.

The argument goes this way. If we assume that incompletely rational action is characterized by the single-minded pursuit of one basic good, then, more often than not, action of this kind will be done at the expense of other basic goods. This explains why the incompletely rational is equivalent to the immoral. Thus, for example, the pursuit of knowledge can easily lead the single-minded to steal books from the library, securing one basic good, knowledge, at the expense of another, civic friendship.[36] It follows that fully rational actions, fully praiseworthy actions, are characteristic of agents less single-minded, more ecumenical in their loves, agents that can pursue one of the basic goods while at the same time neither doubting the goodness of the others nor acting against any one of them. By contrast, agents who act against one of the basic goods proceed with diminished rationality because they ignore one or more of the first principles of practical reasonableness. At the same time their action falls short of the morally praiseworthy because they fail to instantiate one of the basic goods, because they fail to acknowledge that a truly fulfilling human life is one that instantiates all of them.[37] Thus Grisez writes:

> the distinction between moral good and evil is a distinction between ways in which proposed courses of action are related to the whole set of principles of practical thinking. Some proposals comport well with all of the human goods. Others comport well with some of the principles of practical thinking – those which direct action to the goods promised by these proposals – but are inconsistent with or inadequately responsive to one or more others. It is morally good to adopt proposals of the former sort and morally bad to adopt proposals of the latter sort.[38]

Morality, then, is a matter of comporting well in every action with each of the basic goods. Its first principle, which is also a principle of full and unfettered rationality,[39] enjoins openness to all of reason's goods.[40] Still, the first principle of morality is not by itself action guiding.[41] It

---

[36] Grisez, Boyle, and Finnis (1987, 122–125).   [37] Grisez (1983, 130–132, 184–189).
[38] *Ibid.*, 197.   [39] Grisez, Boyle, and Finnis (1987, 121).
[40] In their own words the first principle of morality demands the following: "In voluntary acting for human goods and avoiding what is opposed to them, one ought to choose and otherwise will those and only those possibilities whose willing is compatible with a will toward integral human fulfillment." Grisez, Boyle, and Finnis (1987, 128); cf. Grisez (1983, 184).
[41] Grisez (1983, 189); cf. Finnis, Boyle, and Grisez (1987, 284).

needs further specification in the modes of responsibility, "the intermediate principles which stand midway between the first principle and
the completely specific norms which direct choices."[42] The modes have
negative force. They prohibit unreasonable choices, those inconsistent
with integral human fulfillment insofar as they do not appreciate all of
the basic human goods in all their aspects.[43] As such, they are "requirements of practical reasonableness," which together capture the specific
content of *recta ratio*.[44]

What should we make of this? Well, if the modes of responsibility that
specify *recta ratio* also specify the morally praiseworthy, then we have
good reason to expect that the moral judgments and practices they
recommend measure up to our own, at least for the most part. Some
departures of practice from principle can, of course, be expected.
Indeed, Finnis, Grisez, and Boyle intend the modes of responsibility to
correct our choices, as well as to guide them. However, if the departures
are too numerous, or if they bear upon moral practices and judgments
that we cannot imagine revising, then we have good reason to doubt
that the modes of responsibility in fact yield courses of action that accord
with right reason.

What, then, do the modes of responsibility recommend, what kind of
life, what obligations, prohibitions, and permissions? Finnis, Grisez, and
Boyle reply that together the modes direct us to a life of integral human
fulfillment, where each basic good is instantiated in some measure.[45]
This sort of life, they admit, is an ideal, and yet approximations are
possible. At the very least one can "act for some of the basic human
goods and avoid choosing against any of them."[46] In fact, this is precisely
what the modes, as specifications of the first principle of morality,
demand. Indeed, the moral content of one's identity is largely determined by one's relative openness to the full complexity of the human
good.[47] For this reason the eighth mode, which prohibits acting against
any of the basic goods, bears most of the normative weight.[48] (And this is
as it should be given the understanding of fully rational choice that
Finnis, Grisez, and Boyle advance.) In fact, the other modes are largely
rules designed to prevent the possibility that we might choose against

[42] Grisez (1983, 189).   [43] *Ibid.*, 189; cf. Finnis, Boyle, and Grisez (1987, 283).
[44] Grisez (1983, 251).   [45] *Ibid.*, 222.   [46] *Ibid.*   [47] *Ibid.*, 234–235.
[48] The eighth mode states: "One should not be moved by a stronger desire for one instance of an
intelligible good to act for it by choosing to destroy, damage, or impede some other instance of
an intelligible good" (*ibid.*, 216). The emphasis is upon choice. One should not choose to destroy
one good as a means to another. If, by chance, a basic good is destroyed as a consequence of
choice, this is another matter.

one basic good as a means to achieving another. They are, what the rabbis call a fence around the Torah.[49] When their demands are met the eighth is fulfilled as well, bringing practical rationality to choice and fulfillment to life.

Here troubles begin. For if one must not act against any basic good, then it follows that there are as many absolute moral prohibitions as there are basic goods to act against. Prohibitions proliferate, and at a troubling rate, for it turns out that too many are at odds with our settled moral beliefs and practices. Concerned with locating and justifying the existence of at least some absolute prohibitions, Finnis, Grisez, and Boyle turn out to be too inattentive to the number and variety they have made possible. In fact, they frequently explicate the eighth mode and its ability to generate unconditional rules of rational choice by referring to choices against life and the prohibition against killing, effectively masking the possibility of other, more unacceptable prohibitions.[50] Of course, not all consider killing absolutely prohibited. We have already seen that Aquinas does not. He regards it as an action morally indifferent in its natural species, and thus just and good in some contexts but not in others (*ST* I–II.1.3.3). Still, many of us do consider killing absolutely prohibited, and therefore we cannot say that the prohibition departs from our moral beliefs and practices in a manner that calls for complaint. Widespread disagreement about a prohibition cannot justify revising the moral theory that generates it. Only widespread departure of practice from principle can.

There are, however, other basic goods that could be acted against besides life, and consequently other prohibitions that follow from the eighth mode of responsibility. For instance, "the handing on of life to new persons," is a basic good, which the eighth mode prohibits acting against for the sake of some other good.[51] But does this prohibition make moral sense? Many choose not to marry and have children precisely because they wish to craft their lives around some other basic good, such as knowledge, justice, or civic friendship. Do we want to say that those

---

[49] The first simply demands that one avoid inertia, that one act for the sake of some good. The second and fifth demand that one not act against the basic goods of civic friendship and justice. The third and the fourth demand that one pursue a basic good because it is good and not because achieving it will reduce some emotional tension. The sixth counsels against choosing apparent goods, while the seventh insists that one should not be moved by negative emotions to choose against any of the basic goods.

[50] Finnis, Boyle, and Grisez (1987); Grisez (1983, 216–222, 256–259).

[51] Grisez (1983, 124). Later, Grisez (1993, 567–569) takes the argument to its obvious conclusion. Marriage is a basic good.

who make this choice act viciously because of it? Probably not. In fact, we often find ourselves admiring those who dedicate themselves to knowledge or justice precisely because their lives require a deliberate and regrettable choice against marriage and children. The fact that they sacrifice one basic good for another can, and frequently does, increase the praiseworthy character of the life they have chosen.

Or, consider another example, one we have seen before. Aquinas asks us to imagine a virtuous wife's response to the capture of her thieving husband (*ST* I–II.19.10). In the interests of justice the judge chooses to punish him, effectively taking him from her and ending their friendship that is the principle good of the family. Both justice and friendship are basic goods. If she consents to this choice, she acts against a basic good. If she does not, the result is the same. It appears that the eighth mode of responsibility has bound her in a web of conflicting obligations that she can neither avoid nor fulfill without remainder. In fact, it appears to bind all of us in as many strong moral conflicts of this sort as there are direct conflicts between basic goods. No doubt, Finnis, Grisez, and Boyle intend the eighth mode to preclude moral conflicts insofar as it generates unconditional moral requirements that trump all others. Indeed, Grisez explicitly states that moral conflicts do not exist and that their appearance can be "dissolved by analyzing the human act more closely."[52] In most instances careful reflection of this sort reveals "an error in identifying possibilities or in applying moral principles."[53] If the source of the conflict cannot be found in one of these errors, then it must reside in the mistaken specification of an absolute moral principle.[54] Still, it is not at all clear how these strategies would work in this example. The possibilities and principles are relatively straightforward, the absolute prohibitions relatively clear. Moreover, despite the protests of Finnis, Grisez, and Boyle, most of us find moral conflict of some sort unavoidable, tragedy of some measure inevitable, at least in the short term.

These conclusions connect our two examples and pinpoint the trouble with the eighth mode. Finnis, Grisez, and Boyle insist that conflicts between basic goods should not arise, need not arise, and that choice can proceed without regret, and yet here moral theory distorts moral reality. For of course, we do choose against basic goods, sometimes because the circumstances are such that we must, sometimes because the best and most praiseworthy life cannot be had without

---

[52] Grisez (1983, 299). [53] *Ibid.*, 295. [54] *Ibid.*, 296.

sacrificing some good, and in each instance choice proceeds with regret, with longing for the good left behind.

Happily, Aquinas's alternative approach to conflict among basic goods captures this moral reality quite well. Basic goods can be chosen against because every good besides God is contingent and will therefore be a good object of choice in some circumstances and not others (*ST* I–II.19.10). Thus for example, insofar as the wife acts in accord with her virtue she cannot choose to preserve the friendship found in marriage when her husband is caught thieving. It is no longer a good object of choice because he deserves punishment, not happiness at home. She must, therefore, consent to the judge's choice to punish. In fact, Aquinas would consider failure to consent vicious. In part, because punishment, not friendship, is the good that warrants choice here. In part, because failure to consent also implies failure to recognize that only God's goodness lacks contingency and therefore cannot be chosen against without sin.

Does she consent without regret? Does the contingent goodness of the objects of choice eliminate the misery of her circumstance by eliminating the goodness of the object chosen against? Of course not. While friendship has lost its goodness as an object of choice (*electio*), it remains a good that she can will (*vult*) simply and absolutely. In fact, in cases of this sort Aquinas insists upon a divided will, upon choice tempered by regret. Even as she consents to the judge's choice her will is good only if she also, "wishes him not to be put to death inasmuch as killing is a natural evil" (*ST* I–II.19.10).

Clearly, the contingency of the human good, along with the distinction between *electio* and *voluntas*, offers a more nuanced account of our relation to the basic features of the human good. It also locates the fundamental trouble with Finnis, Grisez, and Boyle's treatment of the natural law. They insist that we ought to appreciate, respect, and be open to the basic goods that are found in the first precepts of the natural law. Aquinas, by contrast, finds no need for such an obligation precisely because he already finds us positively disposed toward those goods. By his lights, Finnis, Grisez, and Boyle have no reason to say in the first principle of morality, "don't fail to consider the goodness of these ends," for in fact we always do, naturally, necessarily. Indeed, Aquinas believes that we could not consider a creature capable of human action who did not regard them as good, will them absolutely, and, in some measure, regret their loss. On the other hand, their contingent goodness prevents him from prohibiting choice against them. We will (*volumus*) the basic goods in all that we do, naturally and necessarily, even as we frequently choose against them (*electamus*) or craft lives that fail to instantiate them all.

(ii) Natural law consequentialism

My dissatisfaction with Finnis, Grisez, and Boyle's treatment of the natural law, both as theory and as exegesis, should now be apparent. Less conspicuous, although there have been hints, is my general agreement with their insistence that the first precepts of the natural law and the first principle of practical reason yield no concrete obligations or prohibitions, at least not by themselves. There is no moral theory here that yields a collection of specific injunctions. Our disagreement turns on the significance of this omission. Finnis, Grisez, and Boyle consider it unfortunate, while I do not. They consider it a failure on Aquinas's part to carry through on his intention to take the first precepts of the natural law and develop a theory of this kind, while I doubt that Aquinas intends to tell us what to do as he specifies those precepts. In the next section I will argue that good reasons warrant his more circumspect aspirations and my more modest exegetical conclusions. In the last, I will offer an interpretation of Aquinas's treatment of the first precepts that takes seriously what he plainly says: that his intention is not to provide guidance for those puzzled about what to do but rather "to consider the extrinsic principles of action," both proximate (first precepts) and distant (God) (*ST* 1–II.90.prologue).

However, before I can turn to these matters I must first address those who, unlike Finnis, Grisez, and Boyle, find in Aquinas's remarks a moral theory that guides as it obliges. Jean Porter, for instance, finds "the norms of morality" and "the content of moral obligation" in the general precepts of the natural law and the first principle of practical reason.[55] Similarly, Ralph McInerny contends that Aquinas's remarks in *ST* 1–II.94.2 specify "reason's natural grasp of certain common principles which *should* [my emphasis] direct our acts."[56]

The exegetical argument is deceptively simple. In *ST* 1–II.94.2 Aquinas specifies the goods to which we are naturally inclined. They are not inclinations we can decide to have or abandon, goods that we can consider desirable or not, and therefore Aquinas does not imply that we

---

[55] Porter (1990, 91, 93). Porter's interpretation of Aquinas's account of the first precepts can be found in her 1990 volume. For evidence that her understanding of his intentions may have changed, and with them, the content of his remarks see Porter (1996). She does not, however, offer a new interpretation of those remarks.   [56] McInerny (1992, 110).

ought to have these inclinations or pursue these goods. Rather his intent is to characterize the theater in which practical reason acts, the various activities that occupy human life, and the various ends that we pursue with nature's necessity.[57]

We do, however, require precepts that tell us how to order our desires for these goods and arrange the activities that we are naturally inclined to pursue. For, of course, they can conflict and frequently do. Aquinas, according to this view, supplies a straightforward answer: "according to the order of natural inclinations, is the order of the precepts of the natural law" (*ST* 1–11.94.2). Both Porter and McInerny take this remark to be, in Porter's words, "the point of the passage," precisely because it implies that Aquinas intends his account of our natural inclinations to yield concrete obligations.[58] It implies that our natural inclinations should have a certain order one to another, and that this order offers a picture of "a normative human life,"[59] what McInerny calls "the good of the whole man."[60] Properly arranged, they provide "an outline of what a human life should properly look like, what goods it will incorporate, and what relations those goods should have to one another."[61] From this outline specific moral norms and principles arise, giving concrete content to the first principle of practical reason by insisting that every human action contribute to the good of the whole man.[62]

For both Porter and McInerny all of this implies that *ST* 1–11.94.2 and its abridged predecessor, *ST* 1–11.10.1, should be considered the conclusion to Aquinas's discussion of human happiness in *ST* 1–11.1–5. There he dismisses a number of goods as potential parts of human happiness and concludes that the imperfect happiness available to us in this life consists in contemplation and practical virtue. However, he does not tell us what a life of virtue entails, neither the human goods it instantiates, nor the order they ought to have one to another. This, they contend, he accomplishes in his treatment of the first precepts. The moral virtues, according to this view, simply direct us to pursue the goods to which we are naturally inclined in the order specified by the norms and principles of the natural law. They are not the measure of a normative human life, but rather the means of securing the one spelled out in the treatise on law.[63]

---

[57] *Ibid.*, 120; Porter (1990, 88).   [58] Porter (1990, 89).   [59] *Ibid.*, 90.
[60] McInerny (1992, 120).   [61] Porter (1990, 90).   [62] *Ibid.*, 89–91; McInerny (1992, 121).
[63] See McInerny (1992, 122); Porter (1990, 87, 97–99). For a similar account of the moral virtues see Grisez, Boyle, and Finnis (1987, 129–130). Indeed, whenever Aquinas's remarks on the first precepts of the natural law are regarded as his attempt to provide a moral theory that tells us what to do the virtues are invariably diminished and belated. They are not the indispensable

Both Porter and McInerny believe that it is a hierarchical ordering of natural inclinations that generates the natural law's norms and principles.[64] Moreover, both locate this order, this hierarchy in the way Aquinas proceeds through the natural inclinations in *ST* I–II.94.2.[65] In a

means of knowing the good, but rather the habits of mind and affection that allow the good that is known by nature to be done with dispatch.

[64] MacIntyre agrees that Aquinas presents a hierarchical ordering of basic goods in *ST* I–II.94.2 that can be known by all "in such a way and to such a degree as to make every individual responsible for not acting upon it" (1988b, 174, 179). He does not, however, believe that Aquinas considers this knowledge easily acquired. Nor does he find Aquinas showing us how to argue from that knowledge to specific moral norms and principles. In this last respect he finds company with Finnis, Grisez, and Boyle: the first precepts of the natural law are not action guiding, at least not by themselves. Nevertheless, he departs from Finnis, Grisez, and Boyle in his evaluation of this state of affairs. He does not consider Aquinas's treatment of the natural law lamentably incomplete. Nor can we imagine MacIntyre having much sympathy for their largely Kantian attempt to complete it. Instead he argues that Aquinas regards the acquisition of the moral virtues as the necessary prerequisite for knowing both the specific ordering of the basic goods and the moral norms and principles that follow from that ordering. Aquinas, by MacIntyre's lights, restricts knowledge of the obligations and prohibitions that follow from the first precepts of the natural law to the virtuous alone (*ibid.*, 174–182).

This is the right exegetical conclusion, or so I will argue below in section 3, and it should motivate MacIntyre to draw another. If the first precepts of the natural law yield no specific obligations apart from virtuous inference, then why should we believe that Aquinas intends his remarks on the natural law to have *this* kind of prescriptive consequence? If the virtues are needed before the natural law can provide moral guidance, then shouldn't we assume that his remarks are motivated by something other than the desire to show how our nature tells us what we should and should not do in particular? For evidence that he is moving toward this assumption, see MacIntyre (1994; 1996, 67–68).

[65] Unlike Porter, who maintains that argument fixes our knowledge of the proper hierarchical ordering of inclinations (1990, 89), McInerny contends that the reasonableness of the ordering is apparent to all, or, at the very least, it could be made apparent with little effort. In fact, it is *per se nota* because it cannot be coherently denied. As such, the basic moral principles that are derived from that ordering are not simply moral norms, they are also criteria of minimal rationality. Thus McInerny argues that every rational agent "can be presumed to know . . . that he ought to act in a way that furthers the good, ought not drink himself blotto, seduce young maids, prevent his kids from learning, and so on" (1992, 124). Later on he mentions prohibitions against suicide, wholesale slaughter, and the like (*ibid.*, 131).

The question, of course, is whether this makes any sense. I suspect that it does not, precisely because we cannot extend the *per se nota* character of the natural law beyond the first precepts without making nonsense of our distinction between the mad and the minimally rational. McInerny implies that failure to know these prohibitions is equivalent to not knowing other *per se notae* propositions, such as the belief that the preservation of human life is good, or that two objects both equal to a third are equal to each other. But the person who acts neither for the sake of preserving human life, nor can imagine circumstances in which it would make sense to do so, cannot be considered a rational agent. Similarly, the person whose knowledge is not governed by rules of simple equivalence cannot be said to know. By contrast, the glutton, the drunkard, and the seducer do have reasons that motivate their actions, that explain what they have done. In this minimal sense, their choices are rational, their actions voluntary. Of course, if they are moved by passions so intense that they do not know what they are doing, we may well call them mad, but passions are not always this strong (*ST* I–II.6.7 and ad 3).

Therefore it seems we cannot find an account of minimally rational human action in the hierarchy of natural inclinations. Better, it seems, to follow Finnis, Grisez, and Boyle and locate that account in the basic goods themselves.

normative human life the lower inclinations that we share with all
creatures ought to be subordinated to those higher inclinations found in
rational creatures alone. This, of course, does not mean that we should
not act in accord with the lower inclinations. As Porter, points out, the
natural law is fundamentally permissive.[66] An action that pursues any
one of the human goods is normally acceptable.[67] Still, the desire for
self-preservation that we share with other species should not impede the
pursuit of knowledge or friendship.[68] We should seek the pleasures of
food and drink, for example, but we should do so in a manner that puts
them to use in the service of these higher goods.[69]

Not as apparent is the fact that the hierarchy of basic goods cuts the
other way in our relations with others. At the bare minimum right
relations with others requires simple well-wishing and nonmaleficence.
We should wish that others achieve all those things that human beings
desire according to the natural law, and we should neither harm the
good they possess, nor interfere with their pursuit of the good they do
not. However, not all obligations are alike. The natural desire for life
and safety generates obligations of nonmaleficence and noninterfer-
rence that trump those that follow from the desire for knowledge or
friendship. Thus Porter writes, "even though we ought to live for the
sake of enjoying higher aims, still, claims that stem from the necessities
of human life are the most exigent claims to mutual respect that we have
on one another."[70] For this reason the natural law does not permit the
pursuit of a higher good by means that impede achievement of a lower
good by another.[71]

According to this account, once we see that Aquinas intends the
hierarchy of natural inclinations to guide action by specifying obligations and prohibitions, we can also see that evaluating a human action –
placing it in its moral species – is largely a matter of finding its place
within the hierarchy. Morally praiseworthy actions will be those that
honor the proper ordering of basic goods, blameworthy actions will be
those that transgress it.[72] We can also see that, hierarchically arranged,
the goods to which we are naturally inclined become a criterion of fully
rational human action, the measure of *recta ratio*. Actions that fit within
the hierarchy of inclinations in the right sort of way are fully rational
precisely because they have found their proper place among reason's
goods.[73]

---

[66] Porter (1990, 144).　　[67] *Ibid.*, 93.　　[68] McInerny (1992, 122); Porter (1990, 144–145).
[69] McInerny (1992, 121, 123–124).　　[70] Porter (1990, 144).　　[71] *Ibid.*, 145.
[72] *Ibid.*, 144–146; McInerny (1992, 121–122).

How shall we evaluate this interpretation of Aquinas's remarks? I suggest we ask whether Aquinas could consent to its normative conclusions. If we can imagine his consent then we are on the way to confirming the interpretation. If we cannot, we have good reason to pursue an alternative.

Consider then Porter's explication of Aquinas's account of killing in self-defense.[74] Aquinas clearly considers defending oneself with violence morally acceptable, and he regards the use of deadly force justifiable in certain circumstances. And yet Porter's interpretation of the prescriptive consequences of his remarks on the natural law make justification elusive. By Porter's lights Aquinas considers self-preservation the most basic natural inclination, precisely because it regards life, the most basic of human goods. As such, the obligation it generates is the most stringent of the natural law's precepts. We cannot will the death of another as a means to some other end. We cannot sacrifice life for the sake of some other good. To do so is murder, which is absolutely prohibited by the hierarchy of basic goods. How then can we protect ourselves justly by intentionally killing another?

Porter believes that Aquinas solves this puzzle by appeal to the natural human inclination that self-defense instantiates.[75] She writes:

an act of self-defense fulfills the most basic criterion for a moral action, namely, that it be in conformity with a rational apprehension of the exigencies of human nature. And because no one has a duty to take more care of another's life than his own, this criterion overrides the criterion that would ordinarily identify the action as murder.[76]

The direct killing of another is unjust when it is done in defense of a basic good other than life. Most intentional killings are murderous in precisely this way. However, when another is intentionally killed in the defense of life the action is just because life is the most basic of basic goods.

Aquinas, I believe, would find this conclusion curious, this interpretation of his remarks odd. This conclusion asks us to believe that we can respond with deadly force when threatened with death but not when

---

[73] Porter (1990, 93, 146); McInerny (1992, 122–132).
[74] McInerny does not consider concrete examples of this sort, and therefore imagining how he would derive concrete moral judgments from the hierarchical arrangement of natural inclinations remains speculative. Nevertheless, since he does insist that the first precepts of the natural law oblige and prohibit conduct only as they are hierarchically arranged, we have good reason to suspect that his conclusions would track Porter's. For hints in this direction see his remarks about exceptions to the secondary precepts of the natural law (1992, 126–127).
[75] Porter (1990, 131).   [76] *Ibid.*, 130.

threatened, say, with an unnecessary lobotomy. Life can be sacrificed for life, but not for knowledge. If my attacker insists that my life is not in danger, only my ability to think and know, then by Porter's lights it would seem that I cannot respond with force that may result in his death, and this seems odd. More significant, however, is the fact that this interpretation enables us to justify actions Aquinas plainly considers vicious. In fact, Porter's interpretation ascribes to him a kind of consequentialism that he considers morally flat-footed precisely because it refers to good outcomes in order to warrant the transgression of absolute prohibitions. Porter contends that Aquinas regards the natural law as a collection of more or less binding prohibitions that together specify "one of the moral foundations of the natural law, namely, 'Do no harm.'"[77] Since these principles permit exceptions the morally significant question becomes one of deciding when harm of this or that sort is acceptable. According to Porter, Aquinas replies that a harmful action is acceptable when the end it seeks is sufficiently desirable, when the outcome it achieves is good enough to warrant the harm done. And he appeals to the hierarchy of natural inclinations in order to distinguish those outcomes that justify intentional harm from those that do not.[78]

The trouble with this interpretation is that Aquinas is clearly unwilling to compromise the prohibition against the intentional use of deadly force by private citizens. It is, he contends, absolutely binding.[79] Of course, he does consider killing lawful when it is directed to the welfare of the common good. For this reason he permits the intentional killing of those who are "dangerous and infectious to the community" (*ST* II–II.64.2), and entrusts the power of this punishment to those charged with the community's welfare (*ST* II–II.64.3). He does not, however, pursue the consequentialist calculations that Porter recommends in order to reach this conclusion. No exception to a prohibition is made here, although a distinction is drawn. Private citizens and public officials have different liberties and obligations assigned to each according to their different tasks and goals. Since the state is charged with the protection of the common good its caretakers are granted powers denied private citizens. Moreover, Aquinas carefully circumscribes the state's power to kill. Only those whose actions indicate that they have departed from the order of reason, away from the dignity of humanity and "into the slavish state of the beasts," can be considered candidates for execution. Clearly, few sinners are beasts of this sort, and therefore Aquinas cautions that

---

[77] *Ibid.*, 143.   [78] *Ibid.*
[79] See *De pot.* 1.1.6.4. I am grateful to Russell Hittinger for pointing out this passage.

"it be evil in itself to kill a man so long as he preserve his dignity" (*ST* II–II.64.2.3).

How then does Aquinas justify the private use of deadly force while insisting that without exception, "it is not lawful for a man to intend killing a man in self-defense"? By distinguishing intended end and accidental consequence. One may intend to repel the attacker and save one's own life by violent means. If one intends this end and uses the violence needed to achieve it, but no more, and if it happens that the attacker dies, his death should be considered an accidental consequence. That is, it may well happen that the violence needed to defend one's life results in the death of the attacker, even as his death was neither intended as an end nor willed as a means to securing safety. And this measure of violence is justified so long as no less is needed to repel the attack (*ST* II–II.64.7).

But what if the unintended consequences are foreseen? What if I know that deadly force will be needed to repel the attacker? How then can Aquinas insist that his death is accidental? This is the standard objection to double-effect reasoning and can be handled by denying what it assumes: that only unforeseen consequences can be unintentional. If you work for me and I let you go because business is slow, knowing that your job prospects are poor, I also know that as a result you will lose your house to the bank. I neither intend this loss as an end nor will it as a means. I wish it wouldn't happen, and yet I know it will. So I act regretfully, knowing that accidental harm will be the consequence of my actions. And in fact, my regret is a necessary, although not sufficient, sign that the harm was done apart from my intention.

We must conclude, then, that Aquinas's own treatment of killing in self-defense is not reflected in Porter's interpretation of his account of the natural law, its goods, precepts, and exceptions, and this gives us good reason to look for a different interpretation. Still, some may find the natural law consequentialism she attributes to Aquinas independently compelling precisely because it offers a way of thinking about moral prohibitions and their exceptions while avoiding the most pressing problem with consequentialism. That is, the hierarchy of goods enables us to sidestep the difficulty of saying how the variety of possible consequences can be compared without a common currency between them.[80] Comparisons are made between levels on the hierarchy, not between good outcomes *per se*. If my actions cause your loss, we do not

[80] Taylor's (1982) treatment of this difficulty remains elegant and compelling.

try to add up benefits and burdens. Rather, we appraise my action by locating the goods lost and achieved on the hierarchy of inclinations.

Nevertheless even natural law consequentialism leaves much to be desired. For it is presented as a universal moral theory, and yet it tends to justify harms that many of us could not. It prohibits defending goods higher on the hierarchy by harming those lower down. By the same token it apparently permits harm to goods higher on the hierarchy in defense of those lower down. If defending my good cannot be had apart from your loss, and if the good in question is lower on the hierarchy than the good you will lose, then it would seem that I can proceed to harm you. Imagine that you and I have been captured by sadistic thugs. They threaten to kill me if I don't lobotomize you. Since knowledge is higher on the hierarchy of basic goods than life, it would seem that I am justified in ending your days as a thinker in order to defend my life. In fact, since every good on the hierarchy is higher than life, and since Porter insists that we are not obliged to sacrifice our life for another, it appears that I would be justified in harming you in every possible way. Indeed, I must, for my life depends on it.

Many, of course, would welcome this outcome, their sentiments about the case confirmed in theory. Many, however, would not. Many would consider this insufficient justification for committing the necessary harms. Whatever their reasons, I think their complaints share a common feature. All find the natural law consequentialism that Porter attributes to Aquinas unable to justify the choices they consider necessary and praiseworthy, and powerless to account for the courses of action they condemn. Since the hierarchy of inclinations is the centerpiece of Porter's view we can further specify their complaint this way: the normative human life that she finds in the hierarchy fails to capture the character of the life they consider normative. Similarly, the secondary precepts and exceptions that the hierarchy generates fail to recommend courses of action that they consider praiseworthy. Aquinas, we have seen, stands in the company of these dissenters. He does concede that some goods are intrinsically better than others, but unlike Porter and McInerny, he does not regard the rough hierarchy that results as a decision machine for the morally perplexed. The goods of the soul are, no doubt, better than the goods of the body, but this fact does not generate a precept that tells us how to resolve the competing demands of body and soul in this or that instance.

2.

Two prominent interpretations of Aquinas's treatment of the natural law fall short. The first because its innovations demand unacceptable departures from our own moral practices. The second because it justifies courses of action that Aquinas could not. Given these outcomes, perhaps we should return to his remarks about the first precepts of natural law and look for a different picture of a normative human life and an alternative list of moral principles, all in the hope of bringing theory closer to judgment. Perhaps. But there is a different possibility here. Since both interpretations assume Aquinas intends his account of the first precepts to provide concrete moral guidance, perhaps we should proceed without this assumption. Perhaps his account follows from entirely different intentions.

The conclusions of chapter two seem to warrant this suspicion. In fact, they indicate that Aquinas has good reason to think that a theory designed to answer doubts about our particular obligations will always escape our reach. If the objects of the will are contingent, good from some points of view but not others (*ST* I–II.10.2; 19.10), and if the will is indeterminately disposed to all things that are good (*ST* I–II.10.1, 4), or nearly so (*ST* I–II.10.2), then the human good is too complex and unstable, and the character of right judgment with respect to that good too diverse and *ad hoc*, for us to think that praiseworthy human action can be captured in a set of precepts that specify rational choice with respect to that good. Indeed, the contingency of the human good makes theory building of this sort a hopeless enterprise. It follows that when Aquinas provides little assistance in deriving obligations and prohibitions from his account of the first precepts of the natural law, he has not abandoned us with an incomplete moral theory, as Finnis, Grisez, and Boyle would have it. Nor has he failed to specify the *per se nota* moral content of the basic goods, as McInerny suggests. Rather he indicates that the complexity of action that accords with *recta ratio* cannot be codified in a simple set of principles. For this reason he repeatedly insists that the judgments of the wise and the virtuous are our best measure of good and praiseworthy action and the only standard of excellence in practical reasonableness that we can, with good reason, hope for in this life (*ST* I–II.2.1.1; 100.1; II–II.49.3; 52.1.1).

Of course, Aquinas admits that there are moral principles, laws that direct us to act in some ways and not others. But he insists that a law is "a dictate of practical reason emanating from the ruler who governs" and is therefore nothing more than an abridgment of his practical deliberations and experience, a mere summary of his conclusions, not an antecedent guide that specifies the course of his deliberations or the content of his judgments (*ST* I–II.91.1). This is just what we would expect given the contingency of the good and the complexity of moral appraisal. For this reason Aquinas maintains that this side of Eden laws are framed to discipline the young and inexperienced, not the wise. Pedagogical intentions govern their use and dissemination. Laws withdraw the young from the "undue pleasures" to which they are inclined and restrain them from evil, "by force and fear" (*ST* I–II.95.1) in order that they might become good (*ST* I–II.92.1). As such, Aquinas does not believe that moral principles specify the content of perfected practical reasonableness. Instead, they constrain agency and shape souls by directing us to some ends and not others (*ST* I–II.92.1). As such, they provide the starting points of action and the proximate source and origin of the moral virtues.[81] They do not guarantee virtue, but rather enclose its training ground, where we come to know the good, desire it because it is, and eventually, to pursue good and praiseworthy courses of action that transcend the demands of principle.

Here one might object that this interpretation of Aquinas's views ascribes to him a kind of purified deontology, where the procedures of autonomous reason are the sole rule and measure of the good. If Aquinas insists that the judgments of the wise are the best measure of the good in this life, one wonders what prevents him from concluding that right reason *creates* goodness. Cris Korsgaard assigns such a view to Kant, who, by her lights, considers a choice and its object genuinely good when each is determined by fully rational procedures, procedures which exhaust the character of a good will and determine its own unconditional goodness. And of course, Kant regards the unconditional goodness of the will as the source of every other good. This means that the objects of the will are good, not in themselves or because of their relation to some other thing, but only insofar as they are the objects of a rational, fully justified, choice. Korsgaard puts the point well: "Value is ... 'conferred' by choice ... Thus the goodness of rationally chosen ends is a matter of the demands of practical reason rather than a matter of ontology."[82]

I think bringing together Kant and Aquinas in this way is a mistake, although distinguishing them with care will help clarify each. Aquinas

---

[81] The ultimate source is, of course, the mind and intention of the lawgiver.
[82] Korsgaard (1983, 183).

certainly believes that the good is located and justified for us by the practical judgments of the wise, but it is not *created*. It cannot be, for of course, even the wise, at times, mistake apparent goods for true, which implies that the truth about the human good resists reduction to their judgments. Aquinas makes sense of this ordinary possibility by referring to the "Sovereign Good," which transcends the fallible judgments of the wise and is nothing other than God's practical judgment about the good (*ST* 1–11.19.9) as it is expressed in the eternal law (*ST* 1–11.91.1). All things act in accordance with the eternal law and acquire their goodness from it, and all knowledge of the human good, both general and particular, is measured by it (*ST* 1–11.91.3.1). It follows that while the judgments of the wise are, for Aquinas, the proximate rule and measure of the human good, the best we can muster in this life, they are not the ultimate rule and measure, which allows Aquinas to refuse all talk of reason creating value.[83] By the same token he refuses to regard the eternal law as "a creature of epistemology," as a standard of truth about the good that can be known apart from participation in actual practices of rational justification, a standard that can be accessed in order to assess those practices.[84] Like Kant, he considers fully rational justification the best path to knowledge of the human good, given its contingency and difficulty, our limited knowledge, and our fallen condition. Like Kant he believes that nothing available to us can assess our justificatory practices except better practices. Nevertheless, he also insists that the human good transcends those practices, and it is not only his theological commitments that compel him to this conclusion. So does his rather ordinary assumption that without a good that transcends us we lose our ability to say that the judgments of the wise can fall short of the good.

Another way of getting to the same conclusion is to ask about the character of the fully rational justification that Korsgaard's Kant considers the source of value. Normally we offer procedural platitudes: be thorough in your inquiry, attend to the particulars, question obvious solutions, etc. And yet, these replies assume normative content, and therefore it is not at all clear how practical rationality can be the *independent* source of value. We say these things because they are abridgments of our account of what makes practical deliberation *good*, a summary of the procedures that have the best chance of achieving the

---

[83] "Human reason is not, of itself, the rule of things" (*ST* 1–11.91.3.2), precisely because practical reason is concerned with matters "singular and contingent," and therefore human judgment and law "cannot have that inerrancy that belongs to the demonstrated conclusions of sciences" (*ST* 1–11.91.3.3). [84] I am indebted to Stout (1988, 34, 259–260).

good as we know it. It follows that *recta ratio* cannot be defined in its own terms, that contra-Kant practical reason cannot be autonomous, at least not in the sense that guarantees the independence of its judgments from everything that we believe about the good. Indeed, practical reason has a moral construal, just as the good is defined in rational terms. Therefore, while the judgments of the virtuous and the wise are the best measure of the good, it is the good, expressed in the eternal law, that ultimately certifies their judgments as fully rational.[85] Finnis, Grisez, and Boyle object to this circularity, calling it vicious precisely because it eliminates all hope for a standard, independent and available, that we can use to evaluate our judgments about each. By their lights, right reason and the good cannot be mutually defining lest we lose our assurance that they are not locked in error.[86] We have seen that Finnis, Grisez, and Boyle secure this assurance by insisting upon the pre-moral character of the basic goods, which together provide an independent standard of practical reasonableness and give morality its original content. We have also seen that Aquinas finds good reason to doubt the pre-moral character of the first precepts. How then does he respond to the charge of circularity?

He accepts it. When practical reason and the good are defined together the circularity is virtuous, not vicious. For it to be vicious we would need good reason to think that many, if not most, of our judgments about the human good could be mistaken, for only then could we suspect that our moral understanding of right reason and our rational understanding of the good have missed their mark together.

---

[85] Korsgaard writes (1983, 183): "The point I want to emphasize here is that the Kantian approach frees us from assessing the rationality of a choice by means of the apparently ontological task of assessing the thing chosen: we do not need to identify especially rational ends. Instead, it is the reasoning that goes into the choice itself – the procedures of full justification – that determines the rationality of the choice, and so certifies the goodness of the object. Thus the goodness of rationally chosen ends is a matter of the demands of practical reason rather than a matter of ontology." Aquinas's point is that "the procedures of full justification" are contentless without an ontology of some sort, for only the good apprehended antecedent to choice can tell us what those procedures look like. Only the good can specify their rationality. Moreover, it is only by imagining a perfect ontology, a perfect list of all the good there is – call it the eternal law – that we can account for the fact that at times our best efforts fail to specify what those procedures demand.

[86] Thus, for example, the judgments of the virtuous cannot be a workable measure of moral goodness, "For ethical reflection is really helpful only if it can examine and criticize the assumptions underlying accepted virtues and vices. Reflection which takes a way of life for granted, as Aristotle, for example, did, fails to overcome the inadequacies in a society's political structure, religion, and so on which prevent its morally good members from attaining, or even accurately conceiving, the true happiness to which their hearts are open." Grisez, Boyle and Finnis (1987, 129); cf. Grisez (1983, 192–193)).

And yet Aquinas finds no good reason to imagine this possibility. In fact, he rules out global skepticism about the good when he insists that we are naturally disposed to know (*intellegere*) its general outlines as a prelude to willing it (*velle*) (*ST* I–II.94.2). Of course, this knowledge does not get us very far. It does not tell us what good in particular ought to be pursued in this or that instance, and thus it does not provide much help in distinguishing wisdom from folly. But it is knowledge enough to guarantee that our confusions about the good will not go all the way down, and this assurance permits us to put aside Finnis, Grisez, and Boyle's worry about the mutual dependence of right reason and the good.[87]

This conclusion brings into sharp relief the differences that divide Aquinas from the interpreters of his efforts considered above. They assume that the character of right reason can be captured by general rules derived in some manner from the first precepts of the natural law. But the good, as Aquinas rightly maintains, is contingent and complex and therefore our right relation to it cannot be captured in general rules of rationality derived from our natural orientation to its most basic outline. This implies that the flexible and manifold deliberations of the wise have the best chance of choosing in a manner that tracks the good in particular, and that the rationality of their judgments must be measured by something infinitely more complex itself, something that could encompass every conceivable statement about the human good that

[87] For a contemporary defense of a similar view see Stout (1988, 13–59). Like Aquinas, Stout believes that the wise can be mistaken about the good, and thus like Aquinas he would have to conclude that it makes little sense to follow Korsgaard's Kant and insist that the good is exhausted by the content of their judgments. However, unlike Aquinas, Stout offers a secular account of practical reason, the good, and moral truth, and therefore he cannot follow Aquinas's solution. That is, he cannot account for the fact that our best practical judgments often fail to capture the truth about the good by locating the independent character of that good in God's eternal law. Instead he asks us to imagine a book that contains every possible true judgment about the human good. Call it "a *Concise Encyclopedia of Ethical Truth*." Stout claims no metaphysical finding here, just an active "philosophical imagination's variation on three themes: the notion that moral truth is one, the hope that the fraction of it we care about is not infinitely complicated, and the realization that it cannot be reduced to what we already know. It is not a handbook anyone can use, even at the end of inquiry . . . Its structure is not that of an encyclopedia. It is a *Phenomenology of Spirit* no chapter of which is the last" (Stout 1993, 230–231). What Stout offers here is best described as a secular, and metaphysically austere, version of Aquinas's eternal law. The *Encyclopedia* serves the same function for Stout that the eternal law does for Aquinas. It accounts for moral truths that transcend the judgments of the wise, and yet its pages list no moral rules that might decide concrete action. Its endless character matches the limitless expanse of God's wisdom and exhausts the nearly infinite variety of possible true judgments about the good. Of course, Aquinas's eternal law originates in the deliberations of a lawgiver, not in the imaginings of philosophers. Still, this theological difference has little practical consequence for those doing the difficult work of distinguishing true from merely apparent goods, precisely because neither the eternal law nor Stout's *Encyclopedia* provides much independent assistance.

tracks the truth. It also implies that our natural orientation toward the basic outline of the human good, recounted in the most general precepts of the natural law, is assigned a quite different role in Aquinas's account of the moral life.

In the next section I will argue that the degree of our participation in the eternal law specifies the character of our practical rationality. The eternal law is nothing but a dictate of God's practical reason, his judgment about the good (*ST* I–II.91.1). As such, our reason is right, its judgments in accord with the human good, when its participation in the eternal law is perfect. When its participation falls short of perfection, our choices remain rational and thus human only insofar as they are knowingly directed to one of the basic ends specified by the first precepts. This means that for Aquinas the first precepts characterize minimally rational agency, not *recta ratio*, the smallest participation in the eternal law that nevertheless preserves our humanity, not the greatest. For now it is enough to see that if the eternal law is the ultimate rule and measure of right reason, then Aquinas has no need for the position many exegetes assume he defends. He has no need for a moral theory that specifies the concrete content of right reason because that content has already been specified by the eternal law.

J. B. Schneewind has argued that moral philosophy moves between two poles in the modern period. At one extreme the standard of moral goodness is located outside of us and the moral life is largely a matter of becoming the sort of person who can conform to its demands. At the other extreme "morality is itself a creation or projection of our inmost nature and that consequently we are naturally both aware of what it tells us to do and motivated to do it."[88] Secularization proceeds as we move from the former extreme to the latter, and it appears that many of Aquinas's interpreters proceed with secular assumptions. Insofar as they ignore Aquinas's insistence that the eternal law is the ultimate measure of *recta ratio*, and thus of good and evil in human action, and insofar as they insist that Aquinas derives normative principles from our nature that can serve as that measure, they appear to read Aquinas's treatment of the natural law with eyes schooled to see the moral life as something that comes into the world as "an expression of ourselves."[89] To be sure, these interpreters locate the origin of our nature in God's will, and therefore the move from one extreme to the next is hardly complete.

---

[88] Schneewind (1990, 18). The remarks come from Schneewind's introduction to the anthology. For an account of the historical progression from the first pole to the second see Schneewind (1997).   [89] Schneewind (1990, 29).

Nevertheless, the impetus is there. If our capacity for moral self-direction is considerable, if the moral law is indeed written on our hearts, then it seems reasonable to imagine good and evil in human action characterized without reference to an extrinsic standard of *recta ratio*. Similarly, it seems reasonable to assume that interpreters could find this kind of treatment of the natural law in Aquinas's remarks only as they proceed without significant reference to what he says about the eternal law.

Of course, following Aquinas and insisting that *recta ratio* is specified by the eternal law provides little comfort to those puzzled about the good that is to be done in this or that instance. And yet, the difficulty, uncertainty, and corrigibility of moral judgment is just what Aquinas believes we should expect. Grace once assured sufficient participation in the eternal law and confident knowledge of the good. This side of Eden, our reason is now "bereft of its vigor," its participation in the divine mind diminished (*ST* I–II.91.6). Given the contingency and complexity of the human good, our confusion about it hardly surprises. Nor does our need for virtue and grace, which together offer the best hope for returning reason to its vigor so that it might again choose in accord with the eternal law.

3.

Since Aquinas regards the kind of moral theory that proposes to answer doubts about obligation as both senseless and unnecessary we have little reason to assume that his remarks on the natural law are designed to provide moral guidance. Instead, we should regard his remarks as a description of human agency, created by God and governed by His Providence, which is precisely what he indicates in the prologue to *ST* I–II.90. There Aquinas tells us that God's law is his concern in the questions that follow, and of course a law is nothing but a dictate of reason that governs the agency of those subject to it (*ST* I–II.90.1). Since Aquinas believes that everything is what it is and not some other thing because of the character of its agency, because of the ends it pursues and the manner in which it pursues them, his treatment of the ends that we apprehend and will with nature's necessity is his account of creation and Providence as they pertain to human beings and human actions (*ST* I–II.91.1–2).

Creation regards the individuation of things, Providence their governance. Both follow from God's practical judgment about the sorts of ends that a creature should pursue and the way it should pursue them, all according to its kind (*ST* 1.22.1).[90] Since a law is a dictate of practical reason (*ST* I–II.90.1.2), a summary of a ruler's judgment about the ends his subjects must pursue (*ST* I–II.91.1), Aquinas maintains that God creates and governs all things by framing laws (*ST* I–II.91.1).[91] The eternal law is the collection of those dictates (*ST* I–II.93.1), and the diversity of creation follows from the diverse ways that God's creatures participate in that law. Thus, everything is what it is and not some other thing because it participates in the eternal law in one way and not another, directed by God's judgment and bound by His law to act for the sake of some ends but not all (*ST* I–II.91.2; *SCG* III.4–5). A swallow, for example, is the particular sort of creature that it is and not an eagle, a fish, or a slug insofar as it participates in God's eternal law according to its kind. Its actions and passions are directed toward certain ends, such as nest building, by certain means, with mud and grass, not sticks, not twine. And a swallow is a good swallow, a perfect instance of the sort of thing that it is, when it achieves all the ends that it naturally pursues as a consequence of its swallow-like participation in the eternal law. Indeed, we say that a good swallow has perfected its nature.

The creation and governance of human beings follows a similar course. God's practical judgment directs us to will certain ends and not others. We will them naturally, which is to say necessarily, and the pursuit of this particular collection of ends is one of the things that distinguishes the agency of our species (*ST* I–II.10.1; 94.2). The other is the manner in which we pursue those ends according to God's law. That is, we act with knowledge (*ST* I–II.91.2). Acting with knowledge entails knowing the ends we are inclined to pursue in a manner that permits deliberation over the means (*ST* I–II.6.1–2). And since the ability to deliberate, to compare one course of action with another, entails a certain indeterminacy of action, we are not bound by God's eternal law to pursue any one of our natural ends or choose any particular course as a means to any particular end (*ST* I–II.10.1; 14.1). That is, acting with knowledge gives human agency an indeterminacy and a diversity not

---

[90] Aquinas discusses Providence by referring to its analogical relation to prudential judgment. There are, of course, disanalogies. The prudent take counsel, while God has no need of "an inquiry into matters that are doubtful." Nevertheless, counsel concludes in "a command as to the right ordering of things towards an end," and this too is the work of Providence (*ST* 1.22.1.1).

[91] "Hence Sacred Scripture ascribes the production and goverance of things to divine wisdom and prudence. Indeed, it is stated in Proverbs (3:19–20): 'The Lord by wisdom hath founded the earth; He hath established the heavens by prudence' . . . And in Wisdom (8.1) it is said of the wisdom of God that 'it reacheth from end to end mightily, and ordereth all things sweetly'" (*SCG* III.10).

found in creatures like swallows that act without knowledge. Indeed, for Aquinas it is precisely because knowledge mediates our participation in the eternal law that we are able to act in all sorts of particular ways, and beyond natural necessity, while swallows have a small repertoire of actions that they must perform insofar as they are swallows. Our ability to act knowingly also explains why we are rational creatures and they are not (*ST* I–II.6.1–2; 91.6). For when pressed we can provide reasons in defense of our choices, reasons that explain what we are doing and why. And of course, rational justification of this sort must refer to ends and means that are known to be good and pursued because of that knowledge.

Aquinas sums up this difference by saying that rational creatures, those who participate in God's eternal law by knowing its demands, act according to the natural law. The natural law, he insists, is nothing "but the participation of the eternal law in the rational creature" (*ST* I–II.91.2). Other creatures, of course, also participate of the eternal law, but not in a rational matter and therefore it cannot be said that the actions characteristic of their kind, their natural actions, are actions done in accord with law.[92] For "a law is something pertaining to reason," and therefore agents can be directed by law only as they know its demands (*ST* I–II.90.1; 91.2.3). Because Providence makes demands upon rational creatures by giving them natural and habitual knowledge of the ends characteristic of their kind, what Aquinas calls *synderesis* (*ST* I.79.12; I–II.94.1.2), they participate in God's practical judgment – in God's eternal law – by becoming provident themselves, by making their own practical judgments as they direct their own actions. And since a law is nothing but a dictate of practical reason, our participation in God's practical judgment is called the natural law in us, whereby we become provident over the actions characteristic of our kind by sharing God's judgment about our proper ends (*ST* I–II.91.2).

Thus to say that human beings act according to the natural law is above all a statement about the formal character of human agency, created by God and governed by His Providence. It is to say, on the one

[92] Aquinas maintains that there are two ways for a thing to participate in the eternal law, by way of knowledge and by way of action and passion. Human beings participate in both ways, creatures without reason only in the latter (*ST* I–II.93.6). The implication is that we are rational animals. We pursue the ends characteristic of our kind with knowledge, and yet we also have animal bodies of a particular sort, and a sensitive appetite that produces passionate responses to the world with a particular natural character. Indeed, without the influence of reason, our sensitive appetite would respond to the world as the natural appetite in irrational animals does, with a natural necessity derived from its participation in the eternal law (*ST* I.82.2.3).

hand, that it is knowledge of the ends to which we are naturally inclined by God's eternal law that moves us to act in ways that are characteristically human. On the other, it implies that human agency is rational precisely because of this knowledge, this judgment we share in common with God about our good. For, of course, the ability to know the ends for which we act entails the ability to provide reasons that make our actions intelligible, reasons that refer to the ends that we naturally and necessarily regard as good and will as such.

Perfection in human agency tracks a similar course. Like a swallow, we become a good instance of the sort of thing that we are by acting in accord with the eternal law and freely perfecting our participation in it. However, a swallow's perfect participation in the eternal law is guaranteed, or nearly so, for only misfortune can prevent it. Providence determines both the specific ends and particular means of its actions and therefore if it manages to act as a swallow, according to its nature, its perfection follows. By contrast, our perfect participation in the eternal law is not even nearly assured. Providence governs our agency with far looser reins. It determines us to general classes of ends while remaining thoroughly agnostic about particular ends and specific means. We have noted this *must* be so if we are to act with knowledge, if our participation in the eternal law is to consist in knowing its demands and acting for the sake of what is known. Now the implication of this ability comes into focus: we can participate in the eternal law in greater and lesser degrees, with more or less perfection (*ST* I–II.93.2, 6). Our relation to the natural law follows suit. Since the natural law is nothing but a rational creature's participation in God's eternal law, our actions will be more or less in accord with the natural law as their participation in the eternal law is more or less perfected.

Of course, every human action, insofar as it is human, must participate in the eternal law and accord with the natural law in some minimal sense. At the very least it must be done with knowledge of one of the ends to which we are naturally inclined, one of the goods that characterize our agency as human. It might also be done to avoid the loss of one of these goods, but no matter. In all that we do the first precept of the natural law is fulfilled: some human good is pursued or some evil is avoided (*ST* I–II.94.2). We can call this bare bones participation in the eternal law minimally rational human action. Why? Because knowing the human good is a prerequisite for acting rationally for the sake of it, and therefore knowledge of the most general character of the human good is the most basic prerequisite for rational, and thus human, action.

Alternatively, actions that pursue specific examples of one of the natural human ends in the right circumstances and by the right means are actions that track the details of the eternal law with greater precision. When this sort of precision is achieved more or less consistently, the agent participates in the eternal law more or less perfectly according to her kind precisely because she chooses courses of action that track the human good as it is characterized in the eternal law (*ST* I–II.93.2). And since action in accord with the eternal law must be done knowingly, with the ability to give reasons why one acts in one way and not another, perfect participation in the eternal law will be the result of perfected rationality. It will be action in accord with right reason. It will also be action in perfect accord with the natural law, which is nothing other than a rational creature's participation in the eternal law.

According to Aquinas, grace perfected Adam's reason and guaranteed his perfect participation in the eternal law. With grace lost and our practical reasonableness disabled (*ST* I–II.91.6), our participation in the eternal law falls short of perfection. So too does our concord with the natural law. For this reason Aquinas insists that every sin is contrary to nature (*ST* I–II.78.3) and to the eternal law (*ST* I–II.71.6). The good is contingent and therefore difficult to know. The will is largely indeterminate and as such does not by nature dispose us to particular goods, neither ends nor means. Our contingent passions distract our reason and distort our judgments about the good. Thus our need for the virtues, moral and theological, which return us to that state where we might know the good, will it because it is good, and therefore choose courses of action in full accord with the eternal law (*ST* I–II.93.6). When our agency is more or less perfected in this way our actions are more or less in full accord with our nature. However, even when our agency falls short of perfection, when reason is less than right, our participation in the eternal law remains sufficient to guarantee that our actions remain minimally rational and thus characteristically human (*ST* I–II.93.2, 6). Indeed, even sinful action is human action. It is done for the sake of one of the ends that we know and will by nature, which is equivalent to saying that it is rational in some minimal sense and thus dependent upon some minimal participation in the eternal law (*ST* I–II.85.1–2; 91.2.1 and ad 1).

It follows that *every* human action is in accord with the natural law, at least in some minimal sense. That is, every human action follows from rational participation in the eternal law, from knowing and willing the good that is characteristic of our kind. Thus Aquinas writes that, every act of reason and will in us is based on that which is according to nature, as stated above [*ST* I–II.10.1]: for every act of reasoning is based on principles that are known naturally . . . Accordingly the first direction of our acts to their end must needs be in virtue of the natural law [*ST* I–II.91.2.1].[93]

This is equivalent to saying that action in accord with the natural law is simply action that is rational and thus human, which in turn is equivalent to saying that it is action that follows from knowledge of one of the ends that Providence disposes us to regard as good and will as such, naturally and necessarily. All human action assumes knowledge of this sort, basic rationality of this kind. For this reason the general ends or basic goods that Aquinas calls the first precepts of the natural law are also first principles of practical reason (*ST* I–II.94.2). We pursue one of them with knowledge if we do anything at all, and we refer to at least one of them when we offer reasons that justify this or that course of action.

Clearly, this is not an account of the general precepts that provides much moral guidance. Concrete obligations receive neither specification nor justification. The content of right reason is neither outlined nor defined. Of course, Aquinas does regard the obligation to do harm to no human being as one of the first general precepts of the natural law, which, like the others, is known without reflection or inference (*ST* I–II.95.2; 100.3). And yet this obligation provides very little assistance as we try to decide what to do in this or that instance. In fact, like the first precepts themselves, this first obligation is, above all, a basic criterion of human action.

The first precepts describe the broad outlines of human agency, rational and voluntary, both good and evil, by specifying "all those things to which man has a natural inclination, are naturally apprehended as good, and consequently as objects of pursuit" (*ST* I–II.94.2). They set us forth as human agents, doing human kinds of things, insofar as they specify the ends that we naturally (and thus necessarily) judge good, will simply, and refer to as reasons for acting. An agent who falls outside of these broad outlines cannot be said to act for the sake of one of the ends that distinguish our agency as human. What they do will be unnatural in the most basic sense. It will not be rational action; it will not be human action. For this reason Aquinas insists that "the precepts of

---

[93] This makes plain that Aquinas's remarks on the natural law are simply an extended commentary on *ST* I–II.10.1. There he argues that the will is moved naturally to certain ends, that those ends act as principles of practical deliberation, and that together they direct us to all those actions that are characteristic of our kind. No mention is made of virtue or vice, good or evil, for it is assumed that human agency as a whole is the object of inquiry.

the natural law are to the practical reason, what the first principles of demonstrations are to the speculative reason" (*ST* I–II.94.2). Just as the principle of non-contradiction is assumed in all human knowing, so too the first precepts of the natural law are assumed in all human action. Just as consistent failure to honor the principle of non-contradiction in belief and inference does not yield false belief, but rather nothing that can be recognized as human knowing, so too failure to act with knowledge for the sake of one of the ends specified by the natural law does not yield vicious action, but rather an event unintelligible as agency.

The prohibition against harming others functions in a similar manner. We have already noted that Aquinas does not think we are prohibited from effecting the loss of another's good. Freedom, property, even life can be taken if the intention and circumstances are right. In short, harm can be just. It follows that the natural law prohibition not to harm is an obligation to refrain from unjust harm. Injustice is the injury we are obliged to refrain from doing, and justice is the good that stands among the others specified by the first precepts. It functions as they do. Imagine a person who does not see the point of refraining from injustice of all kinds. In every circumstance he refuses to give others their due. Don't imagine the clever knave who, on occasion, pursues his own interests by unjust means. Rather, picture the person who *never* acts justly, who never concedes the importance of doing so, and who is never afflicted with remorse when he injures another. We would, I suspect, regard him as mad. Of course, none of this implies that the rest of us fulfill the demands of this absolute prohibition whenever we act. Surely we do not. Surely we injure others with actions rational and voluntary. Like the clever knave we do unjust harm to others in order to achieve some good other than justice that we also know and will by nature. And yet we do so without denying that justice is good, or refusing to will it simply and absolutely, even as we choose against it on occasion.

Caution is required here. The fact that the first precepts do not provide solutions to our puzzles about what we should and should not do, the fact that they simply describe what we in fact do by specifying the ends we in fact pursue no matter what we do according to our kind, does not diminish their status as precept, which, by definition, prescribes that something be done.[94] The first precepts are the conclusions of God's practical deliberations about the ends that give our agency its natural shape and human character. They are His judgments about what *should*

---

[94] " . . . law denotes a kind of plan directing acts toward an end" (*ST* I–II.93.3).

be, and they are promulgated as law insofar as He instills them "into man's mind so as to be known by him naturally" (*ST* I–II.90.4.I) and insofar as they become "the rule and measure" of our agency upon His command (*ST* I–II.90.4).[95] But note, it is God the creator who commands, and thus what He concludes and promulgates in law comes to be according to its measure. With the first precepts of the natural law He creates the human will, the proximate source of human action, by specifying what its most general character should be and will be. Indeed, this is what it means for these precepts of law to be natural. With them God creates the kind of thing that we necessarily are, the kind of agency that distinguishes our kind of thing. It follows that, *quoad nos*, they are not obligations, if by this we mean they are known by us as constraints upon our agency.[96] We feel no duty to do as they command. Rather, the first precepts are known by us as the ends that we, already and always, judge good and will simply as a result of God's command. In fact, insofar as the first precepts are precepts of *natural* law they cannot be received as obligation. Agents must exist as one thing and not another before they can be obliged to do this or that, and it is precisely this specification of our rational nature that God effects by means of the first precepts. He creates us by specifying the natural character of our agency.

Of course, some might ask how a precept promulgated by a lawgiver but not received by the governed as obligation can nevertheless be considered *law*. Mustn't laws coerce? Isn't the person subject to law constrained? Isn't she obliged to pursue an end she might otherwise avoid or ignore? Not always, at least not if we follow Aquinas's lead. Laws direct rational agents to ends judged good by a lawgiver (*ST* I–II.90.I). When those directed show resistance, and when the lawgiver has power and authority, laws can coerce as they are promulgated, but they need not. When a law directs us to an end we know to be good and love because of that knowledge, it is not received as a binding obligation,

---

[95] The fact that Aquinas thinks God creates with law promulgated by command should give pause to those tempted to regard theological accounts of the moral life that begin with divine commands as different in kind from those that begin with the natural law. Aquinas puts this temptation to rest in a remark from the commentary on Job: "For whoever sins is opposed to God when he resists the divine commands, either those which have been handed down in the written Law or those which have been imparted to man's reason naturally" (*Super Iob* 7.155). For a contemporary discussion of this temptation and of reasons to resist it see the essays by Hittinger and Schreiner in Cromartie (1997).

[96] Hibbs (1990) quite rightly points out that talk of obligation *can be* appropriate here, but only insofar as we forego modern usage, which implies the law's constraint and our resistance. For if God obliges us to act according to the first precepts it is only as gentle teacher, as the One who leads us by sweet persuasion to love the human good.

and yet surely it is a dictate of practical wisdom (*ST* I–II.91.3) that must be done by those subject to the lawgiver (*ST* I–II.99.1). The fact that it *will* be done with ease, indeed with natural necessity, does nothing to diminish its status as law. It remains a dictate of practical reason, which is, of course, what law most fundamentally is.[97]

The prohibition against unjust harm offers the one exception to these cautionary remarks. It also confirms them. Unlike the other first precepts of the natural law, the precept, do no unjust harm, is known by us as obligation. It binds and constrains. Justice, at least in this negative sense, *must* be intended in some manner in all that we do, as either proximate or distant end, all according to divine command. However, we are not obliged to regard justice as a good and will it simply, for of course, like the other goods specified by the first precepts, we already do, naturally and necessarily.

Finally, Aquinas does not rank the first precepts or insist that agents with perfect rationality will pursue them in an order specified by the natural law. He does, of course, list the natural law precepts in a certain order, but the hierarchy of inclinations that results does not oblige or prohibit by specifying a normative human life. Rather, it situates human beings under Providence among the rest of God's creatures, displaying at once both the complexity and the unity of the eternal law and the identities and differences among those subject to it. Thus Aquinas follows the order he finds in creation as he describes the ends we are naturally disposed to consider good and desire as such. He begins with our desire to preserve ourselves in being, according to our nature, which we "have in common with all substances." He then moves to those inclinations and activities that we "have in common with other animals . . . such as sexual intercourse, education of offspring, and so forth." He concludes by referring to those inclinations that follow from our rational nature, such as our desire to know the truth, particularly about God, and to live in society (*ST* I–II.94.2).

As such, Aquinas's treatment of the first precepts should not be read as both Porter and McInerny suppose, as a response to *ST* I–II.1–5, as a specification of the human good that the virtuous must pursue if happi-

---

[97] Note, it is precisely the fact that law need not constrain that enables Aquinas to explicate the Gospel as New Law. The New Law instills grace, which enables the faithful to know and love the good that it inscribes on their hearts, and to do so with ease and thus without constraint (*ST* I–II.106.2). He can also distinguish New and Old Law along these lines. The Old is the Law of constraint, the New, the Law of freedom (*ST* I–II.107.1.2), yet both remain law insofar as both are practical directives. This, I suspect, diffuses many of the traditional Protestant complaints with Gospel explicated as law.

ness is to be secured. Rather his remarks should be read as a response to
ST ɪ–ɪɪ.6–2ɪ. In *ST* ɪ–ɪɪ.6–ɪ7 Aquinas develops a moral psychology that
accounts for the voluntary character of our actions. In *ST* ɪ–ɪɪ.ɪ8–2ɪ he
describes the contingency of the human good. His remarks on the
natural law, already abridged in *ST* ɪ–ɪɪ.ɪo.ɪ–2, bring each inquiry to a
close. They conclude the former insofar as they specify the ends that
human actions, rational and voluntary, must, by nature, pursue. They
conclude the latter insofar as they describe the outer limits that our
God-given humanity places upon the contingency of the human good.
Indeed, despite contemporary assertions to the contrary, contingency
cannot go all the way down. It couldn't. A creature that was not directed
to some ends by natural necessity would not be a particular kind of thing
with a particular sort of agency. Indeed, it would not be a creature. It
would be chaos.[98]

4.

If Aquinas's treatment of the natural law is not a moral theory designed
to dispel doubts about obligation, if he does not provide the principles of
rational choice that specify the content of right reason and the character
of virtuous choice, then what relationship between virtue and the
natural law does he assume? The answer comes in three parts.

First, "all virtuous acts belong to the natural law" (*ST* ɪ–ɪɪ.94.3), not
only because virtuous actions are, by definition, rational and voluntary
(*ST* ɪɪ–ɪɪ.58.ɪ), but also because the natural law, by definition, is nothing
but our participation in the eternal law, and virtuous actions participate
in the eternal law in greater measure than actions that fall short of
virtue.

Second, virtue is the proper effect of the natural law (*ST* ɪ–ɪɪ.92.ɪ;
ɪo7.2). The first precepts of the natural law specify what it is to act

---

[98] See R. Rorty (1989, xiii, xv, 7–8, 21, 30, 35, 40–41); Smith (1988, 1–16, 30–53). Rorty and Smith
would probably reply that the contingency of the human good *can* go all the way down precisely
because human beings are not natural kinds of things with a distinctive kind of agency, defined at
creation and governed by Providence. Metaphysical austerity yields radical contingency. Perhaps. But even those committed to a naturalized ontology assume a minimalist account of our
common humanity and a provisional treatment of those goods that distinguish human agency.
Even they must distinguish rationality in action from madness. Indeed if Rorty can say that a
liberal democrat must find Nietzsche and Loyola "mad" because there is no way to see them as
"people whose life plans might, given ingenuity and good will, be fitted in with those of other
citizens," then we can easily imagine him drawing a species specific distinction between human
beings and those animals that do not appear to have life plans that can be identified as human
(Rorty [1991c, 187]). It is this latter distinction that Aquinas marks as he catalogues our natural
inclinations.

rationally, to pursue the goods characteristic of our kind with knowledge. The moral virtues are perfections of our rational powers of action. It follows that "there is in every man a natural inclination to act according to reason: and this is to act according to virtue" (*ST* I–II.94.3). Caution is required here. The remark is modest. Aquinas asserts only this: since the first precepts of the natural law are the origin of every rational human action, both good and evil, they must also be the origin of those actions that follow from our rational powers perfected by habit. There is no indication here that Aquinas believes that action in accord with those precepts makes virtuous action inevitable, or even likely. Rather, his point is that they incline us to rational action, and thus to virtue only insofar as the virtues perfect that inclination. And of course, a natural inclination and its perfection, a power and its habit, are different matters altogether. To know and desire the basic outlines of the human good is one thing. It is quite another to know and choose the good in particular circumstances with the constancy characteristic of virtue. For this reason Aquinas considers the first precepts of the natural law mere "nurseries of virtue" (*seminalium virtutum*) (*ST* I–II.51.1), the "inchoate" beginnings of virtuous habits, nothing more (*ST* I–II.63.1).[99]

Third, while the virtues are the proper effects of the natural law, and thus all virtuous actions, considered as virtuous belong to the natural law, not all virtuous actions, considered as such, belong to the natural law and are prescribed by it. If, however, we speak of virtuous actions "considered in themselves" (*secundum seipsos*), we cannot conclude that all are prescribed by the natural law's precepts (*ST* I–II.94.3; cf. 100.2). Since nature regards those things that are both common and necessary to all, the natural law prescribes acts of virtue that all can know and have good reason to choose. Not every virtuous action is of this sort. We confront a considerable variety of conditions and circumstances in this world (*ST* I–II.94.3.3), and, as a result, we develop a diverse collection of customs and conventions that are conducive to living well in some times and places but not all (*ST* I–II.94.3). Since the virtuous give due attention to the demands of custom and convention in their own time and place, it follows that "certain acts are virtuous for some, as being proportionate and becoming to them, while they are vicious for others" (*ST* I–

---

[99] This account of the relation between virtue and the first precepts, along with the wide scope that Aquinas gives deliberation, effectively eliminates Irwin's (1990a) doubts about Aquinas's treatment of prudence. If the *specific* ends the prudent intend are not set by the first precepts of the natural law, then it cannot be the case that their efforts have nothing to do with disposing themselves to the right ends.

II.94.3.3). Indeed, since human action bears on "contingent matters . . . truth or practical rectitude is not the same for all, as to matters of detail, but only as to the general principles" (*ST* I–II.94.4).[100]

That said, Aquinas does insist that some secondary moral principles are the "proper conclusions" of the first precepts of the natural law (*ST* I–II.94.4). Here he has in mind those obligations and prohibitions found in the old law. Objective, universal, and absolutely binding, they belong to the first precepts precisely because the ends we know and will by nature incline us to approve "at once" what they demand (*ST* I–II.100.1; 98.5). Still, there is no necessity here, for the movement from the first precepts of the natural law to the moral precepts of the old law, from the bare requirements of minimally rational human action to secondary moral principles, is mediated by judgment (*ST* I–II.100.1; 94.4). Of course, it is judgment that proceeds "after very little [*cum modica*] consideration," and therefore most will in fact know the natural law's proper conclusions. By contrast, those less than proper conclusions, those secondary moral principles that cannot be known without "careful consideration," will be available to the virtuous alone (*ST* I–II.100.1). Nevertheless, confusion about secondary principles of all kinds remains a possibility for all of us, the wise as well as the common. "The mind is ready to grasp at once," but the mind, in this instance, is moved by judgment and judgment can fail (*ST* I–II.100.6).

Thus Aquinas writes that, "it is right and true for all to act according to reason: and from this principle it follows, as a proper conclusion, that goods entrusted to another should be restored to their owner." However, not all will know how to derive the prohibition against theft from the criteria of minimal rationality in human action provided by first precepts, or manage to apply it well once it is known. On Caesar's authority Aquinas points out that the German tribes beyond the Danube did not consider theft wrong, "even though it is expressly contrary to the natural law." He speculates that excessive passion, evil persuasions, vicious customs, or corrupt habits may have distorted their judgment. At our distance we can assume that the Germans have overcome these causes and put aside their error, but we cannot conclude that virtuous choices will automatically follow. The prohibition against theft has to be applied in concrete circumstances, where fussy

---

[100] No truth relativism is implied here. Aquinas is simply summarizing the conclusions of our inquiries in chapter two: the good is contingent and its circumstances change. As such, the moral species of an action can change as circumstance and intention do.

details and contingent singulars obscure the good and obstruct practical inquiry, making it difficult to know when to restore property held for another and when to withhold (*ST* 1–11.94.4). Indeed, distinguishing just and unjust takings is rarely easy and the natural law prohibition against theft merely initiates the difficulty. Only virtue can resolve it, and yet a virtuous choice, in this instance or any other, must be made willingly. If, after "slight reflection" upon the first precepts of the natural law the Germans come to know that theft is prohibited (*ST* 1–11.100.3), and if, after reflecting further, they determine that this prohibition can be honored in this instance by restoring this or that piece of property, they will, nevertheless, make a choice that falls short of virtue if they are motivated by threats or rewards and not love of virtue.

It follows that the first precepts of the natural law, by themselves, leave us very nearly morally destitute. They do, naturally and necessarily, without inference or judgment, oblige us to refrain from doing unjust harm, but they do not tell us what acting unjustly in particular entails. They do, upon little reflection, enable us to derive the moral precepts of the old law, but as we have noted, there is no guarantee that reflection will succeed, and when it does, action in accord with the precepts of the old law in concrete circumstances remains unlikely without the perfection in judgment and affection that the moral virtues provide. Since Aquinas insists that the moral virtues cannot be had in significant measure without the theological virtues (*ST* 1–11.65.2), without, that is, "the grace of the Holy Spirit bestowed inwardly" (*ST* 1–11.106.2), and since this gift of the Holy Spirit is the chief element of the New Law, he also insists that action in accord with the proper conclusions of the first precepts of the natural law is largely unimaginable without the "grace instilled in our hearts" by the New (*ST* 1–11.107.1.2). Apart from this grace the first precepts of the natural law cannot tell us how to act virtuously. By themselves they cannot specify the content of the human good that must be pursued in order to perfect our agency and secure our happiness. They cannot tell us what action according to right reason entails. They can, however, specify the general ends that God commands us to know and will by nature, ends that provide the starting points for all deliberation, that circumscribe the broad spheres of intelligible human activity, and that we pursue in all that we do in particular that is rational and voluntary, whether good or evil. As such, they do characterize the effects of His creative practical judgment upon human agency.

These conclusions shed light on a striking feature of Aquinas's moral criticism: the paucity of reference to those things *quae non sunt secundum naturam humanam*. If the first precepts of the natural law spell out, in some more or less specific manner, the content of the human good and the character of the morally praiseworthy, then we would expect Aquinas to resort to the language of nature as he describes good and evil in human action. We would expect him to regard those who pursue sinful courses as acting against nature. This is not what we find. Of course, Aquinas does maintain that sinful actions are unnatural in at least one sense: they fall short of perfect participation in the eternal law (*ST* I–II.78.3). But then all human actions that proceed without the assistance of a full measure of grace fall short, even virtuous actions, which, this side of Eden, are always imperfect. It follows that calling a sinful action unnatural does little to distinguish it, little to place it on the moral landscape. The language of virtue and vice does, and thus Aquinas's frequent resort to it in his moral criticism is hardly surprising.

What *does* surprise is the fact that he considers a small collection of actions both *contra naturam*, in the strict sense, and blameworthy. This puzzles. In the strict sense an action not in accord with human nature is not an action. It is not the sort of thing we do *qua* human kind of thing. It is not done for the sake of an end we know and will naturally by God's law and command. It is not an action to which we could assign a good reason as cause, and thus it would be, quite literally, irrational; more event than action. Oddly enough, Aquinas concurs. That is, those things that are, in themselves, unnatural – cannibalism, bestiality, homosexuality, taking pleasure in eating dirt, coal, and the like – are not, by his lights, intelligible human actions. For him, they carry the mark of fundamental irrationality, indeed, of madness.

No doubt, some might quibble with the composition of his list of abominations, but the obvious examples make the point well enough. Imagine you come across a colleague sitting on the lawn, feasting on spoonful after spoonful of soil. When you ask him what he is doing and he happily replies that he is having breakfast, it is unlikely that you will accept this explanation, content that he's keeping himself in being according to his nature and thus pursuing one of the ends we know and will by nature. Rather, you will doubt the basic rationality and fundamental intelligibility of his actions, precisely because you cannot explain them by referring to any end that the intellect can judge good and regard as a reason for acting. In that event, regarding him as a responsible agent will be difficult if not unjust. Indeed, calling his actions unnatural will not carry the implication of moral criticism but of diagnosis. Aquinas admits as much.[101]

How then does he reach the conclusion that you have witnessed an action not an event, that your colleague deserves blame not pity? First he notes that the unnatural in this strict sense occurs when the ability to pursue human actions has been diminished by some corruption of the natural principles of the species (*corrumpi aliquod principiorum naturalium speciei*). This is as we would expect. Those principles are the ends that give our agency its human character, singular and distinct. Failure to act according to those ends is, in effect, a corruption of our created nature. He then points out that the causes of corruption are many and some can be assigned to the corrupted. So for example, those who take pleasure in eating dirt do so because of an evil temperament (*malam complexionem*). Similarly, those who take pleasure in cannibalism, bestiality, and other such things do so because their souls have been corrupted by some perverse custom (*ST* I–II.31.7; 94.6). In each instance Aquinas considers the consequences that follow these corruptions voluntary and blameworthy precisely because they originate in states of affairs that are themselves voluntary and blameworthy. Of course, it may turn out that we have too little control over temperament and custom to warrant this conclusion, but no matter. The point of significance here is that natural law moral criticism in Aquinas's hands can proceed only when the corrupted nature that causes the unnatural act has voluntary origins. Without those origins there can be no *moral* substance to the charge that the action is against nature, for in that event no action has been done, no step taken into the moral, which, strictly speaking, regards human action simply (*ST* I–II.1.3). But this means that *blameworthy* unnatural actions have ultimate causes that are natural, precisely because natural action in this basic sense is nothing more than action that is rational in the most minimal sense and thus sufficiently voluntary to warrant blame.[102]

By contrast, actions that are rational in ways that surpass this minimal sense, and therefore actions that secure greater concord with the eternal law, are hardly characteristic of our kind east of Eden. Actions of this sort are as difficult as the good is contingent, as arduous as the passions are unruly. For this reason Aquinas insists that we cannot act in a manner that perfects our agency and completes our participation in the eternal law without the virtues, both acquired and infused (*ST* I–II.93.6).

---

[101] *ST* I–II.31.7. *sed contra*: "*quaedam delectationes sunt aegritudinales et contra naturam.*"
[102] For a fuller treatment of Aquinas's views see Jordan (1997).

Many will find this conclusion unwelcome for it implies that we must depend upon the virtues we happen to have, the counsels of the wise, and the grace of God as we choose, judge, and decide. The worry here is not that the fallible and contested character of these resources for moral judgment tempt moral skepticism; it is not the worry that encourages so many to find specific obligations and prohibitions in Aquinas's treatment of the first precepts. As we have already noted the common difficulty and the ordinary uncertainty of our inquiries about the character of the good in this or that circumstance cannot be transformed into the uniquely philosophical worry called skepticism without permitting more confusion about the good than Aquinas allows. Rather, the worry regards fortune's hand upon moral knowledge. If the virtuous alone have consistent knowledge of the good in particular, then it would seem that only those lucky enough to secure virtuous habits will be able to pursue the good with any constancy.

The problem is particularly severe given the external orientation of Aquinas's account of the virtues. For if the virtues are, for the most part, ordered toward success in the world, then the life of virtue will assume acquaintance with the world, which of course, can be acquired only by those lucky enough to have had good teachers and ample experience. Similarly, it is certain that at least some virtuous activities will require some measure of some external goods before they can be pursued at all, let alone successfully. The liberal, for instance, cannot exercise their virtue without at least some wealth (*ST* II–II.117.3). And yet external goods, Aquinas admits, are distributed by fortune (*ST* I–II.2.4; II–II.183.1), which means they are spread among us unevenly and haphazardly. The trouble, of course, or so it appears, is that if certain opportunities to act virtuously presuppose certain measures of fortune's goods, and if virtuous dispositions cannot be acquired without opportunities to act virtuously (*ST* I–II.51.2; 63.2), then it would seem that the uneven and fickle distribution of external goods brings an uneven and fickle distribution of virtue and the happiness it yields.

In both cases, fortune controls access to the life of virtue by controlling access to virtuous activities and habits. And notice, it is precisely because Aquinas's account of the natural law describes the effects of the Creator's practical judgment upon human agency, while at the same time providing very little moral guidance, that fortune becomes unleashed in the life of virtue. For when the natural law is a theory of minimal rationality in action and not a collection of concrete prescriptions available to all, it appears that consistent knowledge of the good is reserved for those with the good fortune that virtue seems to require.

It was the Stoics who, above all, feared fortune's effects upon virtue and happiness. They also intended their accounts of the natural law to provide moral guidance. These, I suggest, are related matters, and together they present new challenges. Earlier I speculated that those modern interpreters of Aquinas who find moral guidance in his remarks on the natural law are motivated by a desire to address doubts about truth in moral judgment, not by fear of fortune. I also tried to say why Aquinas has no equivalent doubts. Noticing that he does not has helped along my alternative interpretation. At the very least it has prevented anachronistic motives from distorting exegesis. But now it appears that securing that alternative interpretation will require that I say, in addition, why he does not share the Stoics's worries about virtue and fortune. Indeed, we have good reason to believe that he may, if only because the Stoics's worries about fortune were as characteristic of his time as skepticism about moral judgment is of ours.[103] And if it turns out that he does share the scope and intensity of their worries, then we have good reason to wonder why he does not share something like their treatment of the natural law.

To that end I need to develop Aquinas's response to a collection of worries about fortune's effects upon the life of virtue. This will be the principle work of chapter five. However, before I can take up that labor I must first complete my account of Aquinas's treatment of virtue, difficulty, and contingency by addressing the other obvious objection to that account: if virtue is unimaginable apart from struggle, then how can it be the surest path to happiness?

[103] Le Goff (1988).

CHAPTER 4

Virtue and discontent

The moral virtues, according to Aquinas, have a functional character. It is the work they do, the function they fulfill, that distinguishes them, that makes them intelligible to us. Attending to his remarks on the contingencies and difficulties the virtuous confront brings this feature into relief. Regarding his remarks on the first precepts of the natural law as a description of human agency, created by God and governed by His providence, enables us to see its significance. For if the natural law is not a moral theory that provides concrete moral guidance, then without the work of the virtues we would neither know the good in particular, nor desire it because of that knowledge.

At this point it seems reasonable to ask whether the life of virtue described in functional terms is desirable, whether happiness can be its ordinary consequence when struggling against difficulties and coping with contingencies are its principal activities, its daily toil. That happiness *should* follow from a virtuous life is an expectation of anyone who assumes – as Aquinas surely does (*ST* I–II.5.8) – what Gregory Vlastos calls the Eudaemonist Axiom: "that happiness is desired by all human beings as the ultimate end of all their rational acts."[1] To this belief is added another: that rational action perfected by the virtues "offers the best prospects for happiness."[2] Again, Aquinas concurs (*ST* I–II.3.2–4). Of course, these assumptions leave most of the interesting questions unanswered. In particular, they fail to indicate whether happiness requires acts of virtue that in fact achieve the collection of goods that the virtuous seek, or whether virtuous action is a good in itself and thus able to bring happiness, either in some measure or altogether, apart from its success.[3] Like Plato and Aristotle, Aquinas maintains that virtuous actions are the principal part of happiness (*ST* I–II.3.2–5; 4.6; 5.4), but not the only part.[4] The ends that the virtuous seek, and at times achieve

---

[1] Vlastos (1991, 203).　　[2] *Ibid.*, 204.　　[3] *Ibid.*

as a result of their efforts, contribute as well (*ST* I–II.3.3.2; 4.5, 7–8). It follows that the virtues must be desirable themselves, both for their own sake and for their usefulness in securing the other things we consider good and desirable.

This answer, however, poses new puzzles about the relation between virtue, success, and happiness. If virtue's work is needed in order to secure a number of other goods that are themselves constituent parts of human happiness, then it seems reasonable to ask whether virtue's efforts can be considered a reliable source of success, and thus, of happiness. The worry here is that success, and therefore happiness, may well depend upon matters the virtuous cannot control, upon fortune good and ill. And if it turns out that fortune does contribute significantly to virtue's success, then we may in fact be unable to say with confidence that virtue offers the best hope for a happy life. We may be unable to assume that something voluntary like virtue is the principle cause of human flourishing.

Even if we assume a favorable solution to these matters, others remain, equally pressing. Can we say that virtue itself is good and desirable quite apart from its ability to bring success? Aquinas, of course, insists that it is, and indeed, it must be if virtue itself is to be considered a part of happiness, let alone the principal part. Nevertheless, it is not altogether apparent how the virtues can be good *per se* given the conclusions of our inquiry so far. If Aquinas in fact offers a functional account of the virtues, we are tempted to conclude that he has reduced virtue's goodness to its effectiveness. If he in fact maintains that the need for virtue arises only when there is some arduous activity (such as pursuing just relations with another) or some good (such as wealth or honor) that arouses passions in us that resist the judgments of reason, passions that make knowing and willing the good difficult (*ST* II–II.129.2; 137.1), then we are tempted to say that the goodness that attaches to the virtues follows exclusively from their ability to cope with these difficulties and achieve the good. Indeed, we are tempted to suspect that insofar as he insists that *virtus est circa difficile et bonum* (*ST* I–II.73.4.obj.2), he is unable to distinguish its goodness from its utility in a difficult life.

Aquinas himself seems to encourage these suspicions by drawing what appear to be conflicting conclusions about the intrinsic goodness of virtuous habits and actions. On the one hand he insists that the virtues are "excellent, not simply, but relatively" (*ST* I–II.66.3.1), precisely

---

⁴ It is Vlastos who insists that Plato and Aristotle agree here. I stand on his authority. *Ibid.*, 205–209.

because they enable us to work well in the right way (*ST* i–ii.56.3), hindering evil and pursuing the good (*ST* i–ii.60.5.4). On the other, he clearly attests to the intrinsic goodness of the virtues. In fact, the best evidence comes in his treatment of courage, where the instrumental character of the moral virtues is most prominent. Expanding upon Aristotle's assertion that "to the brave man fortitude itself is a good: and such is his end," (*ST* ii–ii.123.7. *sed contra*), Aquinas writes that "the proximate end of every agent is to introduce a likeness of that agent's form into something else . . . .Whatever good ensues from this, if it be intended, may be called the remote end of the agent" (*ST* ii–ii.123.7; cf. i–ii.7.3.3). Every agent, not only the brave, but also the just and the wise, act for the sake of their virtue. A moral virtue is "ordained to the act of that virtue" not because the action is directly useful for some other purpose, but rather because it is good that the virtue take form in something else (*ST* i–ii.20.3.2). And what could possibly explain this desire to embody the virtues, to impress their character upon the world, if not that the virtuous consider them intrinsically desirable?

Suppose Aquinas can answer both of these worries. Suppose our doubts about virtue's ability to succeed on its own are resolved to our satisfaction. Suppose further that we manage to show how Aquinas can say that the virtues are good in themselves, desirable as ends and not simply as instruments for the achievement of other goods. Would we then be in a position to say that a virtuous life can in fact yield happiness? Perhaps. But even then it would not be entirely clear what kind of happiness this would be. Indeed, how can it be reasonable to call a virtuous life happy when it is unimaginable apart from struggle and toil?

Aquinas gives us reason to pursue this doubt. Repeatedly, he insists that the happiness available to us in this life that follows from virtue's efforts is imperfect (*ST* i–ii.3.6.1; 5.3–5). It cannot "exclude every evil" (*ST* i–ii.5.3), and therefore it represents only "a certain likeness to true happiness" (*ST* i–ii.5.3.3). Not surprisingly, the evils that it cannot exclude are precisely the contingencies that make good choice difficult: "ignorance on the part of the intellect . . . inordinate affection on the part of the appetite, and . . . many penal ties on the part of the body" (*ST* i–ii.5.3).

Now it may be that these evils cause the happiness available to us in this life to fall short of perfection because the virtues available to us in this life are imperfect themselves. That is, it may be that the virtues, despite their best efforts, do not secure the goods that bring happiness in this life. Their successes against fortune prove too infrequent, their efforts too lame. This possibility will be considered in chapter five. For now, notice that there is another possibility here, and Aquinas points the way, although somewhat obliquely. He remarks that the "many un-avoidable evils" in the life of virtue were set forth by Augustine in *De civ. Dei* xix.4 (*ST* I–II.5.3). When we turn to Augustine's remarks we find him insisting that "the very virtues of this life, which are certainly its best and most useful possessions, are all the more telling proofs of its miseries in proportion as they are helpful against the violence of its dangers, toils, and woes" (*De civ. Dei* xix.4). The fact that the happiness available to us in this life cannot be had apart from virtue's toil "is the plainest proof of the ills of this life," a sure sign that we stand "in the midst of evils or that evils are in us" (*De civ. Dei* xix.4).

The appeal to Augustine's authority puts Aquinas's doubts in plain sight. Moreover, by appealing to Augustine's view in order to frame his doubts Aquinas encourages us to consider the character and signifi-cance of Augustine's influence upon his understanding of virtue and happiness. Aquinas, of course, draws upon Augustine's account of the moral life as he develops his own, but the character of the borrowing is uncertain.[5] Since Aquinas frequently cites *auctoritates* without revising his view in the direction they suggest, the fact that he uses Augustine to spell out his discontents with the happiness virtue yields does not necessarily mean that he adopts Augustine's view. Nor is it certain whether the influence that Aquinas does accept from Augustine will prove compat-ible with his Aristotelian commitments, if only because judgments about compatibility presuppose that we understand what the competing com-mitments actually involve and this, we shall see, does not come easily.

One thing, however, is certain. Aquinas's treatment of the life of virtue *in via*, developed in chapters one–three, *is* largely Aristotelian in outlook. He admits as much (*ST* I–II.3.6.1). But this means that the discontent he shares with Augustine appears to threaten what he as-sumes with Aristotle: that virtue yields happiness. Moreover, it appears that he comes to this Augustinian discontent by Aristotelian means, by regarding the virtues as instruments for struggling against difficulties and dangers of various sorts. This curious state of affairs should cause us to wonder whether Aquinas can have it both ways, whether he can insist with Aristotle that virtue in this life yields "a certain likeness to true happiness" (*ST* I–II.5.3.3) while at the same time voicing Augustinian

---

[5] For two recent accounts see Jordan (1990, 1991) and MacIntyre (1988b, 1990).

discontent with this happiness because of the character of the virtue that is its cause (*ST* I–II.5.3).

We might conclude that he cannot on the grounds that Augustine's conclusion is sound. The life of Aristotelian virtue is in fact a life of misery. We can call it happy if we like, but it will not be the best life that we can imagine. Indeed, its arduousness enables us to imagine other possibilities just as its many ills encourage our complaints. On this reading, being Aristotle's faithful student is both benefit and burden. It brings Aquinas to share Augustine's discontent, but it also prevents him from revising his eudaemonian commitments in order to accommodate his Augustinian conclusions. Indeed, on this reading, both Aristotle and Aquinas should put aside the assumption that virtue yields happiness, or at the very least, they should confess that the happiness virtue secures in this life is not all that happy. Alternatively, we might conclude that the character of human virtue *in via* cannot justify any reasonable discontent with the happiness available to us in this life. In that event, we will need to ask what, if anything, warrants the discontent that Augustine and Aquinas share. If nothing can be found – if they are silent, and if no resources are uncovered that might enable them to answer – then we must encourage both to return to the eudaemonian consensus without complaint. On this reading, Aquinas is a thoroughgoing Aristotelian, or at the very least should be, insofar as his Augustinian discontent with virtue and happiness lacks compelling warrants.

Unfortunately, few interpreters ask Aquinas to respond to the apparent incompatibility between his Augustinian discontent and the eudaemonism he shares with Aristotle, just as doubts about his ability to account for the intrinsic goodness of the virtues rarely arise. These, I suggest, are related matters. Few ask him to justify his Augustinian discontent because most assume that the life of virtue is good and desirable in itself (that is, as an end and not merely as a means for achieving other goods) precisely because its principle part, virtue, is. He is rarely asked to account for the intrinsic goodness of virtue because few notice the emphasis he places upon its usefulness among the evils of this world. Once this emphasis is brought forward, both worries follow. If virtue is principally a tool for hard labor, then Augustinian discontent will make sense, even if its labors, more often than not, yield good. On the other hand, if the virtues can be shown to be good and desirable apart from their effectiveness and in spite of their entanglement with the evils of this world, then there is a presumption in favor of their ability to yield a desirable kind of life. For in that case good accrues by simple possession, happiness in some degree naturally follows, and the burden of proof is shifted to Augustine and his discontents.

The inattention to these matters, has, no doubt, multiple causes, yet I suspect that the most significant is the tendency among contemporary interpreters to think that Aquinas's remarks about the formal relations between virtue and perfection exhaust his treatment of virtue's goodness. The standard interpretation normally begins with a discussion of the general theory of goodness that Aquinas develops in the *prima pars* (*ST* 1.5.3–5; cf. *De verit.* 21.5–6).[6] There he argues that everything is what it is, this thing and not that, only insofar as it possesses a particular set of capacities to act. Each thing is perfected in being, and thus becomes a good instance of the particular sort of thing that it is, when those capacities are exercised consistently and well in the relevant circumstances. A chair, for example, is perfected in being, and as a result becomes a good instance of the sort of thing that it is, only insofar as it is able to perform with excellence the particular capacities that make it a chair and not some other thing. Similarly, Socrates is a good instance of the sort of thing that he is only insofar as he perfects his nature by actualizing his rational capacities, for it is precisely those capacities that distinguish him as a creature of one kind – a human kind – and not some other. The virtues, according to this view, are the habits of mind and affection that make the perfection of Socrates possible by providing him with the ability and the desire to actualize his rational powers (*ST* I–II.55.3; 57.3; 59.4). Virtuous actions are the perfect operations of those powers that make Socrates human. It follows that his good consists in nothing but the virtues and their acts, his happiness in nothing but possessing the virtues and enjoying the perfection they provide.

Notice, once this account is emphasized, the worry about the intrinsic goodness of the virtues is put to rest, and with it every reason to take seriously Aquinas's furtive Augustinian discontent with the happiness the virtues provide. In fact, the sources of discontent – the useful function the virtues fulfill, the instrumental goodness they embody – do not even arise. No mention is made of the difficulties that divide acts of virtue from the goods we hope to achieve, nor of the arduous character of a virtuous life *in via*, nor of the sorrow that attends even the most

---

[6] Porter (1990, 68), for example, considers Aquinas's general theory of goodness the "foundation" of his "theory of morality." For a similar treatment see Stump and Kretzmann (1988). For treatments of Aquinas's account of being and goodness that are not motivated by the need to find the foundations of morality there see the essays by Aertsen, McInerny, and Jordan in MacDonald (1991).

virtuous resolution of moral conflict. Yet without including these features that distinguish human life it is impossible to declare that *human* perfection has been described or that the goodness of *human* virtue has been properly considered. Better to conclude that the conceptual connections that Aquinas draws between virtue, perfection, nature, and goodness do little to help us distinguish human perfections and the goodness they instantiate from the perfections of other kinds of things (angels, dogs, even chairs). In fact, his remarks are largely metalinguistic. They specify the grammatical rules that govern our talk about perfections, human and other. They circumscribe the logical space where talk of this sort takes place. They remind us that when we speak of the virtues we refer to habits that perfect the agency and secure the good of some agent. But they tell us little, if anything, about the specific character of the human virtues or the specific nature of their goodness, both of which Aquinas regards as incomprehensible apart from the difficulties that must be overcome to achieve genuine human goods.[7]

The resulting failure is multiple: the functional character of the moral virtues is bypassed without remark, the intrinsic goodness of the virtues is never doubted, and the possibility that the virtues themselves might precipitate Aquinas's discontent with human happiness *in via* is never imagined. In short, the full significance of both his Aristotelian and his Augustinian inheritance is never considered.

I.

How then does Aquinas account for the intrinsic goodness of the moral virtues in a human life? How can he speak of the virtues and their goodness apart from their usefulness in the life and world we know? If we can elicit his reply to this question, then we will be in a better position to address the apparent incompatibility between his Augustinian discontent with the happiness that virtue brings and the eudaemonism that he shares with Aristotle. For, in large measure, it is the arduousness of the virtuous life that precipitates Augustine's doubt about its felicity. If it turns out that Aquinas in fact cannot consider the virtues desirable apart from the conditions that call for their labors, then Augustine's complaint with the eudaemonian consensus may well place the rest of Aquinas's largely Aristotelian project under judgment. If, on the other hand, he can provide a compelling account of the virtues and their goodness

---

[7] My debt to Burrell's (1979, 3–41) treatment of Aquinas's philosophical grammar is considerable.

without referring to the difficulties we confront as we pursue the good – if, that is, he can assign the moral virtues to Adam in Eden and to the blessed in heaven – then it would appear that Aquinas cannot regard the virtues of this life good *simpliciter*. Rather, they will be good *quoad nos*, given the labor they do in our kind of life. Nor will he be able to rest content with the happiness they are able to secure, for a less laborious virtue and a more leisurely happiness are genuine human possibilities.

Aquinas replies ambiguously. His remarks about the place and character of the moral virtues in forms of life different from our own indicate that he considers the virtues desirable and our need for their work intelligible, precisely because we are a certain sort of creature with a certain collection of needs, limitations, and imperfections. Apart from these conditions, the virtues are unimaginable, their goodness unintelligible. If we were a different sort of creature, one that participated in different sorts of activities, that confronted the world in ways that we do not, and whose agency possessed capacities and limitations different from our own, then we would not need, we would not praise, the moral virtues we know. Indeed, since the grammar that governs *our* talk of the virtues is rooted in the particular details of our creaturely life, it is unlikely that we would be able to speak of virtue in that form of life.

Consider Adam. Because his soul was like ours, because he possessed an animal body like our own, because his pursuits were human, and because he was created in grace, Aquinas concludes that Adam possessed all of the moral virtues (*ST* 1.95.1) and shared our reasons for considering them good (*ST* 1.94.2. *sed contra*; 95.3; 97.3). Consider justice. Justice perfects our relations with others. It enables us to render to each their due, both as individuals and as members of communities (*ST* II–II.58.5; 58.4). And, according to Aquinas, the natural sociability of Eden's inhabitants would have been no less than our own (*ST* 1.96.4). Associations would have formed, relationships established, promises made, goods exchanged, wealth distributed, children raised and so on. The great variety of human interaction that creates and renders intelligible our own need for a general habit by which we accord "each one his due by a constant and perpetual will" (*ST* II–II.58.1) surely would have found expression in Eden's gardens (*ST* 1.95.3). And since just choices are made only after careful consideration of the contingent singulars in the circumstances of choice, it is reasonable to suppose that human beings in the state of innocence would have needed prudence and its work in order to choose justly.

Matters are more complicated when we consider the passions of

Eden's citizens and the virtues of their sensitive appetites. They ate, drank, made love, and took pleasure in each, or would have, had they remained in paradise (*ST* 1.97.3; 98.2 and ad 3).[8] Since temperance is the virtue that generates desire for these pleasures in the right measure and intensity and in the right circumstances (*ST* II–II.141.3–4) it makes perfect sense to say that they would have praised its exercise. However, other sorts of passions are more difficult to imagine in paradise and the virtues that regulate them more difficult to praise. Thus Aquinas cannot imagine penance there, which is sorrow for sin committed, or mercy, which is sorrow for the unhappiness of others, "because sorrow, guilt, and unhappiness are incompatible with the perfection of the primitive state" (*ST* 1.95.3).

Oddly enough, Aquinas gives little attention to courage in his discussion of Adam's virtues, and yet I suspect he would be hard pressed to defend its place in paradise, precisely because Eden excludes the passions and circumstances that call for its work. What would Adam have feared? The conflicts that make our need for courage intelligible and its acts good would have been unknown to him. Disputes, had there been any, would have settled peacefully. His just pursuits would have presented no dangers, for Eden's wealthy and powerful would have coveted justice no less than the rest. Disease, injury, and the infirmities of old age would not have troubled him since his body would have been preserved from every corruption by virtue and grace (*ST* 1.97.1; 97.2.4). Private fears – of betrayal, embarrassment, and the like – would have been unknown since they depend upon moral failures that would have been entirely absent. Fear of poverty would not have hounded him for just relations would have ensured plenty for all. He would not have been concerned with hunger or thirst since "paradise was situated in a most temperate situation" (*ST* 1.102.4), which made the trees of paradise healthy and their fruits plentiful (*ST* 1.96.1.3). Even deadly snakes and stinging scorpions would not have unhinged fearless Adam since all creatures in the state of innocence were subject to his command (*ST* 1.96.1).

Conceding these facts about Adam's lot, Aquinas concludes that courage would have been needed in the state of innocence to moderate daring and hope alone (*ST* 1.95.3.2). But what circumstances would have

---

[8] To the objection that there was no eating or drinking in Eden because defecation, "which is unsuitable to the state of innocence" (*ST* 1.97.ad 3), would naturally follow, Aquinas responds that this inference is unreasonable, because Adam's faecal matter was "disposed by God as to be decorous and suitable to the state" (*ST* 1.97.3).

called for acts of daring? What difficulties would have made hope necessary? Since Adam was threatened with neither injustice in the social world, nor infirmity on the part of the body, nor abuse from the environment, it is hard to imagine what could have precipitated these passions in him. As such, it is difficult to see how Aquinas can assign courage, restricted or not, to Adam. Like mercy, it has no place in Eden, no work to do in the sort of life Adam would have led had he remained.

Aquinas's remarks about God and the blessed confirm this conclusion. Following Aristotle, he argues that God does not lead the sort of life that calls for the work of the moral virtues, at least not as we know them (*ST* I–II.61.5.1; *EN* 1178b9–19). Thus for example, we cannot assign courage and temperance to God precisely because God has neither a body nor a sensitive appetite and thus has no need to regulate fear and desire (*ST* I–II.61.5.1). Nor can we say that God acts justly, if only because He does not participate in buying, selling, or other exchanges that make justice intelligible, its work useful (*ST* I–II.21.1). As for distributive justice, Aquinas admits that God gives to each what they deserve according to their rank, and yet it is as creator that God rules and distributes. His justice is manifest as He gives to each the place they deserve in the *ordo universi* and as He preserves them there with the powers appropriate to their kind (*ST* I–II.21.1). Nevertheless, creating all things and preserving them in being are hardly intelligible activities, and thus we should not think we understand the justice that perfects them. Prudence follows suit. Since God knows all things He has no need to deliberate over doubtful matters, and thus no need for the work of prudence to perfect His knowledge of contingent singulars (*ST* I.22.1.1). Of course, the chief act of prudence is command, not counsel, the ordering of something to some end, not the deliberation that precedes choice (*ST* II–II.47.8). It follows that we can consider God prudent precisely because He orders all things to their proper ends, especially to their last end, which is God Himself (*ST* I.22.1). But again we can hardly make sense of this activity, this providential governance of all creation, and thus we cannot say that we understand the prudence that makes it wise.

No doubt, we can speak metaphorically of God possessing the virtues, and Aquinas concedes as much (*SCG* III.34.5). We can say that "in God the Divine Mind itself may be called prudence; while temperance is the turning of God's gaze on Himself, even as in us it is that which conforms the appetite to reason. God's fortitude is His changeableness; His justice is the observance of the Eternal Law in His works" (*ST* I–II.61.5). Still,

Aquinas doubts that we can know much, if anything at all, about God's form of life (*ST* 1.12.4, 11), and therefore we should not think that metaphorical remarks about divine virtue represent meaningful speech. No form of life is referred to that is, in any measure, like our own, and thus it is not at all apparent how these metaphors bring intelligibility on their own.[9] As Martha Nussbaum puts it in a discussion of Aristotle's account of these matters, in the end we find the divine life "totally, strangely different," and thus assigning moral virtues to it, even metaphorically, seems hollow and misleading.[10]

The godlike virtues "of those who have attained . . . divine similitude" specify this strange difference (*ST* 1–11.61.5). The blessed do not possess "human virtues, that is to say, virtues of men living together in this world" (*ST* 1–11.61.5.2), but rather virtues of a strictly formal nature, virtues without the "quasi-material" content, the passions and the operations, the contingencies and the difficulties, that distinguish our humanity (*ST* 1–11.67.1; cf. *ST* 1–11.61.5.2). Clearly, this is not a life that we know, and these cannot be virtues with which we are familiar, virtues that work to overcome contingencies of various kinds, difficulties great and small. Aquinas can only agree. As a result, he finds he must depict the virtues of the blessed in unfamiliar terms: "prudence sees nought else but the things of God; temperance knows no earthly desires; fortitude has no knowledge of passion; and justice, by imitating the Divine Mind, is united thereto by an everlasting covenant" (*ST* 1–11.61.5).

Together these remarks about forms of life other than our own indicate that for Aquinas human virtues are intelligible because of their place within our life and praiseworthy because of their efforts in it. From this we can conclude that he regards the goodness of the virtues to be an instrumental matter first, an intrinsic matter second. Indeed, if he finds human virtues inconceivable apart from the work they do, then it is unlikely that he can imagine their intrinsic goodness without first speaking of their usefulness. No doubt, he *does* consider them intrinsically good, but his remarks about the conditions that make talk of human virtue intelligible in the first place imply that intrinsic goodness can be imagined only after we have accounted for the work the virtues accomplish in our human form of life.[11]

---

[9] I am indebted to Burrell's account of analogical and metaphorical predication (1979, 55–67).

[10] Nussbaum (1990, 371).

[11] As I noted above, this conclusion makes Hume the obvious conversation partner for Thomists in the modern period. See Hume (1975, 183–204).

2.

Are the virtues intelligible and desirable when the conditions that call for their work vanish? If by this we mean that we can make sense of them apart from the conditions that make our life human, or consider them good apart from the work they do in that life, then Aquinas's answer must be no. Our inquiry so far presents no other possibility. But if the condition that vanishes is the difficulty we experience knowing and choosing the good in a manner that consistently achieves it, then his answer must be yes. For Aquinas insists that those who possess perfect virtue are distinguished by the ease with which they act, the facility with which they cope with contingency in the circumstances of choice and in the passions. Moreover, he assumes that the ease with which the virtuous act has something to do with their ability to consider virtuous actions and habits good and pleasing in themselves.

Following Aristotle (*EN* 1104b3–5) he writes, "he that has a habit of virtue easily performs the works of that virtue, and those works are pleasing to him for their own sake: hence delight [*delectatio*] taken in a work is a sign of a habit" (*ST* I–II.65.3.obj.2, not denied). The virtuous transcend the difficulty that the rest of us experience as we struggle toward the good. They do the work of virtue with ease, and consequently their acts of virtue are pleasing *per se*, good in themselves. Success, of course, remains important, but if the ends the virtuous seek escape their best efforts they are not left destitute for they know their best efforts to be good and desirable in themselves. The ease with which they act, despite various obstacles, and the delight they experience as a result, makes this plain. Moreover, the habits that are the cause of actions, easy and delightful, must also be good and desirable as such. Indeed, ease and delight are the marks of virtue, precisely because they signify a goodness that transcends difficulty.

The connections between the intrinsic goodness of the virtues, the ease with which the virtuous act, and the delight they know as an ordinary consequence of acting as they do are particularly evident in acts of courage. Recall, that the chief act of courage is endurance of dangers that threaten life and limb (*ST* II–II.123.6). This can hardly be pleasant, and yet Aquinas maintains that the courageous have two sources of delight: the end that their acts of endurance achieve and the "soul's delight, in the act of virtue itself" (*ST* II–II.123.8 and ad 2). That delight comes to the courageous who achieve the end they intend is hardly surprising. But it *is* harder to imagine the act itself generating delight quite apart from its success and in spite of the dangers the courageous confront and the pains they endure. In fact, it cannot be imagined without also imagining the facility of their actions. Even the courageous transcend difficulties and dangers, act with ease, and as a result find the habit that is the source of both act and ease intrinsically good. No wonder, then, that Aquinas insists that the courageous act not only for the sake of the dangerous and difficult good, but also for the sake of their habit.

Unfortunately, this talk of ease and delight does not resolve every puzzle about the intrinsic goodness of the virtues. In fact, it generates another: how can Aquinas insist that ease of action is a principal characteristic of virtue, while at the same time maintaining that the human virtues become both intelligible and desirable only in a context of difficulty and need? By maintaining that the virtuous transcend difficulty, Aquinas appears to have cut the tethers that tie the virtues to the human form of life that makes them intelligible and good in the first place. In his shorthand, how can he say that virtue is about ease of action, while at the same time insisting that *virtus est circa difficile et bonum*? But notice, the problem here cuts in both directions. If Aquinas fails to release the virtues from their roots in our arduous life, how then can he speak of their intrinsic goodness? How can he say that the life of virtue is pleasing and desirable *per se* if human virtue itself is unintelligible apart from struggle and effort?

So our dilemma has two horns. The first is a worry about reducing the goodness of the virtues to their ability to cope with difficulty. The other is a worry about the intelligibility of virtue that transcends difficulty. Will it remain virtue that we can identify as human when it transcends those features of human life that make it intelligible and good in the first place? Aquinas captures the dilemma unknowingly, I suspect, when he refers to the virtues that exist apart from every difficulty in the state of innocence. He writes, "it is accidental to temperance and fortitude to subdue superabundant passion, in so far as they are in a subject which happens to have superabundant passions, and yet those virtues are *per se* competent to moderate the passions" (*ST* 1.95.3.1). In the same sentence he insists that the virtues have both everything and nothing to do with superabundant passions and other such difficulties. How is this possible?

Unfortunately, Aquinas does little to resolve this dilemma, and therefore we will have to develop a reply for him. I suggest that we look for assistance in Sabina Lovibond's account of the relation between our natural history and our linguistic practices. Like us, her concern is with the concrete features of human life that make certain practices possible and intelligible. And like us, she is concerned with how it is that those practices come to transcend those features. She asks, how is it possible that our linguistic practices both depend upon and transcend our human capacities, powers, and frailties? She replies this way:

we can point to a certain feature of what Wittgenstein might call the "natural history" of human beings, such that if that feature were absent the relevant language-game would not exist. But once the game is in existence, the concepts that figure in it acquire a measure of autonomy *vis-a-vis* the material circumstances in virtue of which we were able to learn their use. Thus there would be no pain-discourse without pain-behavior – but having learned to talk about pain, we can make sense of the idea that a person may be in pain even though he doesn't flinch.[12]

We can't imagine talk of pain without assuming certain facts about our natural history: that our bodies are pliable, suffer violence, exhibit pain behaviors, and so on. Without those facts there would be no such talk. And yet our talk of pain is not *about* those facts. It is not reducible to talk about the natural history of the body, its frailties, and our observable behaviors, even as its existence depends on these conditions. Of course, novice speakers have difficulty finding pain discourse intelligible apart from that history and those behaviors, but the competent have more liberty. They have mastered the relevant concepts and are free to use them quite apart from the conditions that make the language-game possible and intelligible in the first place.[13]

The connections between virtue, difficulty, and intrinsic goodness can be developed in a similar fashion. On the one hand, the practice of talking about the human moral virtues, a practice that includes locating their intelligibility in our form of life and in the work they do in that life, rests upon certain material facts about our natural history. For Aquinas,

---

[12] Lovibond (1983, 150–151).

[13] The relevant passages from the *Philosophical Investigations* are as follows: "How do words refer to sensations? . . . Here is one possibility: words are connected with the primitive, the natural, expressions of the sensation and used in their place. A child has hurt himself and he cries; and then adults talk to him and teach him exclamations and, later, sentences. They teach the child new pain-behavior. 'So are you saying that the word "pain" really means crying?' – On the contrary: the verbal expression of pain replaces crying and does not describe it" (Wittgenstein 1953, 244).
"But doesn't what you say come to this: that there is not pain, for example, without pain-behavior?" – It comes to this: only of a living human being and what resembles (behaves like) a living human being can one say: it has sensations; it sees; is blind; hears; is deaf; is conscious or unconscious" (Wittgenstein 1953, 281).

two stand out: that unlike other animals we are not ordered of necessity to pursue the particular aggregate of goods that will cause us to flourish in our environment according to our kind, and that we have difficulty knowing and desiring those same goods with constancy. If we experienced no difficulty securing our good and flourishing according to our kind there would be nothing in the natural history of our lives to warrant talk of the virtues, nothing about us that would call for their work.

On the other hand, the fact that there can be no meaningful talk about the moral virtues of creatures like ourselves without referring to certain features of our natural history, features that make the good difficult to know and will, does not make it senseless to speak of the *human* virtues of an agent who knows and desires the good without effort and who therefore consistently accomplishes the good work of virtue with ease. Indeed it is one thing to say that the intelligibility of our talk about the human virtues rests upon certain features of our natural history, quite another to say that our talk is reducible to those features. It is not about them.[14] Once the concept is in use, our talk can transcend its origins. In fact, we have seen that Aquinas considers transcendence of this sort a precondition for our talk of virtue's intrinsic goodness.

To be sure, virtuous lives, not talk of virtue, are Aquinas's principal concern. Nevertheless, the transcendence that Lovibond finds in linguistic practices can also be found in the story of a virtuous life. Consider the process of acquiring a virtue. For novices, acting as the virtuous do is difficult. They struggle to acquire the experience that will enable them to apprehend the good in a variety of circumstances and deliberate over the appropriate means in a variety of contexts. At the same time they struggle against passions that pull them this way and that, threatening their ability to act for the sake of the good that they desire simply. In one instance they summon acts of constancy that match the external actions of the virtuous, only to fall into acts of weakness in the next. Throughout, acting virtuously remains difficult.

And yet, as they struggle to act as the virtuous do, at first failing frequently and only then succeeding with spotty regularity, the work of virtue slowly becomes easier. Their experience with the circumstances in which they act becomes sharper and broader, and their judgment about the good follows with greater speed and ease. After a while, they begin to pursue the goods that the virtuous desire with willful and habitual regularity, and their passions forsake independence and begin

---

[14] I am indebted to Rorty's (1991a, 1991b) discussion of reductionism.

to track their better judgments. Slowly, reasoning and desiring as the virtuous do becomes second nature, and the work of virtue becomes no trouble at all. Just as animals do their work naturally and with ease, they transcend the difficulty that characterizes the agency of their first nature and find that the hard work of virtue has become pleasing and desirable in itself.

If this is a faithful reconstruction of Aquinas's understanding of the relation between virtue, difficulty, and goodness, then I think we can conclude that Aquinas's account of the intrinsic goodness of human virtue is both anti-reductionist and anti-ascetic. By anti-reductionist I simply mean that he refuses to reduce our talk of the goodness of the virtues to our talk about their ability to cope with difficulty, or say that virtue's goodness is nothing but this ability.[15] In fact, Aquinas can imagine neither possibility, if only because he cannot imagine genuine virtue that did not complete its tasks with ease and thus with pleasure. As such, he cannot consider virtue desirable simply because of its usefulness any more than he can believe that our talk of its goodness is exhausted by reference to its function. In short, since virtue is about the difficult *and* the good our moral language must include irreducible talk of each.

By anti-ascetic I mean he refuses to believe that the human virtues and their goodness can be understood apart from their place and function in a human life. Lovibond characterizes asceticism in moral philosophy as the "impulse to escape from the conceptual scheme to which as creatures with a certain kind of body and environment, we are transcendentally related."[16] Aquinas's view is anti-ascetic precisely because he insists that our talk of the virtues must begin with the fact that they are habits of a particular kind of creature, a creature who not only has certain possibilities for agency, but who is also limited in various ways. Some of these limitations he considers natural to our kind, such as our inability to know particulars or future contingents (*ST* 1.85.1, 4). Others he considers effects of our fall from grace – our mortality, our ignorance, our unruly passions, our disordered will. But whatever their distant cause, most follow directly from the fact that human beings possess a certain kind of body that interacts with the world in some ways and not others. Thus he writes,

reason is shown to be so much the more perfect, according as it is able to overcome or endure more easily the weakness of the body and of the lower powers. And therefore human virtue which is attributed to reason, is said to be

---

[15] Rorty, (1991a, 115).   [16] Lovibond (1983, 210).

made perfect in infirmity, not of the reason indeed, but of the body and the lower powers. (*ST* I–II.55.3.3)

Our embodied life makes the moral virtues intelligible and good. Apart from that life they lose their point for us. Indeed, it appears that virtue has value, indeed *more* value, precisely because it is made perfect in infirmity, precisely because it "hinders evil, even as it produces good" (*ST* I–II.60.5.4).

It should also be apparent that for Aquinas *both* the anti-ascetic and the anti-reductionist treatments of the human virtues are needed to account for their intrinsic goodness. A practice, whether moral, linguistic, or other, can, of course, transcend its material base, but that does not make the material base inconsequential for the existence and intelligibility of the practice. In fact, our ability to consider the virtues good apart from their capacity to cope with difficulty presupposes that the moral life is a functional and instrumental matter first, rooted in the particular needs and difficulties of our creaturely existence. Without this material base we could not speak of transcendence at all. But perhaps more to the point, it is unlikely that we could regard the virtues our own or consider them intrinsically good if they *completely* transcended their material base in the difficulties of our human life. Even in transcendence difficulty leaves its traces. The virtuous agent acts with ease and this causes her to take pleasure in her actions and habits, which in turn enables her to consider them good in themselves. And yet, surely much of the pleasure she receives from acting virtuously comes from the fact that she has done something difficult and good well. The delight does not come from the ease of agency *per se*, for in that case she would find pleasure and intrinsic worth in all sorts of tasks she finds simple and mundane.[17] Nor does it come from achieving the good she intends, for this does not always happen. Rather it comes from doing without effort those difficult tasks that are ordered to the good. *This* is what makes virtuous actions and the habits that cause them intrinsically good, satisfying in themselves. Not ease, at least not principally, but rather the fact that difficulty is transcended as the good is pursued.

Oddly enough the best description of the conceptual connections

---

[17] This *is* an agent-relative matter. Most of us don't consider walking difficult and thus by Aquinas's lights there is no reason for us to build a moral practice around it (*ST* I–II.60.5.4). It makes little sense to say that it is the work of virtue that enables me to stroll across the campus. For my grandmother, however, it is a different matter. At ninety-two, stooped and fragile behind a walker, she negotiates hallways and steps with considerable success precisely because of her courage and good judgment.

between difficulty, transcendence, and the intrinsic goodness of the virtues comes from an animal trainer's notebook. In recent years, disagreement has divided the American Kennel Club over jump-height standards. Some hope to lower them in the name of justice and democracy, others insisting, as Vicki Hearne puts it, that "lowering the standards would confer equal rights on dogs who can't jump and handlers who can't train."[18] Reflecting on these squabbles while observing the virtues of a particularly graceful Pointer and his young handler, Hearne remarks:

The dog . . . soared with transcendent ease over jumps twice the height required by the AKC standards. The young man and his dog were overflowing with beauty, and the air around them was full of the light of that exacting joy.

This moment has a background. A year earlier that boy was jerking with sideways bitterness through life, a walking web of cocaine and despair. His discovery, through Koehler's training, of the difficulties of working his dog had given him alternatives.

Exacting joy. An apt description, it seems to me, of the delight that follows from doing something difficult and good well. A perfect description of the sentiments of the agent who knows her actions and the habits that cause them to be good in themselves. Jumping is a good pursuit in a Pointer's form of life and clearing twice the required height *is* a difficult achievement. Consequently when the dog transcends this difficulty with ease, indeed quite literally, it is appropriate to speak of its joy and its desire to participate in this activity precisely because of the intrinsic goodness achieved when it is done consistently and well.[19]

Is this Aquinas's view? It appears to be. For Aquinas gauges the greatness of a virtue and its acts, not simply by referring to the character of the good achieved, but also by referring to the difficulty overcome as the good is pursued. "Virtue is about the difficult and the good: whence it seems to follow that the greater virtue is about what is more difficult" (*ST* i–ii.73.4.obj.2, not denied). And presumably great virtue possesses a greater measure of intrinsic goodness precisely because of its ability to overcome greater difficulties. Thus he contends that Adam's virtuous actions in the state of innocence were less meritorious than ours are, at least in proportionate degree (*quantitas proportionalis*). For "a greater reason for merit exists after sin, on account of man's weakness; because

---

[18] Hearne (1987, 185).
[19] Those with doubts about assigning thoughts of this sort to dogs would do well to consider the rest of Hearne's book. For additional passages in Hearne that connect transcending difficulty with intrinsic goodness, see pp. 86–87, 199, 249–250.

a small deed is beyond the capacity of one who works with difficulty than a great deed is beyond one who performs it easily" (*ST* 1.95.4).[20]

Notice how Aquinas's view of the relation between the difficult and the good in acts of virtue departs from the view that Martha Nussbaum attributes to Aristotle. Nussbaum warns us against thinking that "greater limitedness yields greater possibilities of excellence."[21] She argues that "the fact that I have poor coordination and little natural strength does not open to me possibilities of achievement in tennis that are denied to John McEnroe."[22] Aquinas, it appears, disagrees. Moreover, by insisting that the goodness of a virtue and its acts increase with the difficulty overcome, Aquinas seems better positioned to accommodate our actual sentiments. Despite Nussbaum's objection to the contrary, most, I suspect, would agree that a person who nevertheless manages to play tennis well despite poor coordination, little natural strength, and meager agility achieves a greater good than persons who plays tennis with excellence precisely because they are blessed with natural coordination, strength, and prowess. No doubt, the person whose limitations prevent participation in this, or any similar activity, does indeed have diminished possibilities for excellence, at least in this corner of human life. But Nussbaum's example and our concern regard limitations that make excellent action difficult, not impossible, and in those instances it does seem that judgments about the value of what is done track judgments about the difficulties overcome.

Or consider again Hearne's dog tale. The point of her narrative – its moral consequence – is that "training dogs well is hard."[23] Not because dogs resist training, for Hearne contends that they take to it quite naturally. Rather training dogs well is hard because it is difficult to become the sort of person who can command them with just authority, obey them when appropriate, distinguish false kindness from true respect, and love some thing or activity in a way that will generate a community of common loves with a dog.[24] Obviously, training is even more difficult when drugs and despair diminish opportunity to become this sort of person. When the troubled young man nevertheless trains his Pointer well and the dog executes jumps of great difficulty, Hearne notes that *both* of them radiate exacting joy, precisely because both transcend great difficulties.

---

[20] However, from a different angle, virtuous actions in Eden were more meritorious than ours in exile. Having greater virtue Adam would have performed greater works. Having been made right in grace, he would have acted with greater charity, which is, of course, its own reward, insofar as its very act achieves friendship with God (*ST* 1.95.4). [21] Nussbaum (1990, 372).
[22] *Ibid.* [23] Hearne (1987, 184). [24] *Ibid.*, 42–76, 172–191.

To Nussbaum's credit, she does not regard the connection between the goodness of the virtues and the difficulties they overcome as exalting "struggle itself into an end."[25] Nor does she believe that "human life is best when it is fraught with difficulty."[26] But there is no reason to think that Aquinas's somewhat different treatment of virtue and difficulty entails this sort of muddled-headed romanticism. Indeed, we have already seen him diffuse Amelie Rorty's version of this worry in chapter two. Here he refuses to identify the goodness of the virtues with their ability to cope with difficulty, just as he insists that they acquire their intelligibility and goodness from the end that they seek and not simply from the difficulty they overcome. Virtue, for Aquinas, is about the good as well as the difficult. The virtuous seek the good first. If, as often happens, difficulties must be overcome in order to achieve it, then the intrinsic goodness of their actions and habits is established and enhanced. Still, this enhanced goodness does not give the virtuous reason to ignore the good and hunt after the difficult alone. The difficult and the good are different matters despite their frequent connection in our human life, and thus the virtuous cannot pursue the difficult for its own sake without forsaking their virtue and undermining their chance for happiness *in via*.

3.

It appears then that Aquinas can account for the intrinsic goodness of our virtues, but not apart from their usefulness, not apart from the work they accomplish in our lives. For to speak of their intrinsic goodness we must refer to the transcendent ease with which the virtuous overcome those difficulties that prompt others, those of lesser virtue, to act in a manner that falls short of virtue.

Notice how this conclusion helps us spell out Aquinas's eudaemonian commitments in unexpected ways. Since human happiness *in via* "requires the collection of goods sufficient for the perfect operation of this life,"[27] it follows that the virtues, considered both as goods themselves and as instruments for achieving other goods, will be indispensable for happiness. A life that falls short of virtue will be a life of diminished happiness precisely because it fails to instantiate both kinds of goods: those that the virtues contribute as such and those that they secure as a consequence of their labor. This implies that we cannot give a truthful

---

[25] Nussbaum (1990, 377).   [26] *Ibid.*

[27] *ST* I–II.3.3.2: *requiritur congregatio bonorum sufficientium ad perfectissimam opertationem huius vitae.*

rendering of the goods that constitute human happiness in this life without referring to the difficulties that require virtue's work and generate virtue's complex value. Why? Because that part of human happiness that we locate in the virtues, that measure of goodness, cannot be conceived apart from difficulty struggled against and overcome with ease. Indeed, if the good that attaches to human virtue comes packaged together with difficulty, then so must happiness. As a result, we will be hard pressed to imagine a happy human life, one rich in all those things that we consider good, without difficulty.[28] Or, if human happiness cannot be had apart from the good that virtue itself contributes, then we cannot imagine genuine happiness apart from difficulty and struggle.

This is a remarkable conclusion. The difficulty that threatens human happiness is what makes its fullest measure *in via* possible. And yet, this is not the conclusion we expect from an account of the virtues that puts difficulty front and center. We expect to conclude with Augustine that difficulty and happiness are at odds, that human happiness comes in a life without difficulty, and that as a result the life of practical virtue – that is, the life that copes with the difficulties that hinder our achievement of the good and the best – falls short of the best kind of human life. We expect happiness to be intelligible apart from our ability to transcend difficulty, just as we expect difficulty to be an impediment to complete happiness, not a circumstance within which it is made fully possible, fully intelligible. In short, we expect the happiness that the Aristotelian life of virtue offers to be readily subject to Augustinian discontent, when in fact it is not, at least not in Aquinas's hands.

Aquinas, of course, is not the only interpreter of Aristotle, and others have drawn conclusions more in line with our expectations and Augustine's discontent. For instance, Bernard Yack finds discontent with the happiness virtue brings in Aristotle's remarks about courage and war. War provides opportunities to exercise our courage, and yet Aristotle insists that we should not conclude that human happiness would be diminished in a world without war. "For no one chooses to be at war, or

---

[28] This conclusion about the relation between happiness and difficulty may appear to be equivalent to the relation between mutability and goodness that Martha Nussbaum finds in Aristotle (1986, 318–372), but appearances deceive. Nussbaum argues that various human goods, even virtue itself, become intelligible as goods only after we understand that they can be lost. For her, mutability is an unavoidable aspect of human good, and thus also of human happiness. By contrast, Aquinas follows Augustine and Boethius to the rather ordinary neo-Platonic alternative: mutability diminishes goodness (*ST* i–ii.5.4). Thus his approach to virtue's value is quite different. Changeable things make constancy in the good difficult. The virtues address this difficulty, this contingency, and are valuable precisely because they do. For Aquinas, value accrues as change is overcome, while for Nussbaum, mutability overcome diminishes value.

provokes war, for the sake of being at war; any one would seem absolutely murderous if he were to make enemies of his friends in order to bring about battle and slaughter" (*EN* 1177b9–12). From this remark Yack concludes that Aristotle finds the happiness available to us in this life insufficient, falling far short of the best kind of human happiness insofar as it depends upon the ability of the moral virtues to cope with difficulties and act within circumstances that are themselves undesirable.[29]

This conclusion, however, fails to capture what Aristotle actually intends his remarks about war and virtue to accomplish. He has no interest in encouraging discontent with our possibilities for happiness, if only because he can imagine no other possibilities *for us*. Nor does he mean to imply that we can imagine a form of life where difficulty has no hand in making virtue desirable and happiness intelligible, at least not a life that we could inhabit without sacrificing our humanity. The gods, of course, lead that kind of life, but we cannot. It follows that discontent with the arduousness of virtue is roughly equivalent to wishing for a god's life, and for Aristotle that wish is irrational precisely because that life is unimaginable.

In fact, the best evidence that Aristotle finds a god's life unimaginable comes in his observation that we cannot imagine the gods finding the virtues useful for the kind of happiness they desire. Indeed, we could not recognize that happiness. He writes,

we assume the gods to be above all other beings, blessed and happy; but what sort of actions must we assign them? Acts of justice? Will not the gods seem absurd if they make contracts and return deposits, and so on? Acts of a brave man, then, confronting dangers and running risks because it is noble to do so? Or liberal acts? To whom will they give? It will be strange if they are really to have money or anything of the kind. And what would their temperate acts be? Is not such praise tasteless, since they have no bad appetite? If we were to run through them all, the circumstances of action would be found trivial and unworthy of gods. (*EN* 1178b8–19)

Thus, contra-Yack, Aristotle's remarks on war have a more worldly focus. They encourage us to take heed of the expansive character of virtue. His intent is not to recommend discontent with the human life we lead but rather to warn us against choosing foolishly once we see how virtue, happiness, and difficulty are bound together. His hope is that we will resist concluding that a life of danger and toil should be

[29] Yack (1989, 619–620).

sought out in order to exercise our virtue and increase our happiness.

Aquinas concurs. He finds a simple warning, not dramatic discontent, in Aristotle's remarks on courage and war, and his finding returns us to our puzzle (*In Ethic.*x.11.2100). What then justifies his Augustinian discontent? If it is in fact the case that the intrinsic goodness of the virtues cannot be made intelligible apart from the difficulties we confront, then indeed the happiness that includes the aggregate of all good things cannot be made intelligible without referring to difficulties transcended by virtue. It follows that Aquinas will be hard pressed to justify his discontent with the happiness the virtues provide in this life if it depends, as he implies (*ST* I–II.5.3), upon the ultimate incompatibility of difficulty and happiness.

It is remarkable then to recall that Aquinas finds virtue and happiness in the state of innocence, but not difficulty and work. Indeed, it is remarkable for at least two reasons. First, is it hard to imagine how he succeeds here given his thoroughgoing treatment of virtue, difficulty, and happiness. Second, the fact that he thinks he can succeed implies that it must be the untarnished human happiness in the state of innocence that, above all, generates his discontent with virtue and happiness in exile. As Isaiah Berlin has argued, discontent of the kind that Aquinas imagines, where pessimism about human prospects is global, assumes a comparative judgment, and paradise, it appears, is the point of comparison.[30]

Can he succeed? Above I noted that Aquinas can assign a human form of life to Adam insofar as he pursued goods and participated in activities that we could recognize as human. Similarly, he can say that Adam possessed human virtues precisely because he coped with many of the same contingencies that we confront. However, Aquinas also insists that Adam experienced no difficulty acting virtuously. Citing Augustine (*De civ.Dei* xiv.10), he insists that Adam avoided sin "without struggle" (*ST* 1.94.4). His passions, though contingent in the sense that they arose in response to the world's contingent events, tracked the judgments of right reason without fail and therefore were not particularly troublesome (*ST* 1.95.2). Similarly, the contingent singulars in the circumstances of choice presented no significant obstacles because his practical deliberations were never distorted by unruly passions. In fact, he was established by God in all the knowledge he needed for wise choice (*ST* 1.94.3). As for the acquisition of virtue, the transition from

---

[30] Berlin (1991, 1–48).

knowing and desiring the good with difficulty to pursuing it with greater and greater ease, would have been *ignotum*.

But this means that virtue and difficulty were not bound together for Adam in a common conceptual package, which in turn means that we will not be able to make sense of the intrinsic goodness of his virtues as we do our own. We will not be able to say of him that the delight received from acting virtuously would have come, in part at least, from doing something difficult and good well. And in those rare instances when a chance coincidence derailed his pursuit of the good we cannot imagine him admitting that he nevertheless found satisfaction in the very act of virtue, since that satisfaction depends upon overcoming some difficulty with ease. The fallout, it appears, is that Aquinas cannot make sense of virtue and happiness in Eden, at least not with the functional language of virtue that he inherits from Aristotle. It follows that justification for his Augustinian discontent with virtue and happiness *in via* will require resort to a quite different account of virtue. If justified discontent depends upon the ability to imagine a human form of life where virtue does not cope with difficulty and where happiness does not depend upon this ability, then he must also imagine an account of virtue that specifies its goodness and the happiness it yields without referring to difficulty and work. Since difficulty regards the material content of virtue, it appears that Aquinas needs a strictly formal account of the moral virtues, one that does not distinguish them according to their specific matters, their singular difficulties. Happily, he finds that certain "holy doctors, and also philosophers," speak of the virtues in precisely this way (*ST* 1–11.61.3). Later questions indicate that he is referring to Gregory, Augustine, and Cicero (*ST* 1–11.61.4.1; 65.1; 66.2), each of whom regard the different cardinal virtues as

signifying certain general conditions of the human mind, to be found in all the virtues: so that, to wit, prudence is a certain rectitude of discretion in any actions or matter what ever; justice a certain rectitude of the mind, whereby a man does what he ought in any matters; temperance, a disposition of the mind, moderating any passions or operations, so as to keep them within bounds; and fortitude, a disposition whereby the soul is strengthened for that which is in accord with reason, against any assaults of the passions, or the toil involved by any operations. (*ST* 1–11.61.4)

Two features stand out. First, once the virtues are defined without reference to their specific matters nothing really distinguishes them. Each is simply a general condition of every virtue that can be (and must be) found in all (*ST* I–II.65.1). We no longer find four cardinal virtues perfecting distinct human powers, but rather a single human virtue with a number of general characteristics. Second, virtue here does no work. Or, at the very least, this new account makes it easier to speak of virtue in the absence of those difficulties that call for its labor. For instance, we no longer need the threat of unruly desire for bodily pleasures before we can speak meaningfully of temperance. In fact, we do not even need to refer to disordered passions of any sort, since temperance is not the ability to cope with concupiscence unchecked. It is, rather, the moderation that virtue brings to all operations, not simply or necessarily to our desire for pleasures of the body.

It should be obvious that this account provides Aquinas with a convenient solution to the problems associated with placing the moral virtues in a frictionless paradise. It permits him to speak of Adam's virtue without referring to the work it accomplishes in a life fraught with difficulty. Indeed, he can now place courage in Eden while insisting that subduing fear and daring are accidental to its true character (*ST* 1.95.3.1). What's more, Aquinas can now imagine virtue perfecting agency, instantiating the good, and bringing happiness, not against the resistance of this or that difficulty, but as such. The metalinguistic understanding of virtue, perfection, and happiness that must be assumed in every competing account of virtue becomes substantive itself. Justified discontent with our own virtue and happiness follows naturally.

Less obvious is the fact that this treatment of the virtues is Stoic in its basic outlines. For it is the Stoics who insist that the life of virtue is less a matter of pursuing goods other than virtue, more a matter of securing virtue itself. This tends to make virtue an internal affair; less a matter of moving out into the world, overcoming difficulties of various sorts, and choosing in a fashion that will achieve this or that good, more a matter of perfecting the agent.[31]

Once baptized by Augustine, Stoic virtue finds a natural home in the will.[32] Virtue becomes a singular matter, largely equivalent to having a good will (*De lib.arb*.I.xii.25), one that turns to God and loves Him perfectly (*De mor.eccl.cath*.xv.25; xxv.46). The other virtues are nothing but specifications and confirmations of this goodness, this love. The just are those who will this God and no other (*De mor.eccl.cath*.xxiv.44;

---

[31] Treatments of Stoic virtue can be found in Irwin (1986, 1990); Sandbach (1975, 41–45); Zeller (1962, 257–267).

[32] On the extent and character of Augustine's dependence upon Stoicism in morals see Colish (1985, II:142–238).

xxv.46), while the prudent are those who discern how the will should be turned. Similarly, those virtues that Aristotle locates in the passions, Augustine assigns to the will as protectors of its goodness. And while Aristotle hopes that temperance and courage might perfect our relation to the world by perfecting our passionate responses to it, Augustine simply hopes to make our willing right. With temperance the will restrains lusts and guarantees the integrity of its love (*De lib.arb.*I.xiii.27; *De mor.eccl.cath.*xix–xxi). With courage the will refuses to be shaken and disturbed by fear or pain, each of which threaten to corrupt its love and turn it from God (*De mor.eccl.cath.*xxii–xxiii).[33]

Adam, of course, experienced no such threats, and yet we can continue to speak of his virtues only insofar as we remain within this Stoic language. In this linguistic domain the significance of the virtues follows from their ability to specify the character of a perfectly good will, not in the work they do to produce that character. Thus, Adam's temperance does not cope with burning concupiscence, but rather confirms the goodness of his will with a consequent movement of desire or joy (*ST* 1.95.2). Similarly, courage does not address sorrow and fear, difficulties and dangers, rather it confirms the will's choice with a consequent movement of hope (*ST* 1.95.3.2).

Oddly enough, while Aquinas is explicit about the problem of referring to Adam's virtues in functional terms (*ST* 1.95.3), he is not entirely forthcoming about his solution. While there is little doubt that he resorts to a different account of the virtues when he refers to Adam, he does not concede the need to switch. In fact, he explicitly resists abandoning the functional account at the very moment we would expect him to: when he admits that Adam confronted no difficulties that require virtuous labor. Instead he insists that Adam possessed virtues that work in habit but not in act. His virtues could have overcome confusion about the

---

[33] In these early works Stoic accounts of virtue and will are designed to carry the burden of Augustine's theodicy against the Manichees. By the time that he writes *De civ.Dei.* xix he has found other ways to put his Manichee past behind him (although Julian, of course, doubts his success) and as a result his Stoicism has atrophied. Now he assumes an account that is, in broad outline, Aristotelian. The significance of the virtues lies in their functional character, in their ability to struggle against the difficulties of this life. We have seen how Augustine gives the impression that Aristotelian virtue itself can justify discontent with this life. We have also seen that it cannot, at least for Aquinas. What then explains his discontent? Certainly the alternative that Adam's virtue represents, but perhaps Stoic residues from his youthful efforts play a role as well. Of course, he no longer imagines human virtue and happiness in Stoic terms. His mature understandings of sin and habit have replaced the ease of Stoic virtue with new rigors and disciplines, both earthly and divine. Still, Stoicism could well remain the moral language of comparison and discontent, its virtue marking an ease that we lost as punishment for Adam's sin and for which we yearn in this life of constant struggle.

good and subdued superabundant passion had he been confronted by these difficulties (*ST.* 1.95.3.2). That is, had he been one of us. But of course, he was not, and thus we cannot say that his virtue, like ours, regarded the difficult as well as the good. To say that it would have had he led *our* life simply begs the question, for what we want is a truthful description of his virtue in his life, and for that, it appears, we need an account of virtue that assumes no difficulty, no struggle.

When Aquinas treats the virtues of angels and the blessed he is more forthcoming. He appeals to the Stoic language of virtue and insists that he must:

> we must say that these moral virtues do not remain in the future life, as regards their material element. For in the future life there will be no concupiscence and pleasures in matters of food and sex; nor fear and daring about dangers of death; nor distributions and commutations of things employed in this present life. But, as regards the formal element, they will remain most perfect, after this life, in the blessed, in as much as each one's reason will have most perfect rectitude in regard to things concerning him in respect of that state of life: and his appetitive power will be moved entirely according to that order of reason, in things pertaining to that same state. Hence Augustine says (*De Trin.* xiv.9) that prudence will be there without any danger of error; fortitude, without the anxiety of bearing with evil; temperance, without the rebellion of the desires: so that prudence will neither prefer nor equal any good to God; fortitude will adhere to Him most steadfastly; and temperance will delight in Him Who knows no imperfection. As to justice, it is yet more evident what will be its act in that life, viz. to be subject to God: because even in this life subjection to a superior is part of justice. (*ST* i–ii.67.1; cf. *ST* ii–ii.136.1.1)

The change in moral languages is necessitated by a change in topics. Human virtue is no longer his concern, for angels and the blessed are god-like (*ST* i–ii.50.6; ii–ii.136.1.1). Their virtues dispose them "to an act befitting some higher nature" (*ST* i–ii.54.3). Describing this difference requires a language of virtue altogether different from the functional language that is best suited for capturing the character of human virtue in human lives.

That a Stoic account of the virtues proves useful for describing a form of life that is not our own may well explain Aquinas's resistance to a thoroughgoing and explicit Stoic treatment of Adam's virtues. We can only speculate, but if Aquinas appeals to the Stoic account in order to describe the god-like, then he may resist describing Adam in these terms in order to preserve his humanity. Since Aquinas construes our virtues functionally, failing to treat Adam's virtues in a similar fashion would exclude him from our company. Yet, the momentum is there. Insofar as we can find no connection between virtue, happiness, and difficulty in the state of innocence Adam has already departed from us, his virtues have already been divinized.

Still, we should not make too much of Aquinas's failure to leave Adam's humanity untouched, for the real significance of his discussion of virtue and happiness in Eden lies elsewhere, in the difficulty he has describing Adam's life in the moral languages at his disposal. The functional language of virtue that he inherits from Aristotle, the language fitted to our embodied life in this world, has little purchase on forms of life and varieties of virtue that transcend our own. Transcending that life leaves those virtues behind.[34] It is no wonder then that Aquinas speaks of the god-like virtues of the blessed in the Stoic language of the philosophers and holy doctors, for that moral language enables him to speak of virtue and happiness without referring to the conditions of our embodied humanity. In Adam – who bears the conflicting commitments of paradise and humanity – these competing languages of virtue are brought into relief. His humanity calls for the functional language of virtue that is both appropriate to us and rooted in our form of life. His abode in paradise and his soul made right by grace call for a language of virtue that transcends his humanity. Adam is thus betwixt and between. Standing between us and the blessed, his virtues neither fully human nor fully god-like, he is for Aquinas a problem that exceeds the descriptive capacities of the moral languages at his disposal. For us, however, Adam is less a problem than an exegetical marker, a boundary in Aquinas's work between the functional language of virtue that he borrows from Aristotle and the Stoic language he inherits from Augustine and others. Indeed, Adam's ambiguous character discloses both the different purposes that guide Aquinas's use of those languages and the different relations that obtain between those languages and our merely human form of life.

4.

If we must make sense of Adam's virtue and happiness in order to make sense of Aquinas's discontent with our own, then it appears that both will escape our understanding. Adam's moral life remains opaque,

---

[34] As Nussbaum points out so well (1990, 365–391), transcending human difficulties and transcending our humanity are not only different matters, they are also incompatible desires. See also Kerr (1997).

Aquinas's discontent a puzzle. Does this conclusion call into question the legitimacy of Aquinas's complaint? It depends. If we regard his remarks about Eden as a consequence of natural reason, then the discontent he shares with Augustine stands without support. If, however, we take his remarks to be articles of sacred doctrine, meaningless in themselves, and yet assented to by the believer because of God's gift of faith, then his discontent is warranted, but only by means of God's agency and not by our efforts at understanding. Indeed, we have come to a place in Aquinas's account of the moral life where appeal to the theological virtues is unavoidable. For it appears that it is only with the assistance of God's grace that he can imagine human virtue and happiness apart from difficulty, yearn for a life that is both human and god-like, and hope for that day when it will come. He can qualify our happiness, calling it merely human and thus justifying his discontent, not because he has seen through to an alternative that manages to preserve our humanity, but rather because he trusts God's promises for something better, for a life "when we shall be as the angels . . . in heaven (*ST* I–II.3.2).[35]

However, we also noted that there may well be other sources of Aquinas's discontent with virtue and happiness *in via*, other possibilities for complaint, principally in fickle fortune's influence over the distribution of virtue and its successes. It is to these sources and possibilities that I now turn.

[35] The reference is to St. Matthew's Gospel, 22.30.

CHAPTER 5

Virtue and fortune

It is now commonplace to say that Aristotle considers good fortune useful, if not indispensable, for the acquisition and exercise of the virtues, and for the success of virtuous choices.[1] We have seen that Aquinas borrows from Aristotle as he develops his own treatment of the virtues, and yet he says relatively little about fortune's influence upon the life of virtue *in via*.[2] This reticence puzzles, in part because it seems reasonable to expect Aquinas to address a matter so central to Aristotelian virtue, in part because the field of contingency that fortune generates is the place where virtue works, in part because fortune's effects are hardly benign. If the life of virtue requires good fortune, then the voluntary character of virtuous habits and actions is threatened. So is God's justice, for it appears that Providence, which governs fortune's ways (*ST* 1.116.1), acts as fortune does, offering virtue and its benefits to some, while unjustly denying them to others.

These difficulties cannot be escaped by ignoring them, or so it would seem. We must ask, therefore, whether Aquinas fails to see the problems that fortune creates for his treatment of the virtues, or, alternatively, whether his treatment of the virtues offers reasons that warrant his silence. The possibilities for inquiry are vast, if only because fortune's potential influence upon the life of virtue is as complex as that life. Virtues are acquired, retained, and exercised, and fortune can influence each process in different ways, just as it can affect opportunity to act virtuously and the success of virtuous choices. My inquiry will begin modestly, asking simply this: what kind and what measure of external goods, those distributed by fortune, are required in order to participate in a life of virtue and succeed in its pursuits?

[1] See, e.g., Sherman (1989, 13–55).
[2] Aquinas's interpreters have tended to say even less. For this reason I develop Aquinas's account of the relation between the virtues and the goods of fortune by looking to a number of recent interpretations of Aristotle's account.

I.

Aquinas lists the following external goods: wealth, power, honor, fame, a good country, a good name, and perhaps a few others (*ST* I–II.2.1–4; II–II.108.3).[3] They are instrumental goods that the virtuous must possess in some measure to pursue their activities and achieve their ends (*ST* I–II.2.1; II–II.83.6; 118.1). He writes, "For imperfect happiness, such as can be had in this life, external goods are necessary, not as belonging to the essence of happiness, but by serving as instruments to happiness, which consists in an operation of virtue" (*ST* I–II.4.7).

Often their usefulness to the virtuous is direct, when, for example, they serve as a necessary instrument of a certain kind of virtuous action. The liberal, for instance, cannot exercise their virtue without at least some wealth (*ST* II–II.117.3). At times their usefulness is indirect, their aid to the virtuous mediated by some other condition. For instance, Aquinas warns us that a "man can be hindered, by indisposition of the body, from every operation of virtue" (*ST* I–II.4.6), and, of course, a consistently well-disposed body, one that is healthy and strong and thus able to perform the successful acts of virtue that constitute the happiness available to us in this life, requires a healthy measure of at least some external goods.

They are also distributed by fortune (*ST* I–II.2.4; II–II.183.1), which means they are spread among us unevenly and haphazardly. When this fact is combined with Aquinas's insistence that external goods are instruments of virtue, two distinct problems arise, problems that threaten the voluntariness of virtuous action and the justice of Providence. First, if virtue is the surest path to happiness, as Aquinas insists that it is (*ST* I–II.5.5), and if possessing external goods makes it more likely that virtuous choices will succeed in achieving their ends, and if success in virtue generates a greater measure of happiness than virtue without success (*ST* I–II.20.3; 24.3), then insofar as external goods are distributed by fortune, so is happiness, at least in part. Similarly, if certain opportunities to act virtuously presuppose certain measures of fortune's goods, and if virtuous dispositions cannot be acquired without opportunities to act virtuously (*ST* I–II.51.2; 63.2), then it would seem that the uneven and fickle distribution of external goods brings an uneven and fickle distribution of virtue and the happiness it yields.

In the first case, fortune controls the success of virtue, thus making us wonder whether the virtuous deserve our praise when they succeed. In

[3] I follow Aquinas and use "goods of fortune" and "external goods" interchangeably (*ST* I–II.2.4).

the second, fortune controls access to the life of virtue by controlling access to particular virtuous activities and habits. This in turn makes us doubt the voluntary character of the actions that follow from the habits of fortune's favorites. In both cases, the dependence of virtue upon luck is transferred to happiness. And if it turns out that only the lucky can be virtuous and happy, then it is reasonable to wonder whether Aquinas must conclude that God, who is ultimately responsible for fortune's ways, unjustly tips the scales of virtue and happiness in the direction of some and not others.

How does Aquinas reply? Does he suspect that fortune has scuttled his account of virtue and happiness? Indeed, he does not. For in that event we would expect him to modify that account in one of two ways and he has good reason to refuse both. In the first, external goods are upgraded from instrumental to intrinsic goods. In the second, they are downgraded to indifferents.

It might be argued that there is no escaping the fact that successful acts of virtue depend upon luck and that the happy are fortune's favorites. We should simply accept this conclusion. In fact, because fortune's goods are necessary for both the success of virtue and for the happiness available to us in this life we should not consider them instrumental goods simply. They are, in fact, intrinsic goods, desirable in themselves, and thus indispensable aspects of a flourishing human life. According to this view, which Bernard Yack attributes to Aristotle, if fickle fortune leaves you powerless, impoverished, and friendless, then we cannot consider you happy in *any way*. And this holds even if you have managed to perform many acts of great virtue prior to your misfortune.[4]

Now, it is not my purpose to determine whether this is in fact Aristotle's view of the matter, but I can say why it is not Aquinas's. Unlike Yack's Aristotle, Aquinas does not consider the goods of fortune intrinsic goods, goods that are desirable in themselves because they are necessary constituents of our happiness. They are, rather, instrumental goods for the simple reason that both the virtuous and the vicious consider them useful (*ST* i–ii.59.3). If both despots and democrats require wealth to accomplish their political aims, then why should we consider it good without exception?[5] Indeed, why consider it good apart from its use-value?

[4] Yack (1989, 608–613).
[5] Plato appears to be the source of this influential argument. See *Meno* 87d–89a and *Euthydemus* 278e–282d.

It follows that Aquinas cannot regard the loss of external goods as a fatal threat to happiness. In fact, for Aquinas, nothing short of the complete loss of virtue can eliminate access to happiness altogether. Nor does he consider happiness an all or nothing affair, something that can be had only when all of its constitutive parts are in place. Rather, happiness is an operation according to virtue and can be achieved in greater or lesser degrees according to one's ability to act virtuously (*ST* I–II.3.2.4). No doubt, the wise use of fortune's goods assists the exercise of this ability and the success of virtue's efforts. Nevertheless, even those who have been mistreated by fortune and stripped of the instruments of virtue can count some measure of happiness despite their bad luck in that "act of virtue, whereby man bears these trials in a praiseworthy manner" (*ST* I–II.5.4). Indeed, their happiness will be diminished, but it cannot be vanquished entirely so long as some manner of virtuous action remains possible.

All of this implies that Aquinas need not admit that his account of virtue and happiness has been rendered incoherent by fortune. Indeed, he insists that the measure of genuine happiness available to us in this life is a direct consequence of successful agency, both virtuous and voluntary, and he cannot hold this view while at the same time making luck the decisive element for our happiness (*In Ethic.*I.18.217). He must, then, refuse the intrinsic goodness of fortune's goods and reject the assertion that no measure of human happiness can be had without them.

If Aquinas cannot follow Yack's Aristotle, if he cannot agree that successful acts of virtue always require good luck, that the happy must be fortune's favorites, and that, as a result, external goods are desirable in themselves, then he might try a different tack. He might argue that virtue and happiness can be freed from fortune's reach if external goods can be regarded as irrelevant to a virtuous life. This, in turn, would make it necessary for him to redraw the relations between success, happiness, and the goods of fortune. In particular, he could no longer consider external goods instruments of success in virtue. Nor could he consider them intrinsic parts of the happiness that is the consequence of virtue. With these revisions it would be possible for Aquinas to call the unfortunate both virtuous and happy. Moreover, unlike the solution offered by Yack's Aristotle, this approach retains the constant connection of virtuous choice, success, and happiness, and it does so without threatening the voluntariness of virtuous action or reducing happiness to good fortune.

This is the Stoics' approach, which they develop by redescribing the end that the virtuous seek.[6] The end, the Stoics insist, is not a particular good or an external state of affairs, but simply and exclusively the ability to act virtuously. A successful act of virtue, one that achieves its end, is simply a virtuous choice, and an agent who chooses virtuously chooses an appropriate action because it is appropriate. An appropriate action is an action chosen for the best available reasons and in light of the best information that can be reasonably known. A virtuous action, therefore, is simply a reasonable action that is chosen because it is reasonable.[7] Reason is the standard of appropriateness, according to the Stoics, because it is the principal characteristic of our nature. But note, the standard is not *right* reason, if by this we mean the sort of rationality we expect to find in the experienced and the wise, for all that is required of the virtuous is that they do what is reasonably expected given the knowledge and experience they happen to have.[8]

The Stoics make this point with their famous reflections upon archery. When archers take aim they do not intend to strike the target. In fact, they cannot, since the successful achievement of this end depends upon all sorts of conditions that cannot be controlled (a gust of wind, a violent sneeze), and thus it makes little sense to say that they intend it or that success is properly theirs when the arrow strikes the target. Rather, the end that virtuous archers seek is to do what good archers do: make good shots.[9] If they will this end knowingly, their actions are good, and this holds true even when fortune causes their arrows to fall short of the mark.

Now consider magnanimity. On this view, the magnanimous neither seek the public good as the end of their actions, nor spend large sums of money on noble projects in order to achieve that end. They do not, indeed cannot, pursue the public good as their end because it can be achieved only by choosing external courses of action and establishing external states of affairs; and, of course, externals of this sort, according to the Stoics, are governed by chance, which makes reasoned and systematic pursuit of the public good impossible.[10] They do not require large sums of money, because magnanimity, like every other virtue, simply consists in doing what can reasonably be expected with regard to a particular matter, and even the poor can do this. As T. H. Irwin puts

---

[6] I am indebted throughout this discussion to Irwin (1986, 205–244; 1990b, 59–79) and Rist (1969, 97–111). For evidence that Aquinas is familiar with the Stoic approach see *ST* II–II.125.4.3.
[7] Irwin (1990b, 72).   [8] *Ibid.*   [9] Irwin (1986, 231). Irwin's source is Cicero, *Fin.*3.22.
[10] Irwin (1986, 230–231).

it, the poor man who wishes to act magnanimously will concentrate "on doing what he can to spend large sums of money for the public good; and he can achieve this end even if he has no money to spend at all."[11]

Given that Aquinas's account of the moral virtues highlights the work they do to overcome contingencies confronted in the world, contingencies that make right relations to the world difficult, it is unlikely that he can follow the Stoics down this path. Their revision of virtuous choice construes the moral life as an *internally* oriented eudaemonism, where the good that the virtuous seek is a certain kind of willing. Whereas for Aquinas, the life of virtue is, for the most part, an externally oriented affair. The powers of the soul are "ordered to one another and to that which is outside" (*ST* I–II.55.2). So too are the virtues that perfect them.[12] Temperance and courage, for example, bring our passionate responses to the world's sensible goods and evils into accord with the judgments of right reason. Of course, there is a sense in which a temperate act, for instance, is an internal matter insofar as it includes right affection, but it is not *simply* that. Proper feeling orders our physical attachment to some sensible good and influences the choices we make in relation to it, and as a result alters our practical posture in the world. Of course, it would be a mistake to say that temperate passion can, of itself, move us toward some good (*ST* II–II.60.2). Nonetheless, it can enable us to pursue those worldly goods and states of affairs that justice demands without the distractions of disordered sentiment.

These caveats disclose the complexity of Aquinas's view of virtue's success. The successful achievement of an external good or external state of affairs by good means does not capture it, for the continent and the persevering accomplish that. Rather, it is doing what the constant do while being properly affected by that which is outside. External success, in this sense, is not simply a matter of securing the external good; being properly related to it is also required. But notice, Aquinas holds the complex view precisely because the properly affected act without the distraction of opposing passions, and thus pursue and achieve external goods with greater constancy than the constant. Accordingly, when Aquinas says that a virtue is "that which makes its possessor good, and his work good likewise" the emphasis is upon the good work, to which

[11] *Ibid.*, 233.
[12] Nussbaum's (1988, 170) interpretation of Aristotle's account of the moral virtues reaches similar conclusions. She writes, "interpreters who stress Aristotle's role as theoretician of civic virtue often forget that the Aristotelian virtues are, for the most part, dispositions concerned with the reasonable use of external goods: so they are not 'moral' in the sense of being occupied with a noumenal realm that is totally cut off from or independent of the material circumstances of life."

the goodness of the agent – his praiseworthy habits of knowing and feeling – is ordered functionally (*ST* 1–11.61.1: cf. 56.3)

Justice and prudence follow suit. Justice regards "external action, and also those external things of which man can make use" (*ST* 11–11.58.8). "The practical intellect is ordained to good which is outside of it." Since it is through externals that we communicate with one another, just acts succeed as we make right our own relations to "external actions and things" (*ST* 1–11.3.5.2). Indeed, a person who consistently failed to affect the external world and bring about right relations between himself and others could hardly be called just. Similarly, a person who consistently failed to determine the configuration of those external actions and things that in fact make our relations with others right could hardly be called wise.

Further evidence that Aquinas considers the life of virtue largely oriented toward external success follows from his understanding of what it means to say that the virtues perfect agency and that perfected agency yields happiness. An action is perfected, and thus fully virtuous, only when the good it seeks is actually attained. "The will is not perfect, unless it be such that, given the opportunity, it realizes the operation" (*ST* 1–11.20.4). Consequently, "it is better that man should both will the good and do it in his external act" (*ST* 1–11.24.3). Thus when Aquinas maintains that "happiness is an operation according to perfect virtue" (*ST* 1–11.3.2 *sed contra*; cf. *EN* 1102a5–6), he implies that happiness consists in acts of virtue that actually attain their end through external action. Indeed, the very essence of happiness is not the good itself which we desire, but rather the attainment or enjoyment of that good (*ST* 1–11.2.7; 3.1). The perfect happiness available to us in the company of the blessed is a perfect operation of the intellect where union with God is actually attained in a continuous act of contemplation (*ST* 1–11.3.2–4). Similarly, the happiness available to us in this life is achieved when our periodic acts of contemplation attain the truth by actually knowing it (*ST* 1–11.3.2.4), and when our practical activities that are directed by the moral virtues actually attain "the aggregate of those goods that suffice for the most perfect operation of this life" (*ST* 1–11.3.3.2). Indeed, happiness is an operation according to perfect virtue precisely because it is only an operation perfected by virtue that can consistently achieve that "state made perfect by the aggregate of all good things" (*ST* 1–11.3.2.2).

Of course, Aquinas does, on occasion, make Stoic sounding remarks. At times, he appears to reduce acts of virtue to a certain kind of willing. For instance, he says that the virtuous operation that produces happiness does not proceed "from the agent into outward matter, such as to burn and to cut," but rather is "an action that remains in the agent, such as to feel, to understand, and to will" (ST 1–11.3.2.3). Similarly, when distinguishing virtue from art he notes that, "Making and doing [*facere et agere*] differ, as stated in *Meta*.ix.16, in that making is an action passing into outward matter, e.g., to build, to saw, and so forth; whereas doing is an action abiding in the agent, e.g., to see, to will, and the like" (ST 1–11.57.4). When these remarks are combined with another – that "a moral virtue is ordained to the act of that virtue, which act is the end, as it were, of that virtue" (ST 1–11.20.3.2) – he might be interpreted to imply that the virtuous seek only to feel, know, and will virtuously and that successful acts of virtue simply are virtuous feelings, knowings, and willings. On this reading, the end that the just seek is not a just external state of affairs, but rather to will in one way and not another, presumably justly, and in the full knowledge that willing in this manner is good. Bringing the will to this state is all the success the just desire.

But this reading doesn't hold. No doubt, virtuous action *is* for Aquinas an internal affair insofar as the virtues bring the soul's powers to act in accord with the judgments of right reason. And, of course, acts of this sort occur even when chance intervenes. Nevertheless, these internal acts are, more often than not, directed by the virtues to move external powers to achieve external purposes. Indeed, the moral virtues dispose all the powers of the soul to their proper acts, not simply the will and the other internal powers. "Virtue is a habit by which we work well," writes Aquinas, and this includes the proper working of all those powers that mediate our relation to the world (ST 1–11.56.3). Accordingly, the practical happiness of this life that follows from a consistent exercise of the moral virtues is not an operation that remains exclusively within the agent. Of course, the happiness that follows from the contemplation of truth is an operation of the speculative intellect and as such remains within (ST 1–11.3.5). Nevertheless, in this life, we are best suited to acts of contemplation when our practical intellect and appetites are properly ordered to the external world by the moral virtues. Thus Aquinas says that imperfect happiness consists in acts of the speculative intellect ordained to the good within, and in acts of the practical intellect ordained to the good that is outside (ST 1–11.3.5 and ad 1; cf. ST 1–11.57.1.1).[13]

---

[13] Aquinas writes: "Now virtue causes an ordered operation. Therefore virtue itself is an ordered disposition of the soul, insofar as, to wit, the powers of the soul are in some way ordered to one another, and to that which is outside" (ST 1–11.55.2.1).

Perhaps more to the point, I suspect Aquinas would insist that the Stoic account of virtuous choice makes little sense as it stands. I suspect he would argue that the Stoics frustrate the intelligibility of virtuous action when described without reference to an end external to the substance of the act itself (*ST* I–II.7.4.2). According to the Stoics, the virtuous choose appropriate actions because they are appropriate, and appropriate actions are rational actions. And yet what makes a choice rational if not its relation to the particular end that it is ordered to achieve, in most instances, an external state of affairs in the world? In fact, how would rational choice proceed at all on this view? "Choice," says Aquinas, "is the taking of one thing in preference to another" (*ST* I–II.13.2). And yet if choice is not ordered to the achievement of some particular end by some particular means, why choose one course of action over another? In fact, why choose at all?

Similarly, insofar as virtuous actions are distinguished according to the different ends they seek, how can the Stoics say that an act of justice is different from an act of magnanimity when neither action is ordained to achieve a particular end by particular means? Indeed, insofar as the Stoics have quarantined virtue from luck by insisting that the end the virtuous seek is simply a virtuous choice, it appears that they have either made virtuous choice unintelligible, or, at the very least, reduced the many concrete virtues to a single virtue, airy and mysterious.

Irwin notes that these are the standard complaints with the Stoics' view and that the Latin Stoics reply with their doctrine of the preferred indifferents.[14] Beginning with the Socratic argument that Aquinas also accepts – external goods and external states of affairs can be used for good or evil and thus cannot be good in themselves – they reason to a conclusion he does not: since external goods and external states of affairs are not intrinsic goods they cannot influence the success or the happiness of the virtuous. The virtuous should be indifferent to them while caring for virtue alone. Nevertheless, externals can be valued and desired without referring to their contribution to our happiness. In this respect they can be objects of rational concern. But how? Not as the ends the virtuous seek, since the end of virtuous action is simply to act virtuously. Rather, the indifferents serve as the objective that specifies the activity in which the virtuous seek to act virtuously. Acting magnanimously is the end the magnanimous desire, and they perform this act of virtue and not another only insofar as they seek one indifferent

---

[14] Irwin (1986, 230, 234).

objective – to serve the public good in a grand manner – and not another.

Aquinas, I suspect, would find this reply unintelligible. He would most likely remark that it is impossible for something to be valuable, desirable, and yet indifferent to our happiness. Indeed, something becomes desirable precisely because of its relation to happiness, to our final end (*ST* I–II.1.6). The Stoics retort that nature gives value to the preferred indifferents. They are desirable because they allow us to live and act according to nature, and a life of this sort is valuable in itself and not in relation to some further end.[15]

Clearly, I cannot continue to follow this dispute without saying how Aquinas and the Stoics differ in their respective accounts of "acting according to nature," and this would obviously sidetrack my present inquiry.[16] However, it should be apparent that the Stoics and Aquinas are headed in different directions. The Stoics need an account of natural action with independent normative force, one that can show us why a particular external objective is desirable while others are not without appealing to its relation to some other good, some other desirable end. Aquinas has no equivalent need. For him, everything that is desirable is good, and everything that is good is either good in itself, in which case it is a constituent of happiness itself, or good because of its relation to happiness or one of its constituent parts.

Still, Aquinas could point out that the internal orientation of Stoic virtue prevents us from saying that virtuous action is genuinely excellent, qualitatively better than more common kinds of agency. Their account makes it possible for the young and the inexperienced to act virtuously, while Aquinas insists that they cannot (*ST* I–II.95.1). Of course, he does admit that their external actions may occasionally track the good and the best, either because of good fortune or because the circumstances of choice present no serious difficulties, but these cases are exceptional. The virtuous, on the other hand, act with excellence consistently, and at least in part, the difference is their experience with the world (*ST* II–II.49.1). In fact, experience must be the difference, for virtuous actions are directed toward making right our various relations to the world and to each other, and this, according to Aquinas, can be achieved only by those with a firm understanding of what good relations are like and a stable grasp of the contingent singulars that make them difficult to achieve (*ST* II–II.58.1).

---

[15] *Ibid.*, 236.   [16] For an excellent account of the Stoics' view see Striker (1991).

As such, the young and wealthy and well meaning, for instance, cannot act magnanimously because they do not know what the public good requires. If they were advised by the wise about the character of this good they would be ignorant of the means to achieve it, both virtuous and effective. If they were told how it might be achieved they would be unprepared for the unpredictable contingencies that would inevitably arise and foil their progress. The Stoic sage, on the other hand, does not seek to achieve a particular end by a particular external means and thus inexperience with the world is no impediment to virtue and success. Virtuous action, for him, consists in choosing as well as can be expected, which simply means choosing after a thorough consideration of the knowledge and experience he happens to have. It follows that even those endowed with little understanding of the world and meager experience with its ways can act as the virtuous do.

Irwin points out the irony here. The Stoic sage is virtuous precisely because he knows all that is required to act virtuously. Normally this is taken to mean that his knowledge and experience are vast, but now we see that the knowledge needed to act virtuously may well be insignificant.[17] In fact, the most consistently virtuous sage may know very little. For if he acts virtuously only after a reasoned consideration of the knowledge available to him, then it would seem that he has a greater chance of acting virtuously when he has less knowledge to consider.

2 .

If Aquinas has good reason to resist modifying his treatment of virtue and happiness in either of these two ways, then how does he respond to the charge that fortune's control over external goods threatens his treatment of virtue and happiness with incoherence? He casts doubt upon the assumption that generates the problem. He maintains that God supplies all human beings with the external goods they need to participate and succeed in a life of virtue. The best evidence that this is in fact Aquinas's view comes when he asks whether it is unlawful to be solicitous about temporal goods. He answers that it is when our fear of being without a sufficient measure is excessive, and he then provides three reasons for putting aside this fear.

First, since God has supplied us with the goods of the body and of the soul without our solicitude, we have reason to believe that He will

---

[17] Irwin (1990b, 72).

provide us with temporal goods as well. Second, since we know that God provides animals and plants with the external goods they need to flourish according to their kind, we have good reason to trust that God watches over our needs with similar attention and care. And lastly, because God is providential, and thus able to care for our temporal needs, we have reason to believe that He will (*ST* II–II.55.6). Aquinas offers an identical view when he asks whether we can merit external goods as gifts of grace. He replies that when external goods are considered instruments of virtuous action they fall directly under merit and that God provides all human beings, "both just and wicked, enough temporal goods to attain everlasting life" (*ST* I–II.114.10; cf. *ST* I–II.5.5.1).

Now, caution is required here. Aquinas is not arguing that our worry about fortune's control over access to virtue is wrong-headed simply because God, and not fortune, governs the distribution of external goods. Indeed, we have already noted that he regards fortune and Providence equivalent causes that *we* happen to distinguish only because God's providential purposes transcend our knowledge (*ST* I.116.1). Our ignorance makes fortune's effects compatible with providential planning. Thus, the fact that divine Providence controls the distribution of external goods does nothing to undermine their status *for us* as goods governed by fortune's whim.

Rather, the argument is that all human beings have been provided with a sufficient supply of external goods to lead a life of virtue. It is a simple factual claim, nothing more. The trouble, of course, is that it is difficult to see how *this* can be an intelligent reply to our worry about fortune's effects on virtue and happiness. Indeed, it would be the best reply if it were true, yet all agree that external goods are distributed unevenly, and that it is often the case that we do not possess the external goods that we need in order to act, all things being equal, in the ways and contexts we would prefer. The reply is particularly puzzling given the dire material conditions of Aquinas's own age.[18] How, then, can he smugly reply that Providence provides us with the external goods we need in order to pursue a virtuous life?

---

[18] Le Goff (1988, 229–254). Of course, not every inequity in the distribution of external goods is directly caused by fortune. I may farm a dry and rocky quarter because there has been no rain for many years, or it may be because all the rich and fertile lands have been confiscated by the local despot. Aquinas is well aware that sin creates losers in a zero sum game. Excessive love of external goods is a principal cause of sinful action, and inequitable distribution of externals is one of its effects (*ST* II–II.118.1.2). Nonetheless, if tyranny deprives me of the wealth and power I need to act virtuously, fortune still has a hand in my privation. For it is certainly my misfortune that a despot should rule the land at a time when he could have this effect upon my life.

The easiest, but also the most unsatisfactory, way to understand this curious remark is to point out that Aquinas considers fortune's goods unnecessary for the beatific vision that is our perfect happiness. Since contemplation is the activity in this life that most resembles that blessed vision (*ST* I–II.3.5), it stands to reason that those who spend more time in contemplation will need fewer of fortune's goods (*ST* I–II.4.7). And, since, Aquinas believes that contemplation offers the surest path to the imperfect happiness of this life, we should not be surprised when he says that external goods are always in sufficient supply.

However, this approach ignores what Aquinas explicitly maintains: that in this life our animal bodies require care and attention for contemplation to proceed without distraction. The contemplative intellect cannot find its proper focus when a diseased body, a demanding stomach, and an empty purse interrupt with their complaints (*ST* I–II.4.6), complaints that cannot be answered without participating in a variety of practical activities that cannot be pursued successfully without external goods in some measure (*ST* I–II.4.7). So although the contemplative life may well require a relatively smaller portion of fortune's goods than the active life, Aquinas gives us no reason to believe that destitution and want are conducive to it.

Perhaps, then, it is better to admit that Aquinas does not defend his reply directly. He is truly silent. Nevertheless, I think a defense can be developed for him that is faithful to his account of the moral virtues and to his understanding of their place in a flourishing human life. Progress here requires three assumptions. First, the conclusions of chapters one and two are largely correct. Aquinas does, in fact, construe the moral virtues functionally. Their work makes them intelligible. This does not imply that he doubts the intrinsic goodness of virtuous habits. Nor does it conflict with his insistence that virtuous actions are pursued because they are good in themselves and not simply because they are useful for the achievement of this or that end. However, it does mean that Aquinas cannot make sense of the virtues without referring to the function they fulfill in our human form of life. Second, an act of virtue can be great in two ways: either by achieving a great and noble good, or by coping with some great difficulty (*ST* I–II.60.5.4). Lastly, when Aquinas says that external goods are useful to the virtuous he does not simply consider them instruments of success in virtue. Their usefulness also consists in their ability to create opportunities for the virtuous to exercise their virtue. Wealth, for instance, is not simply an instrument of the just, whose actions bear on external matters and thus often require financial resources in order to be successful. It also generates opportunities for the liberal to make good use of their virtue (*ST* I–II.117.3). These three assumptions enable us to argue that Aquinas considers the relation between external goods and virtuous action thoroughly ambiguous. Indeed, once this ambiguity is established we can begin to see how reasonable his insistence is that Providence provides a sufficient supply of external goods for a life of virtue and how sensible his silence regarding fortune's threat.

Consider physical appearance. We might assume that one must have the good luck of being relatively attractive in order to encounter opportunities that call for acts of temperance. John Cooper assigns this view to Aristotle:

if one is physically quite unattractive not only will one's sex life, and so one's opportunities for exercising the virtue of temperance, be limited in undesirable ways (you may still have sex, given the circumstances, with whom you ought, and when, and to the right extent, and so retain and exercise the virtue of temperance, but the effects of this kind of control will not be as grand as they would be if you really had a normally full range of options) . . . People will tend to avoid you, so that you will not be able to enter into the normally wide range of relationships that pose for the virtuous person the particular challenges that his virtue responds to with its correct assessments and right decisions. Such a person, let us assume, may in fact develop all the virtues in their fully perfected form and actually exercise them in ways that respond appropriately and correctly to his circumstances; but the circumstances themselves are restricted by his ugliness and the effects this has on others, so that his virtue is not called upon to regulate his responses and choices in all the sorts of circumstances that the more normally attractive person would face, and so its exercise is not as full and fine a thing as that more normally attractive person's would be.[19]

Whether this interpretation tracks Aristotle's actual view is beside the point. My concern is Aquinas's response to Cooper's Aristotle, and I think he would consider the argument useful, but also muddled by the simplicity of its vision. Why should we assume, he would most probably ask, that the attractive have a greater need for temperance than the physically unattractive or the ordinary? If temperance is needed to cope with desire for bodily pleasures, desire that make it difficult for us to choose well (*ST* II–II.123.1; 129.2; 141.2,4), why should we assume that only the attractive find themselves in circumstances that elicit concupiscible desires of sufficient strength to threaten their pursuit of the good? Those who are exceedingly unattractive, and as a result find their

---

[19] Cooper (1985, 182–183).

amorous intentions frustrated at every turn, may well be in constant need of great acts of temperance. In fact, it is very likely that without this virtue their perpetually unfulfilled desire for physical affection will constantly threaten to derail their judgments about the good and the best.

However, all we can say is probably and perhaps. It is only likely, and never certain, that the ugly and the beautiful will frequently find themselves in opportunities that demand great acts of temperance. In fact, the number of additional contingencies involved in the production of frustrated desires and amorous temptations are so numerous that even the most general judgments about an agent's opportunities to act temperately are presumptuous. Health, wealth, and local custom will all exert some influence, as will character, class, and achievement. Would Alcibiades have frequently found himself in circumstances that required great acts of temperance if he had not been an aristocrat, a war hero, and a witty dinner companion? Perhaps not. A poor, cowardly, and dull Alcibiades would have probably attracted few suitors and therefore found himself in no more need of temperance than the rest of us.

Yet even this is difficult to conclude, for it may turn out that the rest of us, those who are neither beauties nor beasts, may in fact find ourselves in need of great acts of temperance. Socrates, for instance, was neither praised for his physical beauty nor decried for his hideousness, and yet his intelligence and wit, the constancy of his character, and the beauty of his soul, made him beloved by many and created numerous opportunities for great and noble acts of temperance.

These reflections display the ambiguous relation between a particular external good and a particular kind of virtuous action and they make Aquinas's curious assertion that all possess a sufficient measure of external goods to pursue a life of virtue intelligible, perhaps even sound. The beautiful will find no more opportunity for temperate action than the ugly or the common. Nor will they alone find need for great and noble acts of temperance. No doubt the work that temperance does for each will differ – moderating concupiscence in some, challenging insensitivity in others – but all will find themselves in need of its labors both ordinary and great. Moreover, this ambiguity occurs whenever the instrumental character of some good generates opportunities action. Consider children. Cooper argues that according to Aristotle,

a childless person or one whose children are bad people will find his virtuous activities impeded, even though he retains a firm grasp on those qualities of character that constitute the virtues, because, again, he is forced to put them into effect in circumstances that do not give his virtues their normal scope. One central context for the exercise of the virtues is in the raising of children and the subsequent common life one spends with them, once adult, in the morally productive common pursuit of morally significant ends. If this context is not realized in one's life then, Aristotle would be saying, one's virtuous activities are diminished and restricted.[20]

Again, Aquinas would certainly agree with Cooper's remark as far as it goes, but unfortunately it doesn't go very far. If the virtues cope with those difficulties that hinder our achievement of the good and the best, then one might argue that the parents of bad children require greater and more frequent acts of every moral virtue than the parents of good children. But even this conclusion would be presumptuous. Who is in greater need of virtue, parents whose children elicit excessive pride or those whose children bring sorrow? It is almost impossible to say.[21]

To be sure, Aquinas does contend that certain passions are naturally stronger than others and therefore more able to hinder our deliber-

[20] *Ibid.*, 183.
[21] This reply bears on another matter. According to Cooper (*ibid.*, 188–195), Aristotle regards all things besides virtue as instrumental goods, even children. He thinks this allows Aristotle to agree with Socrates, that only virtuous action is good in itself and the chief constituent of happiness, without maintaining – as the Stoics do – that all things besides virtue lack goodness and are therefore unable to add or subtract to happiness. He's mistaken. If the virtuous desire well-raised children simply for the opportunity they provide to act virtuously in the future, then why should we think that failure in this endeavor will diminish happiness? In fact, failure may increase it, since it is quite likely that poorly raised children will provide them with an equal, if not greater, opportunity for future acts of virtue. Perhaps it is better to say, then, that Cooper's Aristotle has provided us with no reason to believe that failure to achieve some good will affect happiness in one way or another, and this, of course, is precisely the Stoics' view when they call all goods besides virtue indifferents.

   The suspicion that Cooper transforms Aristotle into a *de facto* Stoic receives additional confirmation once we notice that reducing all things besides virtue to instrumental goods has the same befuddling influence upon action description as the Stoics' strict internalism. I argued above that the Stoics cannot tell us why an agent pursues one course of action and not another when they insist that the only good the virtuous seek is virtuous choice itself. In a similar manner, Cooper's Aristotle cannot provide a compelling account of virtuous action when he insists that the virtuous pursue some good only insofar as it provides opportunities for further acts of virtue. If the virtuous desire well-raised children simply for the opportunity to act virtuously in the future, then they lack sufficient reason to pursue *this* course of action and not another, since both well- and ill-raised children provide opportunities to act virtuously. In short, both Cooper's Aristotle and the Stoics characterize the end that the virtuous seek in a manner that makes it impossible for us to assign reasons to agents that will make their actions intelligible.

   Ultimately, both the Stoics and Cooper's Aristotle share a simple mistake. Both are unable to account for our ordinary sense that many goods besides virtue have some measure of intrinsic goodness. It is this, I suspect that compels Aquinas to divide up the moral world quite differently. By his lights, only external goods have instrumental value simply, while only God and happiness have unconditional value. All other goods, including children, are a mixed lot, good in themselves, but also useful, perhaps indispensable, for the pursuit and achievement of other goods (*In Ethic.*1.18.217–222).

ations. Anger, for instance, he considers, of all the passions, "the most manifest obstacle to the judgment of reason" (*ST* 1–11.48.3). Thus we might be tempted to say that children who frequently slight their parents and goad their anger create a greater need for virtue than children who elicit only sorrow or pride (*ST* 1–11.47.2). But this is a temptation to avoid. All things being equal anger may well be a more difficult passion than others, but things are rarely equal, for of course the difficulty of a particular passion varies with its intensity. Once this is taken into account ranking passions according to difficulty becomes a hopeless project. Which passion calls for greater acts of virtue, intense sorrow or mild anger? How could we say?

Again, it is certainly true that child rearing and the common life of the family create contexts that demand the exercise of the virtues, and it may well turn out that bearing their misfortune well is the only way for a particular childless couple to act virtuously. Nevertheless, there are "various pursuits in life . . . found among men by reason of the various things in which men seek to find their last end" (*ST* 1–11.1.7.2), each potentially complex and difficult, each demanding acts of virtue, both common and great, for the good to be achieved within them. The childless are denied one significant opportunity to act virtuously, but only one. They could just as well participate in the common life of a religious order, a university faculty, a neighborhood group, a church, an extended family, a softball team, or a social reform movement. The list is almost endless and all have the potential to be as important and difficult as raising children, and thus in general requiring no more and no less virtue. It is groundless, therefore, as well as a failure of imagination, to say that the virtuous activities of the childless are diminished and restricted.

These examples allow us to see that Aquinas is able to sidestep our worry about fortune's control over access to a life of virtue and insist that Providence provides only because he assumes that there is no good answer to the question, "what quantity and variety of external goods are needed to lead a virtuous and happy life?" The moral virtues cope with the difficulties we confront as we seek the good (*ST* 11–11.137.1), and both the presence and the absence of external goods call for the work of the virtues precisely because both create opportunities for action and difficulties that must be addressed. As such, the absence of any one external good from a particular human life does not necessarily diminish opportunity to act virtuously. In fact, opportunity may be increased. Similarly, the presence of any one external

good may in fact create some opportunities for virtue only as it extin-
guishes others.

Still, it might be argued that misfortune can diminish or eliminate the
opportunity to participate in a particular sort of virtuous activity when
participation presupposes the possession of a particular external good.
Consider liberality and wealth. The impoverished have neither the
opportunity nor the instruments to act virtuously in precisely this way.
Aquinas can hardly disagree, and yet when he considers the plight of
those who have nothing to give and no opportunity for virtuous action
beyond enduring their poverty he implies that their numbers are few (*ST*
II–II.117.1.3). Even the poor have *some* wealth that needs to be put to good
use and that calls for the work of the virtues, and in particular the work
of liberality (*ST* II–II.117.1.3; 117.3.3). Aquinas writes that "it belongs to
liberality before all that a man should not be prevented from making
any due use of money through an inordinate affection for it" (*ST*
II–II.117.3.3). Poverty, like great wealth, tends to cause affection for
money that is both inordinate and strong and thus those who have little
will be in great need of liberality. Indeed, when they make good use of
their wealth, their actions are great and praiseworthy despite the relative
poverty of their means (*ST* II–II.117.1.3).

The great advantage of this view is its ability to make the uneven
distribution of external goods inconsequential for access to virtuous
pursuits, thus limiting, in some measure, fortune's effect upon virtue and
happiness. It also honors a simple truth about human life. Most of us
face a mixed distribution of external goods, both of quantity and variety,
and as a result most of us are provided with the opportunity to act
virtuously in a diversity of contexts and with a diversity of instruments.
We do not all share the same contexts and opportunities, but most of us
are provided with a range of options that require the full exercise of the
virtues. Indeed, it is precisely because fortune generates a diversity of
contexts for each of us that we *must*, according to Aquinas, give full
exercise to our virtues if we are to achieve the happiness available to us
in this life (*ST* I–II.4.7).

Other outcomes are also worth noting. If this treatment of Aquinas's
account of the goods of fortune is correct, then we must hear nothing
remarkable when he declares that we should care little for external
goods (*ST* I–II.87.7.2) and that the life of virtue requires but a few things
(*ST* II–II.117.1). In both remarks he simply insists that Providence provides. If both the presence and absence of external goods equip us with
opportunities to act virtuously, then excessive care for them seems

unwarranted as even a small measure should provide sufficient opportunity. But this does not imply that a virtuous life *must* assume a small measure, since the virtues can be had and exercised in both plenty and in want.

Of course, at this point, we might be tempted to conclude that there is no way to choose between a life flush with external goods of all kinds and a more common life of mixed blessings. Both lives offer opportunities to act virtuously and secure happiness, and thus it appears that we have no grounds to prefer the fate of fortune's favorites. But this would be a mistake. Better to say that good fortune is best, fortune that not only provides opportunity for virtuous action but also encourages it. Bad fortune, on the other hand, creates opportunities to act virtuously but is not conducive to success because the difficulties that it creates and the acts of virtue it demands are too great. The fallout of this is that we cannot determine whether fortune's gifts are blessings or burdens, at least not without prior knowledge of the character and circumstances of the agent in question. Is it good fortune to win a flush lottery jackpot? It depends. New opportunities to act virtuously will certainly arise, but it may be that the character of the one who wins is such that she cannot cope with the new difficulties these new opportunities present.

Still, we want to say that, all things being equal, the person who hits the jackpot is better off because of it, and I think Aquinas would agree that there is something right about this desire. External goods are useful to the virtuous not just as opportunities for action, but also as instruments of success; and instruments of success in the hands of the virtuous will yield good, at least for the most part. Thus, when we count new found wealth a blessing we express our hope that it will be used for good, that the person blessed possesses virtue of such strength that she will act virtuously in plenty as well as in want. Similarly, when we decry the tyrant who leaves his people destitute, we do not lament lost opportunities for virtue, for the poor and powerless are rich in those. Rather, we oppose their diminished access to the instruments the virtuous need to achieve those goods that constitute a flourishing human life. Our complaint is not with their access to virtue but to happiness that is complete and secure. Of course, we know nothing of their virtue and therefore we do not know whether they would use fortune's gifts to pursue the goods that the virtuous desire, but this is our hope.

Here the two worries distinguished at the start of the inquiry converge. While Aquinas refuses to believe that fortune distributes opportunity to act virtuously he appears to concede that it does distribute happiness. This seems reasonable. Fortune's control over the instruments of success in virtue does offer some a greater chance for happiness, others less. Nevertheless, these are matters of degree and we have not yet determined the extent to which Aquinas regards the happiness of the *virtuous* subject to fortune's twists and turns. This question will have to wait. There are other matters related to fortune's control over access to virtue that must be addressed first.

3.

By Aquinas's lights, the uneven distribution of fortune's goods does not yield an uneven distribution of opportunities to act virtuously. Nor, as his reflections on liberality indicate, does he think that fortune's whim controls access to particular kinds of virtuous activities, if only because the demands of virtue are normally proportionate to the means available. But Aquinas is not out of this thicket of complaints yet. He construes liberality in terms general enough – making good use of wealth – to accommodate fickle fortune. Even the poor can make good use of their modest means. But what about the large scale virtues? He concedes that both magnanimity and magnificence demand considerable resources and therefore it appears that only the wealthy and the powerful have the opportunity and the means to acquire and exercise these virtues (*ST* II–II.129.8; 134.3).

As before, fortune seems to threaten the voluntariness of virtuous action and distribute virtue and happiness according to its fancy. This time, however, its threats are mediated through Aquinas's insistence that the virtues are mutually connected (*ad invicem connexae*). By this he means that they enable one another. They offer indispensable assistance to each other in their respective labors. As such, an agent must possess all the virtues perfectly in order to possess any of them perfectly (*ST* I–II.65.1). The trouble, of course, follows from the participation of the large-scale virtues in this society of mutual aid. If they are needed in order to possess any of the virtues, then it appears that only those whom fortune has blessed with the wealth and power of a tyrant will be able to act virtuously at all. In short, fortune undermines the voluntariness of virtuous action and distributes access to virtuous habits circuitously, by means of the connections that obtain among the virtues.

Aquinas finds this problem so puzzling that he proposes three different solutions and so difficult that he fails to develop any of them with sufficient care. We shall have to fill in the detail. Doing so we will find that only one of the three satisfies. The other two free the virtues from fortune's domain more successfully, yet they are unacceptable insofar as freedom is won at the expense of the distinctiveness of the large-scale virtues.

His first solution is the least satisfactory of the three. He begins with the common assertion that both magnanimity and magnificence bear on something great. The magnanimous act virtuously in great undertakings of every sort and pursue virtuous courses of action only insofar as they are great (*ST* II–II.129.1,4; 134.2.2); while the magnificent pursue great undertakings, usually great public works, that can be achieved in the external world by great expenditures (*ST* II–II.134.2.2). Magnanimity regards great and difficult actions simply, while magnificence regards such actions in a determinate matter, namely in external production (*ST* II–II.134.4.1). He then argues that, "an act may be called great proportionately, even if it consists in the use of some small or ordinary thing, if, for instance, one make a very good use of it: but an act is simply and absolutely great when it consists in the best use of the greatest thing" (*ST* II–II.129.1).

The direction Aquinas is headed should be obvious. Those who lack the riches, power, and friends necessary for undertakings that are in fact great may still act magnanimously by making the best use of the resources they do possess (*ST* II–II.129.8.1,3). Similarly, those incapable of the great expenditures needed for accomplishing acts of magnificence considered simply, "may be able to do so in things that are great by comparison to some particular work; which, though little in itself, can nevertheless be done magnificently in proportion to its genus; for little and great are relative terms" (*ST* II–II.134.3.4). The conclusion is clear: since little and great are relative measures all may possess and exercise the largescale virtues. As such, the unity of the virtues cannot be a conduit through which fortune determines access to every virtue and sabotages the voluntariness of every virtuous action.

The trouble with this argument is that it takes the relativity of little and great too far and thereby threatens the distinctiveness of the large-scale virtues. Of course, in a community of paupers those with relatively more wealth than the rest can act magnificently in relation to their fellows. But so long as there are other available frames of reference, other standards of excellence to judge the greatness of their actions, the locally magnificent will sooner or later discover how far their actions fall short of genuine greatness. We might say, "they were as magnificent as they could be," but the caveat implies the tacit conclusion that their

actions forsake true greatness. Moreover, there is something suspicious-
ly paternalistic about saying that the impoverished can act magnificently, for it seems to imply that their poverty is of no consequence; that it
cannot divide their capacity for great expenditures that serve the common good from the capacities of those whom fortune has blessed with
substantial means.

It follows that actual greatness *must* distinguish the large-scale virtues
if they are to embody distinctive kinds of human excellence, and
therefore unlike the liberal, the magnanimous and the magnificent
cannot make do with what they have. The poor and the powerless may
well act virtuously given their resources but they cannot participate in
great undertakings or make great expenditures. As T. H. Irwin puts it
(borrowing an analogy from Aristotle), a shoe might be the best that can
be made from shoddy leather without being a very good shoe.[22]

Aquinas's second solution is better, but not much. It turns on the
difference between possessing a virtue and exercising it, and is offered as
a direct response to the worry about the large-scale virtues, the goods of
fortune, and the unity of the virtues. Regarding magnanimity Aquinas
writes,

> the mutual connection of the virtues does not apply to their acts, as though
> every one were competent to practice the acts of all the virtues. Wherefore the
> act of magnanimity is not becoming to every virtuous man, but only to great
> men. On the other hand, as regards the principles of virtue, namely prudence
> and grace, all virtues are connected together, since their habits reside together
> in the soul . . . Thus it is possible for one to whom the act of magnanimity is not
> competent, to have the habit of magnanimity, whereby he is disposed to
> practice that act if it were competent to him according to his state. (*ST*
> II–II.129.3.2)

Aquinas's remarks concerning magnificence are nearly indistinguishable (*ST* II–II.134.1.1).

What does it mean to possess a habit and yet be unable to exercise it?
Aquinas doesn't say, but I think we can construct an answer for him
from the one hint he does give. "The chief act of virtue," he writes, "is
the inward choice, and a virtue may have this without outward fortune"
(*ST* II–II.134.3.4). Elsewhere Aquinas tells us that choice is an act of the
will and can be of two sorts: complete and incomplete. A "complete act
of the will is only in respect of what is possible" (*ST* I–II.13.5.1). And,
since it is impossible for those who possess the large-scale virtues to

---

[22] Irwin (1990b, 65–66).

choose courses of action in accord with those virtues without healthy measures of a number of external goods, we can safely assume their *interior electio* is an incomplete act of the will.

An "incomplete act of the will is in respect of the impossible; and by some is called *velleity*, because, to wit, one would will [*vellet*] such things, were it possible" (*ST* I–II.13.5.1). It follows that those without great resources can nevertheless possess the large-scale virtues insofar as they are positively disposed toward the acts of those virtues. Although they are unable to will complete acts of magnanimity and magnificence, incomplete acts of the will are within their range. That is, they are capable of interior choices that they would complete and actually translate into magnanimous and magnificent courses of action if fortune provided them with the relevant resources.

The problem with this solution is making it work within Aquinas's externally oriented account of the virtues. What sense can be made of an inward choice of the impossible when Aquinas insists that choice is ultimately oriented toward the external and the possible? Consider the fact that choice is preceded by rational apprehension of the end that ought to be pursued and practical deliberation over the means that will achieve it (*ST* I–II.15.3). These two acts of practical rationality are the linchpin of at least a portion of this second solution, since Aquinas maintains that prudence is at least partly responsible for bringing the large-scale virtues to those who cannot exercise them. Therefore, if we wish to know whether it is possible for those without great external resources to possess the large-scale virtues by incomplete and inward choice, we need to look at the place of prudence in acts of magnanimity and magnificence.

Recall that the *opus prudentis* is needed to cope with the contingent singulars in a circumstance of choice (*ST* II–II.47.3), many and various, that make it difficult for us to apprehend the good that ought to be pursued as an end and to choose the good course of action that will be a proper means to that end (*ST* I–II.14.1–3; II–II.47.1 and ad 2). The prudent do this work well, in part because of their experience with similar circumstances (*ST* I–II.14.6; II–II.49.1). More often than not the contingent singulars they confront have arrangements and relations that are familiar, and as a result the difficulty of their labors is much diminished. It follows, then, that those who are habitually disposed to pursue great projects and to make large expenditures that serve the common good will need experience with the contingent singulars associated with these enterprises in order to acquire the familiarity that makes choice good. Aquinas appears to share this conclusion. Commenting on Aristotle's remark that the magnanimous act slowly and with caution (*EN* 1125a13–16), he argues that they must proceed with all due care, for "the magnanimous man is intent only on great things; these are few and require great attention, wherefore they call for slow movement" (*ST* II–II.129.3.3). And I think we can assume that great attention is needed in those circumstances of choice where experience is also required. Both make it possible for the magnanimous to choose well despite the many contingent singulars that make good choice difficult in great undertakings.

From these reflections I think we can concede the possibility that some can possess the large-scale virtues without actually exercising them, in particular, those who once possessed great resources and as a result acquired the experience of the magnanimous and the magnificent. We can imagine them saying, "I would choose *this* way, as the magnificent do, if I only had the means." I suspect, however, that we will find it difficult to imagine those who have never possessed great resources making internal choices that accord with the choices of those who actually possess and exercise the large-scale virtues. They will lack the necessary experience. The person who hits the lottery jackpot, for instance, cannot act magnificently, at least not right away, because she has never pursued great ventures and she knows nothing of the great expenditures required to conclude them successfully.

Aquinas appears to regard liberality in just this way. He writes, "those who, having received money that others have earned, spend it more liberally, through not having experienced want of it, if their inexperience is the sole cause of their liberal expenditure they have not the virtue of liberality" (*ST* II–II.117.4.1). Why then should he think something different with respect to magnificence? Since the lottery winner has had no previous opportunity to pursue great public works that require great expenditures and no previous demand to reflect in a concrete way upon the large-scale needs of her fellows, she will undoubtedly have little idea how to proceed.[23] And even if she understands that the common good would in fact be served at this time and in this place by restoring a neglected city park, her inexperience with financing, city officials, safety regulations, local political feuds, etc., would most likely derail her choice of appropriate means.

Moreover, the role practical wisdom plays in unifying the virtues and

---

[23] Irwin (1988, 63).

shaping the passions guarantees that the effects of inexperience are not merely cognitive. The lottery winner's inexperience not only makes it impossible for her to offer prudential judgments about the kinds of great undertakings that will actually serve the common good, but it also prevents her from being rightly affected toward money, the material object of magnificence (*ST* II–II.134.3). Perhaps she was destitute before her win and as a consequence has a great love of money. Now she knows no want, and yet her inexperience with excess may cause her affection for wealth to continue as before. A strong and habitual desire that perhaps in the past hit virtue's mean now surpasses it and causes her to love immoderately. In short, her inexperienced passions make it too arduous for her to spend large sums on great endeavors that serve the common good, and thus her magnificence is hindered (*ST* II–II.134.3,4). If this scenario is a reasonable possibility, why then should we assume that she *could* have made internal choices before her win that track the actual choices of the magnificent?

So we can sum up the trouble with Aquinas's second solution this way: by construing the latent or tacit possession of large-scale virtues in terms of incomplete and internal choice Aquinas has failed to honor his own treatment of choice. Choice bears on contingent singulars, and therefore magnanimous and magnificent choices, even of the incomplete and internal sort, demand experience with those particular contingencies that hound great projects and expenditures. Still, the best way to characterize Aquinas's confusion is to recall his own remarks about the relation between virtue and difficulty. The work of a distinct virtue is called for and made intelligible only when a distinct difficulty that needs addressing is located (*ST* II–II.137.1). Virtue, Aquinas insists, is not only about the good desired; it is also about the difficulties that must be overcome in order to desire that good constantly and achieve it regularly. The large-scale virtues are needed because of our difficulties with great measures of honor and money. Both are desirable, and thus our passions for each often create a powerful resistance to the judgments of right reason (*ST* II–II.129.2; 134.2 and ad 2; 134.3). Aquinas maintains that the virtues associated with ordinary measures of these goods are insufficient for the difficulties associated with large measures; in part because our passions intensify when directed toward large sums and great honors, but also because the proper use of these goods – for great public works – presents practical difficulties that surpass those associated with the proper use of ordinary measures and thus call for different kinds of experience (*ST* II–II.129.1; 131.2.1). Accordingly, when Aquinas argues that those who have never possessed large measures of external goods can nevertheless possess the large-scale virtues without exercising them, he seems to deny the distinct cognitive and affective difficulties that large measures and great projects create for us and that make the large-scale virtues both distinct and necessary. In short, he can make the large-scale virtues available to all only by ignoring the difficulties that make them necessary and intelligible as distinct virtues in the first place.

Aquinas's third solution is the most compelling of the three. It manages to make the uneven distribution of the goods of fortune matter less for the possession of the large-scale virtues, and therefore it prevents fortune from using the mutual connections among the virtues as a means of controlling access to them. Nevertheless, it comes with costs, for it fails to resolve the puzzle in a manner that leaves all the original pieces untouched.

Responding directly to the dilemma the large-scale virtues create for the unity of the virtues Aquinas writes,

> But there are some moral virtues which perfect man with regard to some eminent state, such as magnificence and magnanimity; and since it does not happen to all in common to be exercised in the matter of such virtues, it is possible for a man to have the other moral virtues, without actually having the habits of these virtues, – provided we speak of acquired virtue. Nevertheless, when once a man has acquired those other virtues he possesses these in proximate potentiality [*in potentia propinqua*]. Because when, by practice, a man has acquired liberality in small gifts and expenditures, if he were to come in for a large sum of money, he would acquire the habit of magnificence with but a little practice: even as a geometrician, by dint of little study, acquires scientific knowledge about some conclusion which had never been presented to his mind before. Now we speak of having a thing when we are on the point of having it, according to the saying of the Philosopher: That which is scarcely lacking is not lacking at all. (*ST* i–ii.65.1.1; cf. *ST* ii–ii.129.3.2; 134.1.1)

When the liberal possess magnificence *in potentia propinqua* it is not actually possessed. Rather, it is nearly possessed and easily acquired because of its similarity to liberality. Liberality and magnificence are kindred virtues, first cousins perhaps, related in concern and divided only by fortune and a share of experience so small that it is easily had with a bit of practice. Consequently, nothing significant prevents those who do not possess large sums of money from possessing all the virtues, since the magnificence they lack is so similar to the liberality they enjoy that its absence has little influence upon the condition of the other virtues.

But notice, Aquinas does not dissolve the difference between large and small expenditures. Nor does he say that when fortune brings great resources that the large-scale virtues necessarily follow. Rather the claim is that the habits of mind and affection required to make large expenditures well are not much different than those possessed by the liberal. The skills of the liberal transfer easily to the contexts occupied by the magnificent because the difficulties that need addressing in those contexts are similar, differing in magnitude but not in kind. And if the contexts of action are similar, then inexperience should not be a problem, since the experience required to act liberally make acts of magnificence a quick study. The liberal person who hits the lottery jackpot cannot pursue magnificent projects immediately, but she can soon enough. In short, the difference between liberality and magnificence makes no difference. It is as if the liberal already possessed the ability to act magnificently, or at least nearly so.

Clearly, Aquinas walks a fine line here. Wishing to preserve the connections among the virtues from the scattering effects of the uneven distribution of fortune's goods, he diminishes the distinctiveness and the significance of the large-scale virtues. But he knows he cannot take this solution too far and risk collapsing the large-scale virtues into their counterparts among the ordinary virtues. So he insists that only those truly experienced with the proper use of great resources can actually possess magnanimity and magnificence. What makes this solution compelling is its ability to secure all the original pieces of the puzzle. Unity among the virtues is retained and fortune leashed without dissolving the distinct need the large-scale virtues fulfill, without making their work unintelligible. What makes this solution succeed is the fact that Aquinas has weakened the relative strength of the claims made on behalf of both the unity of the virtues and the distinctiveness of the large-scale virtues. In the other two solutions Aquinas retains the unity of the virtues by sacrificing the distinctiveness of the large-scale virtues. Here, both are diminished but neither eliminated, and they are diminished together. One does not need to possess *all* the virtues in order to possess any of them precisely because the large-scale virtues are not *all* that much different from their ordinary counterparts.[24]

---

[24] Of course, some might ask whether an account of the virtuous life that preserves a place for the large-scale virtues manages to preserve its Christian character. Christians normally wish to make the distinction between little and great projects and expenditures independent of available resources. For Aristotelians, this muddies the distinction between little and great precisely where it ought to be clarified. The easiest way to resolve this conflict in points of view would be to exclude the large-scale virtues from a Christian account of the moral life. Aquinas's first two

4.

Puzzles remain. If it is one thing – indeed, a rather easy thing – to possess a measure of external goods that is sufficient to secure opportunity to act virtuously, it is quite another to have in hand the measure one needs for success in virtuous choice. As we have noted, success in virtue is subject to fortune's disruptions in all sorts of ways, quite apart from the distribution of external goods, largely because the virtuous so frequently hope to rearrange the world that fortune rules. Here the difficulty is that fortune's control over success in virtue casts doubt upon our ability to praise the virtuous when they succeed and upon Aquinas's ability to maintain that virtue is the principle cause of happiness, its absence the principle source of misery. How does Aquinas respond? Imagine the following.

If I promise to visit an ailing friend, then all things being equal, justice demands that I keep my promise and make the three day journey by sea. If it happens that my ship is blown off course by a storm or is boarded by pirates, or if some other calamitous coincidence obstructs my progress, then I will fail to honor my promise. I will fail to succeed in virtue. Assume that I made all the relevant precautions to avoid such mishaps and thus cannot be charged with negligence. It follows that I fail to succeed in acting justly simply because of a fortuitous coincidence of my agency with certain states of affairs in the world over which I have no direct control. If, on the other hand, good fortune blesses me with favorable winds and currents, pirates occupied elsewhere, and hull-splitting storms that skip around but never across my route, then I will succeed in honoring my promise. As with my failure before, it appears that my success here follows from my luck with the circumstances.

The Stoics, we have noted, regard examples of this kind as conclusive evidence against both the voluntariness of virtuous action and the dependence of happiness upon virtue; conclusive, that is, when action is ordered toward external success and when happiness is said to follow as the virtues succeed. They respond by redescribing what it means for an act of virtue to be successful, hoping in turn to insulate virtue and happiness from fortune's effects. Aquinas resists, largely because he understands the relations between virtuous action, contingency, and

---

attempts to solve the problem of access to virtue that fortune and the unity of the virtues create in conjunction with magnanimity and magnificence indicate that he is tempted by this approach. Nevertheless, an account of the moral life that wishes to be both Christian and Aristotelian must find a place for the large-scale virtues, and thus the obvious need Aquinas has for his third solution.

fortune quite differently. The key here is Aquinas's assertion, developed in chapter two, that the virtues perfect agency by causing us to attend to the contingencies in the circumstances of choice that influence the goodness of potential means. In fact, of the three possible kinds of circumstances – necessary, contingent, and fortuitous – only contingent circumstances influence the goodness of the potential means in a way that both calls for the work of the virtues and makes their efforts possible. Necessary circumstances of choice do not because they cannot change and therefore cannot make the goodness of the potential means uncertain or the deliberations that precede choice difficult. On the other hand, changes in the circumstances of choice that are due to fortune cannot be the object of prudent deliberation because there is no rule or principle that governs their haphazard and singular occurrences. Infrequent, irregular, and thus unpredictable, there is no way for us to deliberate over their influence upon the goodness of a potential means. Of course, the virtuous can guard against the threat of disruption by fortune, and indeed justice may well demand this sort of advanced preparation, but they cannot predict its ways, and thus they cannot choose according to any knowledge of it (*ST* ii–ii.95.1; *In Perih.*1.13.9).

By contrast, contingent circumstances can be the object of prudent deliberation precisely because they obtain for the most part (*ST* ii–ii.95.1; *In Perih.*1.14). This enables those experienced in the ways of a particular set of contingent circumstances to reduce "the infinity of singulars to a certain finite number which occur as a general rule" (*ST* ii–ii.47.3.2). When the prudent possess knowledge of this sort they will choose well, for they will know that the relevant circumstances influence the goodness of the potential means (goodness which of course includes its effectiveness) with a regular, although uncertain, constancy. They will proceed with confidence, but also with caution:

of the evils which man has to avoid, some are of frequent occurrence; the like that can be grasped by reason, and against them caution is directed, either that they may be avoided altogether, or that they may do less harm. Others there are that occur rarely and by chance, and these, since they are infinite in number, cannot be grasped by reason, nor is man able to take precautions against them, although by exercising prudence he is able to prepare against all the surprises of chance, so as to suffer less harm thereby. (*ST* ii–ii.49.8.3)

A number of conclusions about the relation between virtuous action, success, and happiness follow.

First, since the virtuous cannot be expected to cope with fortune they cannot be blamed when it interferes and success escapes them. I could not know that my ship would happen upon a storm and send it three days off course, and consequently I cannot be blamed for failing to honor my promise. Complaint would be groundless. What's more, if the virtuous are not blameworthy when misfortune undermines their success, then we have every reason to consider their choice virtuous and good despite its external failure (*ST* I–II.20.4).[25] It is for this reason that Aquinas insists that good and evil are principally attributes of the will (*ST* I–II.19.1).

It follows that Aquinas does not equate virtue and success, at least not strictly. Still, his understanding of contingency and fortune permits us to say that he regards virtue and success as *largely* equivalent. Because it is misfortune that divides virtue and success, its disruptions will be infrequent. Similarly, because the contingencies in the circumstances of choice that could influence the goodness of the means possess a constancy that makes them intelligible to the virtuous, and because the virtuous give due attention to these contingencies, we can expect them to make choices that normally succeed in achieving the good. Of course, Aquinas admits that fortune's play in the external world makes deliberation and choice difficult (*ST* I–II.14.1), but it is precisely this difficulty that prudence is ordered to overcome, and Aquinas thinks that the prudent normally succeed in this effort, at least for the most part (*ST* II–II.44.1,3 and ad 2).

Notice how this conclusion helps resolve whatever doubts linger about Aquinas's insistence that Providence provides a sufficient supply of external goods for a life of virtue. Because the moral virtues are externally oriented, and because virtuous choices normally succeed, we should not be surprised to find that the virtuous normally possess a measure of external goods that satisfies their desire. For the most part – that is, unless misfortune intervenes, which of course it rarely does – they will have secured the external goods they need, both to participate in a variety of virtuous activities and to give them a good chance of succeeding in those activities they actually pursue. Nor should we be surprised, therefore, when Aquinas remarks that "nature does not fail man in necessaries, although it has not provided him with weapons and clothing, as it provided other animals, because it gave him reason and hands,

---

[25] My concern here is fortuitous coincidences that prevent the chosen means from achieving the good, but the same reasoning applies when the concern is the culpability of accidental consequences. When choice proceeds from a consideration of all the due contingencies in the circumstances of choice and successfully achieves the good, the unwanted accidental consequences that follow are involuntary and thus cannot undermine the praiseworthiness of the choice. Aquinas's discussion of accidental death is particularly relevant (*ST* II–II.64.8).

with which he is able to get these things for himself" because the virtuous will make good use of nature's gifts and obtain what they need (*ST* I–II.5.5.1). Similarly, since the virtuous seek to establish just external relations among neighbors near and far, we should not be surprised to find that they frequently succeed in distributing the goods of fortune according to the norms of justice.[26] And of course, in many instances (although not all), when virtue makes right the uneven distribution of fortune's goods it also smoothes fortune's uneven distribution of happiness among the virtuous.

In many respects these conclusions are unremarkable. They reaffirm what most interpreters concede: that Aquinas's moral vision is comic and not tragic. However, the means employed to stand with the consensus *are* remarkable, for we have not yet referred to the divine grace that directs all things to good, and by whose assistance the virtuous find happiness even when their external actions fail disastrously. This is the normal route to comic conclusions, and I shall appeal to it soon enough, but the life of virtue is, for Aquinas, largely comic even without the assistance of grace. The virtues work. They cope with contingencies that hinder the achievement of some external good or state of affairs, and they normally succeed. Miserable failure is not an impossibility for them, and as we shall see, success in virtue does not guarantee happiness. And yet the misery that follows from the failure of the virtuous to achieve the ends they desire is as infrequent as the misfortune that is its cause.

It follows that the life of virtue and the happiness it generates is hardly fragile. Although vulnerable in many ways and unavoidably subject to undoing because of virtue's inability to cope with misfortune and because of its dependence upon goods that are subject to fortune's control, the happiness that follows from the life of virtue is remarkably hardy. The virtuous can cope with the contingencies that hinder their pursuit of the good. They can do little about misfortune beyond preparing for its effects, but happily it is infrequent, and when it does disrupt their practical rationality is agile enough to return them to the hunt. The virtuous, it appears, do not stand "on the razor's edge of luck," but rather upon a broad highway they have constructed for themselves out of the contingencies they confront.[27]

---

[26] I am indebted to Cooper (1985, 194–195).

[27] The phrase is Nussbaum's (1986, 80), who finds a quite different treatment of virtue and luck in Aristotle, one that highlights fragility and tragedy. Whether Nussbaum's exegesis warrants her conclusions has been a matter of debate. See a series of papers on *The Fragility of Goodness* published in *Soundings* (winter, 1989), especially those by Ruprecht and Bruns.

Second, contrary to the Stoics' view, the successes and failures of the virtuous cannot be attributed to fortune, at least not for the most part. As a result, we have every reason to consider virtuous choice the principal cause of virtue's success in the world. The virtuous attend to the regularities in the circumstances of choice, they read the contingencies that may influence the goodness and the effectiveness of the means, they consult the wise and the experienced, and they choose after a full consideration of this carefully gathered wisdom. When the regularities hold, success follows, and the good is achieved precisely because of this effort. Of course, those who fall short of perfect virtue will frequently fail to attend to the relevant contingencies, and for Aquinas this includes all of us *in via*. In these instances, choice will follow from an incomplete understanding of the play of contingency and fortune in the circumstances of choice, and fortune may well have a hand in the success or failure of the action. Nevertheless, the Stoics' complaint has to do with the influence of fortune upon the external success or failure of *virtuous* action, and Aquinas's reply is that virtue normally excludes its influence.

The Stoics, on the other hand, argue that the virtues are a necessary cause of external success but never a sufficient one. Good luck must be added, since success follows only when chance does not interrupt the normal flow of contingent singulars that the virtuous assume when they choose. But is it good fortune that causes the regularities to hold? Is it fortuitous when something that normally happens in a given set of circumstances actually comes to pass in those circumstances? If I normally walk to work without being struck by lightning, does it make sense for me to enter my office and declare, "How lucky I am not to have been struck by lightning today"? Of course not, this regularity regularly holds and thus there is no good fortune involved when I arrive unharmed each day. Similarly, when the virtuous find regularities in the contingent circumstances of choice and choose in accordance with their knowledge we have no reason to call the success that follows the consequence of good fortune.

Of course, if I just escape being struck by lightning, if it shatters the sidewalk a hundred paces ahead, I would undoubtedly comment that the success I experience that day is my good fortune. Would I say this with good reason? On the one hand, no, since what normally happens did happen, and there is no good fortune in this. Therefore my success is no less voluntary and praiseworthy than it would have been if I had not skirted with disaster. On the other hand, yes, of course I can say that I was fortunate, but harmlessly and only as a manner of speaking. When an irregularity arises in the normal progression of contingent singulars, an irregularity whose occurrence I can neither predict nor control, then a contingent circumstance whose constancy I count on and assume shows itself to be contingent. That is, I am forced to confront how unlucky I might have been if things had been slightly different. It demonstrates to me in a dramatic fashion precisely what I have been trying to argue by more common means: that it is no luck at all when the regularities hold, but only when they do not.[28]

Third, and lastly, Aquinas's understanding of the relation between virtue, contingency, and fortune gives us no reason to think that the happiness of the virtuous is largely a consequence of good fortune. Since virtuous choice, and not fortune's favor, is normally the source of external success, then it must also be the most common source of human happiness. Of course, virtuous action that fails to succeed will also result in some happiness insofar as some good is achieved simply by choosing virtuously, bearing the consequences of failure well, and persevering in the good that was not achieved (*ST* I–II.65.3.2; 123.6; 136.1; 137.1). And, indeed, these diminished forms of happiness follow directly from virtuous choice. Nevertheless, a full measure of the happiness available to us in this life will require virtue's frequent success, and if the argument so far is sound, the success that generates happiness is largely the result of virtuous choice. Nevertheless, because fortune *can* (though infrequently) affect happiness, either by derailing acts of virtue, or by bringing us to the good when our virtue fails, Aquinas cannot bring himself to call the happiness of the virtuous voluntary and praiseworthy. Only actions can rightly receive these appellations (*ST* I–II.6.1).

What then accounts for the persistent belief that the happiness of the virtuous is substantially dependent upon good fortune, that virtue and success are somehow opposed?[29] In part, I suspect, it follows from the persistence of the mistaken belief we have just considered: that success in

---

[28] Aristotle comments on these mental games we play: "chance is called good when the result is good, evil when it is evil. The terms 'good fortune' and 'ill fortune' are used when either result is of considerable magnitude. Thus one who comes within an ace of some great evil or great good is said to be fortunate or unfortunate. The mind affirms the presence of the attribute, ignoring the hair's breadth of difference" (*Ph.*197a25–30). Aquinas's commentary: "And since being deprived of a good is included in the notion of evil, and being deprived of evil is included in the notion of the good, then when one is a little removed from a great good, he is said to be unfortunate if he misses it. On the other hand, if one is close to a great evil and is freed from it, he is said to be fortunate. This is so because the intellect takes that which is only a little removed as if it were not removed at all, but already possessed" (*In Phys.*II.9.223).

[29] Yack's (1989, 607–629) remarks are a good example. So are Kant's remarks in the *Foundations of the Metaphysics of Morals* (395–396).

virtue normally requires good fortune. In part, it is due to an analogous mistake: that happiness is sustained by fortune's blessings, not by the work of the virtues. In part, I suspect it is due to the stubborn ambiguity we find in the relation between happiness and success in virtue. In the world we inhabit, the virtuous soon discover that the achievement of one good frequently brings the loss of others. And whether success yields sorrow or a full measure of happiness often depends upon the fact that choices are made in moral contexts that the virtuous have neither chosen nor control.

The problem is not strong moral conflict, where the goods that bring us to our proper flourishing generate mutually exclusive and yet binding obligations in certain instances, for as we have noted, Aquinas denies that the virtuous confront dilemmas of just this kind. Rather, the worry follows from the fact that the virtuous succeed in a fallen world. Too often they live among thieves and knaves and within social and political arrangements ordered by despots and fools. Frequently, they can do little to change these arrangements or their place within them, and thus more often than not their successes precipitate the loss of other goods, perhaps even torture and imprisonment, instead of "an aggregate of all good things."[30] This in turn makes the measure of happiness they happen to experience subject to fortune in two ways.

When the measure is great they are surprised by their good fortune, by the fact that there is no guarantee that success in virtue will end tragically, even in a fallen world. There is no certainty that the just will languish in jail when tyranny rules. The point here is not that tyrants can be duped, for of course they can and the virtuous may be obliged to try and when the deception succeeds the happiness that follows is clearly a consequence of virtue. Rather, the point is that, with luck, the just may well escape persecution despite their successes and enjoy a measure of happiness that is commensurate with their hopes. But that is just what we should expect in a world ruled by the whim of tyrants and the cowardice of bureaucrats and not the constancy of the virtuous. For the most part, the virtuous can count on success having its costs, but good fortune may surprise them.

When the measure is little, when they get what the just in an unjust world expect, they decry their misfortune precisely because they can imagine a moral world where tyrants and bureaucrats do not rule. They can imagine being born into circumstances that would, for the most

---

[30] Consider the plight of poor Boethius from whom Aquinas borrows this phrase (*ST* I–II.3.3.2; *De Consol.*III.2).

part, yield them a measure of happiness commensurate with their virtue. This is what makes their unhappiness so miserable. Not tragically miserable of course, for with the assistance of charity they can bear their sufferings well for the sake of that perfect happiness where they are united with God, but relative to what they can reasonably hope for in this life (*ST* II–II.23.7–8).[31]

So we should amend the third conclusion about the relation between virtue, success, and happiness this way: when the world is ordered by justice, the happiness available to us in this life follows from successful acts of moral virtue. In such a world the success of the virtuous will rarely result in the loss of other goods. That is, in a just world, the relation between success and happiness will be equivalent to the relation between virtuous choice and success. Both pairs will be largely equivalent, divided only by fortune's interruptions, which, by their very nature, occur infrequently. The trouble with this amendment, however, is that it renders harmless one way in which happiness depends upon fortune while generating another, more troubling dependence. If the happiness of the virtuous depends upon the existence of a just moral order, then it appears that their happiness can be considered a direct consequence of their virtue only when they have the good fortune of being born into a just moral community, and yet this is something they can neither predict nor control.

Happily, this kind of fortune associated with birth does not run all the way down. Indeed, it *is* good fortune to be born into a just moral community, but fortune cannot sustain its justice. This requires the work of the virtuous. Similarly, a just moral community is the sort for which the virtuous work and hope and pray for the assistance of grace, and thus the effects of an unfortunate birth can be righted. Of course, the virtuous are not guaranteed success in either endeavor. Sustaining a just moral community is difficult work, and creating one out of entrenched tyranny often requires the efforts of generations. So the good fortune of good birth does matter, and it may, for a time, diminish the ability of virtue to generate happiness. But insofar as the virtuous persist in these difficult goods and exercise that part of courage that Aquinas calls perseverance (*perseverantia*), a just community may arise from their efforts, in which case the happiness they know will be their own (*ST* II–II.137.1).

---

[31] For an account of the pragmatics of charity, of how the virtuous bear suffering well for the sake of their future friendship with God, see Tilly's (1991) excellent treatment of martyrdom in the early church.

5.

The threat fortune poses to the causal connections Aquinas assumes between virtue, success, and happiness, like the threat it poses to the just distribution of opportunity to act virtuously, is more apparent than real. In each instance, confusion about the character of virtuous agency and the extent of its dependence upon fortune generates the worry. In each instance a solution unfolds as we better understand the relations between the virtues and those things subject to fortune. Nevertheless, these solutions assume virtues already in place, and Aquinas's account appears to make their acquisition largely fortuitous. He insists that our knowledge of and desire for the basic outlines of the human good, although natural and necessary, provide only the meagerest beginnings of virtue (*ST* I–II.63.1), and he contends that prudent choice presupposes considerable experience with the contingent singulars that make choice difficult. It follows that the virtues cannot be had without the aid of wise teachers and rich experience (*ST* II–II.49.3), and of course access to each is a matter of good fortune. One not only needs to be born into a moral community with traditions and resources that encourage the development of wise teachers, one also needs to be lucky enough to have access to them and the time and leisure to benefit from their wisdom and experience. Healthy measures of time and leisure normally presuppose equally healthy measures of wealth and power. And although we noted that in the right circumstances the virtuous may well have considerable control over their access to these goods, those without virtue will have little. For them, birth not only controls access to moral communities where virtue flourishes, but also to the wealth and power one needs in order to benefit from the good company of others.

Of course, Aquinas does admit that some have bodies that offer certain benefits or burdens to one or more of the soul's powers, disposing them to act either well or ill. Since it is virtue that perfects those powers we can refer to those benefits as natural virtues. Thus, "one man has a natural aptitude for science, another for fortitude, another for temperance: and in these ways, both intellectual and moral virtues are in us by way of natural aptitude" (*ST* I–II.63.1). From this one might assume that it is fortune's control over the genetic lottery that is the real threat to Aquinas's account of the virtues, but this would be a mistake. Like those dispositions that we all share as a result of our natural knowledge of the human good, those natural virtues that some possess are inchoate. There is an inclination to virtue, but no real virtue itself.

Indeed, like all things natural, inclinations of this kind are determined to one act not many, while acquired virtues are not determined to one particular action but to "various modes, in respect of various matters . . . and according to various circumstances" (*ST* I–II.63.1). As a result, those with a natural inclination to a particular act of virtue can do that act well when conditions remain simple and constant. When conditions change, however, they cannot adjust and strike the mean again, and ironically, it is often their inchoate virtue that generates the conditions that precipitate their failure. Thus the blind horse with plenty of speed stumbles terribly precisely because its natural talent makes its lack of perfection a liability (*ST* I–II.58.4.3).

Therefore, like the rest of us, those with a natural inclination to a particular kind of virtuous action need training, experience, and assistance if they are to acquire genuine virtue. They need a moral community that can take their natural inclinations, whether shared with the rest of us or uniquely their own, and transform them from narrow and inflexible dispositions into generous perfections. They need wise teachers and rich experience and a sufficient supply of external goods. They need a fortuitous moral inheritance.

The worries that follow are now familiar. If virtue is needed for happiness, both as constituent and instrument, it appears that each is distributed by fortune when the things needed to acquire virtue are securely in fortune's hands. And if virtue cannot be had without fortune's assistance, how then can we regard what the virtuous do as voluntary and praiseworthy? Aquinas insists that we can (*ST*II–II.58.1), but the warrants for his confidence need spelling out against these doubts. In particular, we need to consider how the virtuous lay claim to their moral inheritance, accept what is useful in it, transform or reject what is not, and as a result make fortune's gifts their own. Courage is the key, for there is a direct connection between acting courageously and acting in a manner that is voluntary and thus praiseworthy, a connection that holds even when the action arises from habit and when the habit arises, at least initially, from the good fortune of being raised in a moral community that nurtures courage and sustains the courageous. That is, laying claim to one's own character, giving it shape and thereby making it one's own, is an ordinary condition and a common consequence of courageous action. Aquinas, of course, considers this true of every virtuous action. What then distinguishes those called courageous? Only this: the best way to see the voluntary character of an action that arises from a settled habit is to notice that it is ordered to overcome some

difficulty. Since courage regards great dangers and extraordinary difficulties it compels our attention to the relations between habit, difficulty,
and voluntariness. The other virtues, by contrast, cope with more
commonplace obstacles, and thus display the voluntariness of virtuous
action less vividly (*ST* II–II.129.2).

Recall for a moment some of the details of Aquinas's discussion.
Courage regards sensible goods that are difficult to achieve because they
endanger other goods that we hold dear, principally life and limb. This
prospect arouses fear, which in turn discourages us from pursuing the
dangerous and difficult good that we ought. Unless, of course we are
courageous. In that event, our fear of losing something good as a
consequence of pursuing some particular obligation will be moderate.
Courage is the virtue that habitually disposes us to respond in this way,
to pursue the good that right reason dictates despite discouraging
dangers and fears.

All of this implies that those with genuine courage have their attention fixed upon a number of goods all at once: the difficult good whose
pursuit justice demands as well as the goods that are threatened as the
pursuit proceeds. It also implies that those confronted with a circumstance that calls for courage are in fact caught between a collection of
competing goods and conflicting passions. Just states of affairs are, of
course, good and desirable. This is undeniable. But it is equally undeniable that pursuing a just cause frequently threatens other things that we
consider good. Conflicting emotions naturally follow. Desire for the
difficult good pulls in one direction, fear of loss causes retreat in another.
What is distinctive about the courageous is their ability to confront this
complex context reflectively. Indeed, they must. If the courageous are
those who are able to pursue the good that right reason dictates despite
the fact that doing so threatens some other good, then it follows that
their courageous actions presuppose reflection upon the relative merits
of at least some of the goods they love steadfastly and will habitually.

Consider the rescue of the Danish Jews during the Second World
War.[32] It appears that the Danes resided in a cultural and political
context that encouraged most to regard religious and ethnic affiliation
as irrelevant for civic friendship and many to regard their fellow citizens
as neighbors who required protection when threatened. For the Danes,
care for the citizen-neighbor was a good that justice required, and like

---

[32] According to Gutman (1990, 1799), of the 7,800 Jews in Denmark at the start of the war, 7,220
were secreted off to Sweden, 475 were deported (although most returned), 50 died in the camps,
50 were hid in Denmark, and 10 were killed in Denmark itself.

most of us who consider some thing good by force of habit, the Danes probably willed this good unreflectively. However, when the Nazis intervened, they were, quite literally, compelled to see that willing the good of their Jewish neighbors was incompatible, at least in this instance, with habitually willing their own. They were forced to reflect upon the character of their moral inheritance and to consider how habitually willing some goods and not others would actually affect their lives. And since justice, according to Aquinas, disposes us to pursue some goods (presumably those that will consistently give our neighbors their proper due) and not others, we can say that the Nazis' attack upon their Jewish neighbors compelled Denmark's gentiles to reflect upon the account of justice that they had inherited and to which they had consented without deliberation.

Clearly, acting courageously in this instance presupposed reflection of just this sort. We would not call the Danes courageous if their actions did not put their lives and welfare at risk, and it is difficult to imagine pursuing a life threatening course that did not prompt reflection on the relative value of the goods pursued and threatened. In fact, Aquinas insists that when the unreflective respond to danger as the courageous do, they do not deserve praise, for their actions are but semblances of truly virtuous conduct (*ST* II–II.123.1.2). Of course, he does not believe that deliberation precedes every act of courage. When dangers are sudden the courageous act without forethought (*ST* II–II.123.8). Nevertheless, dangers confronted and overcome tend to prompt retrospective reflection on what was felt and done by force of habit. In these reflections the courageous will not simply ask whether the object and intensity of their fear tracked their judgment about the relative worth of the goods pursued and endangered, but they will also ask whether that judgment, solidified in habit, is best, all things considered.

The point of significance should be plain. It is this kind of coerced reflection that enables one to take the habits of mind and affection that were fortune's gifts and make them one's own. Reflection accomplishes this feat either by confirming the goodness of those ends one is disposed to love by habit in a judgment that they are in fact good and desirable, or by casting doubt upon the goodness of those ends as objects of intention in this instance. In either case a moral inheritance is transformed, perhaps even recreated, as judgments are made about its moral content. And note, it is a particular kind of reflection and a particular sort of judgment that marks courageous action, frees it from the contingencies of birth and circumstance, and guarantees its voluntary character. When the truly courageous among Denmark's gentiles concluded that their Jewish neighbors deserved rescue despite the grave risks involved, they did not simply choose one course of action over another or express their preference for some ends and not others. Had their reflections proceeded no further we could not, by Aquinas's reckoning, count them among the courageous, their actions being mere semblances of virtue. Indeed, this judgment would remain even if their reflections had brought them to put their own lives at risk for the sake of praiseworthy ends and no other, even if they had managed to participate with no thought of petty honor, sensual pleasure, or private gain (*ST* II–II.123.1.2).

By contrast, genuine courage requires a more thorough going assessment of one's moral posture in the world, of the habits one happens to have, of the ends one happens to pursue. Comparing the relative worth of this end or that is not enough. Reflection must also confirm the importance of courageous actions and habits in the best kind of human life. It must generate the conclusion that a life devoid of courageous action is not worth living, that a cowardly self is not worth having given the difficulties, dangers, and frailties that constantly hound us. It follows that the truly courageous Danes participated in the rescue precisely because they believed their chances of leading a noble and honorable life, one qualitatively better in kind than other possibilities, would be forever sacrificed by refusing to assist a group of fellow citizens in need. Refusal, they concluded, would transform them into the cowards they regarded with contempt, into the sort of people who have little chance of leading a praiseworthy and fulfilling human life precisely because they do not see the point of acting courageously. It follows that the truly courageous not only lay claim to the moral inheritance that bears directly upon immediate courses of action. They also transform their whole moral posture from something largely given into something confirmed by judgment, and thus their own. They move themselves, not without assistance from the culture they have inherited and the context of action they inhabit, and yet not because they are compelled by culture and context. Moreover, they act as they do precisely because they have assessed the place of courageous conduct in human life as a whole. By contrast, those who fail to act among the courageous fail to move themselves *simpliciter* (*ST* I–II.68.2) precisely because they act without this kind of knowledge.

As always, Aquinas assumes a theological context throughout. He assumes that with the love of charity the truly courageous direct their intentions, both proximate and remote, to God (*ST* II–II.123.7; I–II.65.2). He assumes that with the benefit of the Holy Spirit's gift of courage they act confidently and without fear, certain that they will finish whatever difficult work they begin and mindful of the insignificance of the goods they put at risk when compared to the everlasting life they hope to achieve (*ST* II–II.139.1). He also assumes that like the rest of our moral inheritance this gracious assistance is given with fortune's necessity. Nevertheless, because charity is infused with faith (*ST* I–II.62.4), and because the gift of courage is given with the gift of counsel (*ST* II–II.139.1.3), the truly courageous act knowingly, reflectively. Of course, their knowledge of the place of courageous action in a happy and praiseworthy human life differs from the knowledge mustered by those with courage untouched by grace. It follows from reflection motivated by the promptings of the Holy Spirit, not by fear, and it includes hints of our final end, of God's wisdom and will (*ST* I–II.68.2; II–II.68.4.3). Still, it is knowledge all the same, and by Aquinas's lights all that is needed is reflective knowledge of the end in the agent who acts in order to secure the voluntary character of what is done (*ST* I–II.6.1–2).

Of course, not all virtuous actions are species of courage, despite the difficulties that the virtues generally regard. Nor should we assume that every virtuous pursuit of one good necessarily entails threats to another. Given these caveats, one might suspect that reflection on established dispositions and judgments cannot distinguish virtuous agency generally, that laying claim to inherited habits is a matter for the courageous alone, but this suspicion misleads. The virtues act together and are therefore connected (*ST* I–II.65.1). As such, when the courageous are compelled by circumstance to reflect upon the merits of their moral inheritance, their whole moral posture toward the various goods at stake in that circumstance falls under inspection. Our example bears this out. Before they could decide to aid their Jewish neighbors, Denmark's gentiles had to consider the relative merits of the difficult and dangerous goods that fall under courage, the goods of neighbor, family, and self that fall under justice, and the goods and evils of the body (in particular, those that generate pleasures and pains) that are the objects of temperance. Before the Nazi invasion their attitude toward these goods may well have been relatively unreflective, a matter of habit determined by custom. After the occupation this became impossible, reflection on the relative worth of each unavoidable. In turn, the habits and actions that followed reflection could no longer be considered mere accidents of history, at least not simply. The habits now carried the mark of those who chose according to them, the actions now followed from beliefs and sentiments that the agents had claimed for themselves.

Perhaps most significantly, reflection of this sort is the ordinary work of prudence, presupposed in every virtuous action. In contexts that call for courage this work is literally compelled, and the compulsion makes it apparent. Nevertheless, Aquinas considers it indispensable even in those circumstances where the prudent choice of one good does not immediately threaten another, precisely because he does not imagine that choice can proceed well without reflection upon the relative merits of a number of ends that are habitually willed and frequently intended. For an end is not simply an end, it is also a means to some other end, perhaps many (*ST* I–II.13.3). As a result, deliberation over the most effective means to a proximate end and reflection upon the achievement of that end will, more often than not, encourage reflection upon the desirability of a number of ends near and far. And since deliberation is normally over things that are uncertain, prudent reflection will normally consider the consequences of failure, which in turn generates reflection on the desirability of the end sought and the goodness of virtue itself apart from its successes.

This leads Aquinas to conclude that it is not only the virtuous who reflect upon their moral inheritance as they choose, but the rest of us as well. In fact, reflective knowledge of the ends we will and intend by habit is, Aquinas believes, the distinguishing mark of the voluntary agency that we attribute to human beings as such. An action is voluntary when it is caused by knowledge of the end in the agent who acts (*ST* I–II.6.1). An action that is fully voluntary – as opposed to the incompletely voluntary that is characteristic of children and animals – follows from perfect knowledge of the end. Perfect knowledge of the end entails, "knowing it under the aspect of end, and the relationship of the means to the end" (*ST* I–II.6.2). Knowing the relationship between means and ends, knowing, that is, how to deliberate, is what distinguishes the voluntariness of our agency from that of irrational animals. They have knowledge of the ends they seek, but they can neither deliberate over this or that means, nor choose one and not the other. Rather, the means they employ are determinate and few, and as a result they move to the end they apprehend "at once" (*ST* I–II.6.2).

We do not. Our deliberations slow us down. They also enable us to know the ends we pursue reflectively, that is, "under the aspect of end" (*cognoscitur ratio finis*). This, in turn, helps us distinguish the fully voluntary action of adults from the imperfectly voluntary action of young children.

Children, of course, do manage to consider and choose. Even toddlers confront decisions: apple juice or orange, red shorts or green, go with Mom or stay with Dad, play with trucks or read a book, and so on. But what toddlers can't do, and won't do until they are somewhat older, is reflect on the relative merits of this or that end. They cannot ask how the various ends they happen to pursue stack up, one to another. They cannot rank them as more or less important. Their immature deliberations do not lead them to this kind of reflection. Their fears cannot compel them to it. As a result they have no self-conscious realization that the pursuit of any particular end is normally one option among others. It is for this reason that Aquinas equates the fully voluntary with the self-reflective knowledge that follows from mature deliberation:

now judgment is in the power of the one judging insofar as he can judge about his judgments; for we can pass judgment upon the things that are in our power. But to judge about one's own judgments belongs only to reason, which reflects upon its own act and knows the relationships of the things about which it judges and of those by which it judges. (*De verit.* 24.2)

Young children and animals cannot make judgments about their own judgments. By contrast, when inherited habits encourage us to judge a certain end as worthy of pursuit, we can step back and compare it to other ends, its goodness to theirs. In fact, we normally pursue second order judgments of just this sort as a consequence of deliberating over the means.

It should now be apparent that Aquinas considers the voluntary a species of the rational. Not the perfected rationality that is characteristic of the virtuous alone, but the minimal rationality that is characteristic of our kind. By regarding the voluntary as consequent upon the ability to deliberate in a manner that yields second order judgments Aquinas implies that it is the ability to give reasons that justifies acting in one way and not another that is the characteristic mark of ordinary human freedom. Indeed, in most instances, a satisfying answer to, "why did you do that?!" not only entails reasons that justify the means chosen but also reasons that justify the end pursued.[33] Reasons of this latter sort come only as the agent situates the intended end in relation to others, which of course cannot be done without second order reflection. It is for this reason that Aquinas commences his whole discussion of voluntary

---

[33] The caveat is essential, for of course, some objects of the will are, in a given context, so obviously good that our desire for them cannot be justified. All justifications would fail precisely because all would appeal to reasons for acting less certain than the reason provided by the objects themselves.

agency in the *prima secundae* by citing Damascene's remark that "the voluntary is an act consisting in a rational operation" (*ST* I–II.6.1.*sed contra*). It is for this reason that he concludes that "the whole root of freedom is located in reason" (*De verit.* 24.2).[34]

This is a remarkable conclusion, and a number of equally remarkable consequences follow. First, human freedom becomes unimaginable apart from reflection upon the human good, which means that Aquinas's treatment of the voluntariness of human agency (*ST* I–II.6) must be read together with his discussion of the natural law (*ST* I–II.90–95). Reasons are given in the hope that actions will be made intelligible. Actions become minimally intelligible when it is made plain that they are done for the sake of ends that human beings can recognize as good. By Aquinas's lights good reasons of this minimally decent variety will inevitably refer to one of the human goods that we know and will by nature, simply and absolutely. Agents that do not refer to one of these goods fail to explain their actions precisely because they fail to refer to ends that human beings can consider good and desire because they are. Their reasons fall short of even minimal decency because no connection is made between what they have done and the good that they are presumed to know and love because they are creatures of a particular sort. Since no such connection is made, what they have done cannot be regarded as human action, rational and voluntary.

Of course, minimally decent reasons for acting are hardly good reasons. At the very least, they are not good enough, for the explanation they provide hardly satisfies. Why? Because the human good is multiplex, and thus human actions become intelligible only after we know why the agent found this end more desirable than other possibilities. And this greater measure of intelligibility comes only as the conclusions of the agent's second order deliberations are offered in the explanation. Once this level of intelligibility has been reached, we can continue to distinguish good and bad reasons, but the difference will be between reasons that compel consent and those that do not. Here all reasons explain but not all convince. You will probably be able to explain why you rob banks. You may even be able to explain how thieving fits into your account of the best kind of human life. Indeed, you must carry your second order reflections this far if we are to count your actions your own, and not the consequence of habit inherited from fortune. But it is unlikely that you will be able to convince me that this collection of ends,

---

[34] For more on Aquinas's treatment of voluntary agency see Bowlin (1998).

this account of the best life, deserves consent. My own second order reflections bring me to different conclusions. I may even decide that you would have consented to my view had you carried your own reflections a bit further. But no matter, our concern is the voluntary character of what you have done and only second order reasons of *some* sort are needed to establish that.

Second, if free agency is a matter of acting for reasons that are good enough to explain what was done, then it need not be the case that an agent must have been able to do other than he did before we can count his action free. Knowing the good and pursuing it because of that knowledge is the mark of freedom, not the ability to turn the will away from that good. No doubt, the ability to do otherwise often accompanies actions that we consider free, but it need not. If the end I know and desire is sufficiently good, if it stands head and shoulders above all others that I might pursue in this instance, then convincing you that I acted for its sake should explain what I have done. If its overwhelming goodness makes it impossible for me to imagine acting differently, nothing follows. Surely not the loss of my free agency.

Lastly, this conclusion enables Aquinas to dismiss the objections of those who find voluntary agency incompatible with creation and Providence. Since both entail God moving us to pursue some general ends but not others (*ST* I–II.6.1.3), both appear to cast doubt upon the freedom of the agency they cause. But Aquinas insists that appearances deceive. We are moved to pursue an end only after we know that it is good (*ST* I–II.9.1). Knowledge of the good always precedes desire of it, and of course it is knowledge of some end judged good that is, for Aquinas, the principal condition of the voluntary. Thus, while we are inclined by our nature to seek knowledge and self-preservation (*ST* I–II.10.1), we can nevertheless regard the actions that pursue them as free precisely because they presuppose judgments about the goodness of these ends. By the same token, the blessed can be considered free agents even though they are inclined by God to a specific end by specific means (*De verit.* 22.8; 24.8). Their actions are fully determined, and yet they nevertheless act freely because they are moved by knowledge of a good that has no peer. Insofar as this knowledge provides reasons that explain what they do we can locate the origin of their agency in themselves, in their knowledge of the human good.

Notice how this compatibility between the necessity that is implicit in creation and the free agency of human creatures is roughly equivalent to the compatibility between habits formed by tradition and the voluntary character of the actions that they cause. In both instances we are inclined to some ends and not others by something external, something beyond our control, either God or tradition. And in both instances it is self-reflective knowledge of those ends that certifies the resultant agency as voluntary. Indeed, when God is the source of habit the two problems converge while the solution remains the same (*De verit.* 22.8; *ST* II–II.23.3). When grace inclines us to an end that transcends our nature by infusing us with the habit of charity (*ST* II–II.23.2), faith guarantees the voluntary character of our acts of love by providing assent of the mind to the object of charity (*ST* II–II.4.7), which is none other than God's goodness, our final happiness (*ST* II–II.23.4.2; 23.5).

Epilogue
Hope and happiness

One pressing puzzle remains. If Aquinas's relative silence about the threats that fortune poses to his account of virtue and happiness makes sense given the details of that account, what then explains his noisy discontent with a life of virtue threatened by fortune, burdened with contingency (*ST* I–II.5.3)? No doubt, the life of virtue is a life of struggle. No doubt, fortune can disrupt a virtuous life and diminish human happiness in all sorts of ways. Nevertheless, in Aquinas's hands the virtues prove too well suited to these challenges for discontent to follow without explanation. Worry about fortune seems out of place, complaint with the happiness the virtuous are able to secure seems unjustified. How then can he remain discontent and what prevents him from following discontent, as the Stoics do, to an account of virtue and happiness that removes each from fortune's reach?

As before, it is Adam's virtue that provides the point of contrast that generates both the complaint with the happiness virtue brings in this life and the hope for something better. In Eden the acquisition of virtue was assured by the grace that was its principal cause (*ST* 1.95.1, 3), just as opportunities to act virtuously and grow in virtue were plentiful, never once impeded by the absence of external goods. In fact, no good was "wanting which a good-will could desire to have" (*ST* 1.95.2). Food was plentiful (*ST* 1.96.1.3) and the climate always temperate (*ST* 1.102.2). The body was strong (*ST* 1.96.1.3) and free of defect, fault, or disproportion (*ST* 1.96.3). Death and disease were unknown (*ST* 1.97.1), as were slavery and tyranny (*ST* 1.96.4). Dangerous animals slept at Adam's feet (*ST* 1.96.1). Plants and inanimate things proved no hindrance at all (*ST* 1.96.2).

By the same token, success in virtue was virtually guaranteed, not only by the full measure of external goods, those indispensable instruments of virtue, but also by the knowledge that successful choice assumes. Adam "was established by God in such a manner as to have

213

knowledge of all those things for which man has a natural aptitude . . . whatever truths man is naturally able to know" (*ST* 1.94.3). This is not to say that he was born with perfect knowledge, but rather that knowledge in Eden was easily acquired (*ST* 1.101.1). Of course, there are all sorts of things that we are unable to know, things that may bear upon the success of virtuous choice: future contingents, the secret thoughts of others, perhaps even the number of pebbles in a stream, and the like (*ST* 1.101.1). Adam was no different, even while in Eden. But even this limitation was made inconsequential by divine guidance, which guaranteed that Adam was not "deceived in a matter to which his knowledge did not extend" (*ST* 1.94.4.5).

And finally, the principal source of Adam's happiness, the contemplation of the divine through its intelligible effects, was neither impeded nor distracted by his passions. Created *in gratia*, Adam had perfect dominion over them (*ST* 1.94.1), and as such they were only "consequent upon the judgment of reason," never once elicited by the shifting character of "exterior things" (*ST* 1.95.2).[1]

To be sure, Aquinas does concede that if Adam had not sinned, some of Eden's inhabitants would have been stronger, more beautiful, more knowledgeable and experienced than others. Strict equality would not have obtained. However, he also insists that these different fortunes would not have been the result of defect or fault in body or soul and thus would not have translated into fundamental differences in virtue or happiness (*ST* 1.96.3).

Our lot is much different. Although our virtues are well suited to cope with fortune's twists and turns, they are not perfect and therefore they cannot master misfortune as Adam's did with God's assistance. Storms, disease, drought, and exile can scuttle even the best of our efforts. Unwelcome coincidence between competing goods can produce intractable conflicts that even the most virtuous among us cannot untangle. Acquiring virtue can be made difficult by the circumstances of birth: wise teachers may be absent, the body may be weak, basic needs may go unmet. And virtue acquired can be put aside in circumstances that make vicious courses of action too tempting or virtuous courses too frightening. It can also be lost altogether in circumstances that encourage moral apathy or that impede nearly every opportunity to act virtuously. Of

---

[1] A passion can be consequent upon the judgment of reason in two ways. First, by way of redundance, when a passion follows the movement of the will and confirms its intensity. Second, by way of choice, when one chooses to be affected by a passion that will enable the will to reach its object more promptly (*ST* 1–11.24.3.1).

course, we have noted that opportunity normally abounds, despite fortune's fickle distribution of those goods that are the instruments of virtue and the source of opportunity. Most will possess goods of fortune in sufficient measure to participate in a variety of virtuous activities. Opportunities remain even when the measure is low. The ordinary as well as the beautiful have need of temperance. Even the poor have some wealth to spend well, some need to exercise their liberality and to lay the foundation of future magnificence. No doubt this assumption makes sense most of the time. But what about those instances when misfortune bears down with such force that endurance is the only possible activity, the only sphere of action for virtue to shine? Surely cruel fortune prevents the genuinely powerless – the victims of torture, abuse, or profound disability – from participating in nearly every variety of virtuous activity. Surely the thoroughly destitute among the virtuous lament their inability to act as those with virtue *and* good fortune do.

So virtue might not be established, might be lost if it is, might lie fallow if it remains, or might be unsuccessful when it acts, and all because of misfortune. This is the uncertain state of our virtue this side of Eden. This is the unpredictable and imperfect happiness it yields. Since Adam's virtue and happiness in Eden represent other possibilities, since he once stood free of fortune's effects, and because Aquinas assumes that God made us for that life and not ours, he can follow Augustine and lament our lot (*De civ.Dei.* xix.5–9). And yet without this alternative perspective it is unlikely that he could generate much legitimate discontent. His trust in Aristotelian virtue is too keen for that.

This puts Aquinas awkwardly in between confidence that the virtues can succeed against fortune on the one hand, and discontent, perhaps even despair, over their fragility, on the other. He cannot revise his treatment of the virtues in the manner the Stoics suggest, effectively eliminating their exposure to luck, for this would not only ignore his confidence in unreconstructed Aristotelian virtue, it would also deny the reality and consequence of our fall from grace – that virtue and happiness are in fact exposed to misfortune in ways that can undo each. Nor can he simply rest content in his Aristotelian commitments and maintain that the virtues do well enough against fortune's challenges, for this would ignore the obvious – that virtue in Eden does far better. And of course it is this fact that gives him grounds to find fault with what he has, to yearn for something more, and to tempt Stoic revisions of his largely Aristotelian treatment of the moral virtues. His actual response, if we can call it that, resides between these two alternatives, and since hope is the mean between confidence and despair we should not be surprised to find Aquinas's reply in his treatment of the theological virtues.

That Aquinas regards the theological virtues in general, and charity in particular, as indispensable for the possession and exercise of genuine moral virtue is, of course, indisputable. The ordinary explanation for the claim refers to one of the formal requirements of virtue in general and to the relations that obtain among the moral virtues in particular. Since the moral virtues are habits that perfect ourselves and our agency in the practical matters of this life, it follows that perfect moral virtue must direct us to our perfect good, our final end, our highest happiness. Since Aquinas assumes that our final end surpasses the reach of our human nature, he concludes that, strictly speaking, perfect virtue cannot be had without charity. For it is charity that disposes the will to that supernatural end and therefore enables the practical intellect that is perfected by prudence to deliberate well with respect to it (*ST* I–II.65.2; II–II.23.7 and ad 2). Since the other moral virtues cannot be had without prudence (*ST* I–II.58.4–5; 65.1), its labors mediate the effects of charity upon the rest. It directs them to the last end, and thus, quite literally, imprints charity's form upon their acts (*ST* II–II.23.8).

There is, however, another possible explanation. Perhaps Aquinas insists that perfection in virtue is unimaginable without charity in order to respond to at least some of fortune's ill effects upon the life of virtue this side of Eden. The best evidence that we can regard his efforts in this way follows from the fact that charity induces Stoic modifications of the moral virtues that are infused with it, effectively eliminating fortune's authority over virtuous habits and actions, and by implication, its influence over the happiness of the virtuous. Consider temperance. The distribution of wealth and power may determine access to pleasures of the table, and yet the need to moderate desire for these pleasures obtains in both plenty and in want, and thus the opportunity to act temperately accompanies both conditions. Fortune has little, if any, purchase here. Still, it has none at all upon those blessed with the perfected temperance infused together with the rest of the theological virtues. Their desire for the pleasures of the table is no longer measured according to the rule of human reason, which dictates desire for food that will neither harm the body, nor hinder the use of reason, nor injure those who deserve regard (*ST* I–II.63.4; II–II.146.1). It is, rather, fixed according to the divine rule, which directs the temperate to subject the body "by abstinence in food, drink, and the like" (*ST* I–II.63.4). Clearly, all can participate in this activity, those rich in fortune's goods, and those impoverished.

Or consider patience and perseverance. Both are integral parts of endurance, which Aquinas considers the principal act of courage (*ST* II–II.123.1). The patient bear hardships well, without sorrow in deficiency or excess (*ST* II–II.136.2 and ad 1). They suffer some evil in the present, some good lost, without inordinate sadness (*ST* II–II.136.4.2), and those with perfect patience do so with the assistance of God's grace. While false patience bears evil for the sake of lesser goods, normally bodily pleasure of some sort, true patience endures hardship for the sake of the greatest good, fellowship with God and the blessed (*ST* II–II.136.3.1). Since charity allows the patient to love these goods above all, it also allows them to endure the loss of every other good (*ST* II–II.136.3). Their sorrow is moderate because the good they have lost is insignificant when compared to the Supreme Good their wills *already* embrace in love. The persevering, by contrast, endure the difficulties and disappointments of virtuous deeds delayed, and they do so without excessive fear of weariness or of failure on account of the delay (*ST* II–II.137.1; 137.2 and ad 2). And yet, like patience, Aquinas considers true perseverance an infused virtue, its work unthinkable without the habitual gift of grace that turns the will in love to God. For it is this love of charity that allows the persevering to persist in the proximate ends of virtue for the sake of its ultimate end (*ST* II–II.137.4). And, as with patience, the work of perseverance is needed precisely because misfortune has disrupted the life of active virtue. Nevertheless, in each instance, courage transformed by charity does not enter the world and alter its character. The patient and the persevering do not overcome contingencies and confront difficulties in order to bring about some state of affairs. Their virtue is not active in this sense. Instead they wait, not simply for a change in fortune and a chance to resume activity; indeed, not principally, for of course, they know their fortune may not improve. Instead they "endure throughout the whole of life" (*ST* II–II.137.1), standing unmoved in the midst of dangers and waiting upon the end of their days for a world that exceeds fortune's reach (*ST* II–II.137.3). In a sense, they are already there. The courageous endure the disruption of their agency in this life only with God's gracious assistance, and it is precisely God's grace that transforms courage into a habit whose acts remain within the agent who possesses it, and thus whose success cannot be disrupted by fickle fortune.[2]

In fact, this is true of every moral virtue, perfected by grace and

---

[2] Hauerwas (1993, 256–260) treats these virtues in a similar fashion but for a somewhat different effect.

transformed by charity. Each is ordered to two ends, one proximate and determined by reason, another that is "remote and excelling, namely God" (*ST* II–II.17.1). When their acts fall short of achieving the proximate end they nevertheless succeed in achieving the distant. Indeed, they must, for charity not only moves the virtuous to act for the sake of the distant end, it also guarantees that every act of genuine virtue "attains God Himself that it may rest in him" (*ST* II–II.23.6). Consider, for example, acts of justice done out of charity for the sake of our final end. In each instance the remote end of action is achieved without fail, for charity is an act of love and as such implies union with its object (*ST* II–II.23.6.3). It follows that success in justice perfected by charity – that is, success in achieving its distant end – is a rather simple matter. All that is needed is a will disposed in love toward God, and with God's gracious assistance the just succeed in bringing about this turn of the will "with ease and pleasure" (*ST* II–II.23.2). No doubt, a will disposed in love toward God by charity may nevertheless fail to act in accord with this love. Mysteriously, the will can turn away from any good that it knows and loves, even the greatest and the best, and the habitual grace bestowed in this life does not repair this illness (*ST* II–II.137.4). But that said, insofar as the just do manage to choose in accord with charity, they will in fact succeed. They will in fact act among the saints and angels in the household of God (*ST* I–II.63.4).

Virtue whose completed act is nothing but a certain state of the will, success in action that is assured, at least with respect to the final end, and fortune made inconsequential, at least for the most part – these are the marks of Stoic virtue that Aquinas imprints upon the moral virtues, infused by grace and perfected by charity. Of course, the caveats are important. Aquinas does not imagine that charity works a complete Stoic overhaul of the moral virtues. A proximate end is still desired and more often than not its pursuit remains subject to disruption by misfortune. Thus, for example, those with justice perfected by charity may well be guaranteed a measure of success, and thus of happiness, that is proportionate to the measure of their union with God. Nevertheless, it is still quite possible for misfortune to trip them up short of their proximate ends, and their happiness may be diminished accordingly. Indeed, if the course of action that Denmark's gentiles had taken to rescue their Jewish neighbors had been thwarted by misfortune of some sort – by an insufficient supply of external goods, a freak coincidence of events, or the like – we would surely consider their happiness incomplete. If, despite their earthly failures, God's grace had brought their just choices to supernatural success, we would not say that their happiness had been restored untarnished for their neighbors were dead, tyranny was left unchecked, and their own lives were at risk.

Here Aquinas stands plainly between theologically motivated discontent with Aristotelian virtue that is periodically subject to fortune's disruptions and confidence that it does well enough against fortune's threats most of the time. The discontent leads him to imagine a kind of virtue that escapes fortune's reach and whose success requires nothing beyond a turn of the will toward God. The confidence prevents him from recasting the moral virtues in these terms alone, even those perfected by charity. The ends intended by the virtuous are not simply internal states of the will. Virtuous action does not remain exclusively within the soul, but ventures outward into fortune's domain where, happily, it succeeds most of the time. Still, one suspects that Aquinas can maintain his confidence in Aristotelian virtue and refuse to follow theological discontent to radical recasting precisely because grace guarantees the successful achievement of the remote end of virtuous action. Misfortune may obstruct the proximate ends of justice but never the friendship with God that charity secures. Secular Aristotelians have no equivalent transcendent consolation, but then, nor do they have theological sources of discontent. They do not have Adam's perfect virtue tempting comparison and complaint with our own. They do recognize that misfortune disrupts the life of virtue now and again, and yet as we have seen, these disruptions are too infrequent to justify reconceiving virtuous action as the Stoics recommend.

It follows that silent resignation is all that the secular Aristotelian can offer when fortune's hand lays heavy upon the life of virtue. Is Aquinas tempted by such a reply? One might suspect that he is. He *is* silent about the distribution of virtue, both natural and infused. He does, in fact, say very little about the fate of those who have been prevented by circumstance from acquiring the moral virtues. He is taciturn about virtue that has been lost or corrupted by the worst kinds of misfortune – poverty, torture, abuse. He does remind his readers that we are largely ignorant of the ways of Divine Providence, the true source of all things that happen here by accident (*ST* 1.116.1), and that we know nothing at all about the intentions of the Holy Ghost, who infuses virtue "according as He will" (*ST* 11–11.24.3). Still, we should not conclude that these replies amend his confidence in Aristotelian virtue with a sigh about its failures. He is not recommending that we consent to our ignorance, accept fortune's control over our lot, and concede without complaint when lives are crushed and virtue scattered. Perhaps the secular Aristotelian can muster this kind of asceticism, but it is unlikely that Aquinas can. The freedom from misfortune that Adam knew and the happiness he enjoyed precludes this response.

But what alternative might replace asceticism? For Aquinas it must be hope, for only hope can address the discontent that the comparison with Adam generates. It is not hope that Providence dressed in fortune's jacket will treat us gently, for hope, by definition, regards the consequences of our agency. We hope for something that we might achieve by our own doings, and there is little that we can do to affect Providence. Rather, it is the eschatological hope that comes only with the assistance of God's grace; the hope that stretches forth toward the most difficult of goods, the fellowship of everlasting happiness (*ST* I–II.17.2–3). That fellowship will be characterized by peace, by concord between friends, and by freedom from those external hindrances that might otherwise threaten virtue and happiness (*ST* II–II.29.1–3). It follows that to hope in this way entails yearning for a happiness that transcends fortune's reach. And yet, because hope cannot be without charity (*ST* I–II.65.4), and because charity entails not only love of God but also friendship with Him (*ST* I–II.65.5), genuine acts of hope, in a sense, already achieve that happiness (*ST* II–II.17.1). Success is guaranteed, the difficult good achieved, in the very act of hoping. Or, more precisely, those who hope already attain God, on whose help they lean, even as they yearn for that perfect heavenly fellowship that they expect to have (*ST* II–II.18.4) even as it escapes them now (*ST* II–II.17.1.3).

This is, of course, a Stoic rendering of Christian hope. Described in these terms there is no chance that fortune might interfere with the hopeful. This is hardly surprising. If, as I have suggested, Aquinas in fact thinks his treatment of the infused and theological virtues provides a response to his discontent with the virtue and happiness available to us in this life, then this is what we would expect. It *is* remarkable, however, that he appeals to Stoicism so late and in such a circumscribed fashion. Only the infused and theological virtues receive a Stoic rendering. The moral virtues that are, as he says, fitted to our nature and to our life in this world, do not (*ST* I–II.63.4). When explicated in the moral language Aquinas inherits from Aristotle their exposure to fortune is not sufficient to warrant Stoic rethinking. It is only as Adam's virtue precipitates discontent with ours that Aquinas turns to Stoic treatments of virtue and agency for assistance. Again, this is what we would expect, if, as I have suggested, he regards different moral languages as so many tools for describing different features on the moral landscape and for addressing the problems that accompany this or that description.

Perhaps more to the point, Aquinas's circumspect use of Stoicism shows us what kind of tool he thinks it is, and how narrowly he regards its function. He uses it to address the difficulties that his theological commitments create for his account of virtue and fortune in the same breath that he describes those virtues that fit us for a life with "the saints and the household of God" (*ST* I–II.63.4). Without those commitments, and without the need to explicate those otherworldly virtues, Stoicism would have remained in his tool box. There it remains for the secular Aristotelian, and there it should remain in ours, unless of course, we share Aquinas's theological commitments and his discontent with virtue that misfortune can defeat or dislodge. In that event, we may need it in order to give an account of our hope for something better.

References

Alston, William. 1985. "Divine–Human Dialogue and the Nature of God." *Faith and Philosophy* 2: 5–20.

Annas, Julia. 1993. *The Morality of Happiness.* New York: Oxford University Press.

Anscombe, G.E.M. 1981. "Modern Moral Philosophy." In *The Collected Papers of G.E.M. Anscombe.* Vol. III. Minneapolis: University of Minnesota Press.

Aquinas, Thomas. 1948–50. *De Malo.* Vol. VIII, *Opera Omnia.* New York: Musurgia.

1950. *Summa Theologiae.* 4 vols. Turin: Marietti.

1952. *On the Power of God.* Translated by the English Dominican Fathers. Edited by L. Shapcote. Westminster, MD: Newman.

1952–54. *The Disputed Questions on Truth.* 3 vols. Translated by R.W. Mulligan, J.V. McGlynn, and R.W. Schmidt. Chicago: Henry Regnery.

1953. *Quaestiones Disputatae.* 2 vols. Turin: Marietti.

1962. *Aristotle: On Interpretation: Commentary by St. Thomas and Cajetan.* Translated by J.T. Oesterle. Milwaukee: Marquette University Press.

1963. *Commentary on Aristotle's Physics.* Translated by R.J. Blackwell, R.J. Spath, and W.E. Thirlkel. New Haven: Yale University Press.

1961. *Commentary on the Metaphysics of Aristotle.* 2 vols. Translated by J.P. Rowan. Chicago: Henry Regnery.

1967. *Liber de Veritate Catholicae Fidei contra errores Infidelium.* 3 vols. Turin: Marietti.

1965. *On The Virtues in General.* Translated by R.P. Goodwin. In *Selected Writings of St. Thomas Aquinas.* Indianapolis: Bobbs-Merrill.

1968. *On Being and Essence.* 2nd rev. edn. Translated by Armand Maurer. Toronto: Pontifical Institute of Mediaeval Studies.

1975. *Summa Contra Gentiles.* 4 vols. Translated by A.C. Pegis, J.F. Anderson, V.J. Bourke, and C.J. O'Neil. Notre Dame: University of Notre Dame.

1981. *Summa Theologica.* 5 vols. Translated by Fathers of the English Dominican Province. Westminster, MD: Christian Classics. Reprint (New York: Benzinger Brothers, 1948.)

1989. *The Literal Exposition on Job: A Scriptural Commentary Concerning Providence.*

Translated by A. Damico. Classics in Religious Studies 7. Atlanta: Scholars Press.

1995. *On Evil.* Translated by Jean Oesterle. Notre Dame: University of Notre Dame Press.

Aristotle. 1984. *The Complete Works of Aristotle.* 2 vols. Edited by Jonathan Barnes. Princeton: Princeton University Press.

Augustine. 1872. *On the Morals of the Catholic Church.* In *Writings in Connection with the Manichaean Heresy.* Vol. v of *The Works of Aurelius Augustine, Bishop of Hippo.* Edited by Marcus Dods. Translated by Richard Stothert. Edinburgh: T. & T. Clark.

1874. *On Marriage and Concupiscence.* In *The Anti-Pelagian Works of St. Augustine,* vol. II. Vol. XII of *The Works of Aurelius Augustine, Bishop of Hippo.* Edited by Marcus Dods. Translated by Peter Holmes. Edinburgh: T. & T. Clark.

1950. *City of God.* Translated by Marcus Dodds. New York: Modern Library.

1953. *Earlier Writings.* Translated by John H.S. Burleigh. Philadelphia: Westminster Press.

1955. *Later Works.* Library of Christian Classics, vol. VIII. Translated by John Barnaby. Philadelphia: Westminster Press.

1991 *Confessions.* Translated by Henry Chadwick. Oxford: Oxford University Press.

Baier, Annette. 1985a. "Doing Without Moral Theory." In *Postures of the Mind.* Minneapolis: University of Minnesota Press.

1985b. "Theory and Reflective Practices." In *Postures of the Mind.* Minneapolis: University of Minnesota Press.

Barad, Judith. 1988. "Aquinas's Assent/Consent Distinction and the Problem of Akrasia." *New Scholasticism* 62: 98–111.

Berlin, Isaiah. 1991. *The Crooked Timber of Humanity: Chapters in the History of Ideas.* Edited by Henry Hardy. New York: Knopf.

Berns, Laurence. 1984. "Spiritedness in Ethics and Politics: A Study in Aristotelian Psychology." *Interpretation* 12: 335–348.

Blumenberg, Hans. 1983. *The Legitimacy of the Modern Age.* Translated by Robert M. Wallace. Cambridge: MIT Press.

Bourke, Vernon. 1974. "Is Thomas Aquinas a Natural Law Ethicist?" *The Monist* 58: 52–66.

1983. "The Synderesis Rule and Right Reason." *The Monist* 66: 71–82.

Bowlin, John. 1998. "Psychology and Theodicy in Aquinas." *Medieval Philosophy and Theology* 7/2: in press.

forthcoming. "Sieges, Shipwrecks, and Sensible Knaves: Justice and Utility in Butler and Hume." *Journal of Religious Ethics.*

Bradley, Denis J.M. 1996. *Aquinas on the Twofold Human Good: Reason and Happiness in Aquinas's Moral Science.* Washington, DC: The Catholic University of America Press.

Brown, Peter. 1988. *The Body and Society: Men, Women, and Sexual Renunciation in Early Christianity.* New York: Columbia University Press.

Bruns, Gerald. 1989. "Tragic Thoughts at the End of Philosophy." *Soundings* 72:

693-724.

Burrell, David B. 1979. *Aquinas: God and Action*. London: Routledge & Kegan Paul.

1984a. "God's Eternity." *Faith and Philosophy* 1: 389-406.

1984b. "Maimonides, Aquinas, and Gersonides on Providence." *Religious Studies* 20: 335-351.

1986. *Knowing the Unknowable God: Idn-Sina, Maimonides, Aquinas*. Notre Dame: University of Notre Dame Press.

1988. "Aquinas's Debt to Maimonides." In *A Straight Path: Studies in Medieval Philosophy and Culture*. Edited by R. Link-Salinger, J. Hackett, M.S. Hyman, R. James Long, and C.H. Manckin. Washington, DC: The Catholic University of America Press.

1990. "Aquinas and Scotus: Contrary Patterns for Philosophical Theology." In *Theology and Dialogue*. Edited by Bruce Marshall. Notre Dame: University of Notre Dame Press.

1993. *Freedom and Creation in Three Traditions*. Notre Dame: University of Notre Dame Press.

Cessario, Romanus. 1991. *The Moral Virtues and Theological Ethics*. Notre Dame: University of Notre Dame Press.

Colish, Marcia. 1985. *The Stoic Traditions From Late Antiquity to the Early Middle Ages*. 2 vols. Leiden: E.J. Brill.

Cooper, John. 1985. "Aristotle on the Goods of Fortune." *Philosophical Review* 94: 173-196.

1987. "Contemplation and Happiness: A Reconsideration." *Synthese* 72: 187-216.

Cromartie, Michael, ed. 1997. *A Preserving Grace: Protestants, Catholics, and Natural Law*. Washington, DC: Ethics and Public Policy Center; Grand Rapids: W.B. Eerdmans.

Darwall, Stephen. 1995. *The British Moralists and the Internal "Ought": 1640-1740*. Cambridge: Cambridge University Press.

Davis, Grady Scott. 1992. *Warcraft and the Fragility of Virtue: An Essay in Aristotelian Ethics*. Moscow, ID: University of Idaho Press.

Dent, N.J.H. 1984. *The Moral Psychology of the Virtues*. Cambridge: Cambridge University Press.

Elster, John. 1984. *Ulysses and the Sirens: Studies in Rationality and Irrationality*. Rev. edn. Cambridge: Cambridge University Press.

Finnis, John. 1980. *Natural Law and Natural Rights*. Oxford: Clarendon Press.

1983. *Fundamentals of Ethics*. Washington, DC: Georgetown University Press.

Finnis, John, Joseph Boyle, and Germain Grisez. 1987. *Nuclear Deterrence, Morality, and Realism*. New York: Oxford University Press.

Frankfurt, Harry. 1971. "Freedom of the Will and the Concept of a Person." *Journal of Philosophy* 63: 5-20.

Frede, Michael. 1980. "The Original Notion of Cause." In *Essays in Ancient Philosophy*. Minneapolis: University of Minnesota Press.

Fuchs, Josef. 1983. *Personal Responsibility and Christian Morality*. Translated by

William Cleves and others. Washington, DC: Georgetown University Press.

Gallagher, David. 1991. "Thomas Aquinas on the Will as Rational Appetite." *Journal of the History of Philosophy* 29: 559–584.

Grisez, Germain. 1983. *The Way of the Lord Jesus Christ*. Vol. 1 of *Christian Moral Principles*. Chicago: Franciscan Herald Press.

1993. *Living a Christian Life*. Vol. 11 of *Christian Moral Principles*. Chicago: Franciscan Herald Press.

Grisez, Germain, Joseph Boyle, and John Finnis. 1987. "Practical Principles, Moral Truth, and Ultimate Ends." *American Journal of Jurisprudence* 32: 99–151.

Gutman, Israel, ed. 1990. *Encyclopedia of the Holocaust*. 4 vols. New York: Macmillan.

Hacking, Ian. 1985. "Styles of Scientific Reasoning." In *Post-Analytic Philosophy*. Edited by John Rajchman and Cornel West. New York: Columbia University Press.

Hall, Pamela M. 1994. *Narrative and the Natural Law: An Interpretation of Thomistic Ethics*. Notre Dame: University of Notre Dame Press.

Harak, Simon. 1993. *Virtuous Passions: The Formation of Christian Character*. New York: Paulist Press.

Hasker, William. 1983. "Concerning the Intelligibility of God as Timeless." *The New Scholasticism* 57: 170–195.

1985. "Foreknowledge and Neccesity." *Faith and Philosophy* 2: 121–157.

Hauerwas, Stanley. 1993. "The Difference of Virtue and the Difference It Makes: Courage Exemplified." *Modern Theology* 9: 249–264.

Hearne, Vicki. 1987. *Adam's Task*. New York: Knopf.

Heinaman, Robert. 1988. "Eudaimonia and Self-Sufficiency in the Nicomachian Ethics." *Phronesis* 33: 31–53.

Herman, Barbara. 1985. "The Practice of Moral Judgment." *Journal of Philosophy* 82: 414–436.

Hibbs, Thomas. 1990. "A Rhetoric of Motives: Thomas on Obligation as Rational Persuasion." *The Thomist* 54: 293–309.

Hittinger, Russell. 1987. *A Critique of the New Natural Law Theory*. Notre Dame: University of Notre Dame Press.

Hume, David. 1975. *Enquiries Concerning Human Understanding and Concerning the Principles of Morals*. 1777. Edited by L.A. Selby-Bigge. 3rd edn., with text revised and notes by P.H. Nidditch. Oxford: Clarendon Press.

Incandela, Joseph. 1986. "Aquinas' Lost Legacy: God's Practical Knowledge and Human Freedom." Ph.D. diss., Princeton University.

Inwood, Brad. 1985. *Ethics and Human Action in Early Stoicism*. Oxford: Clarendon Press.

Irwin, T.H. 1986. "Stoic and Aristotelian Conceptions of Happiness." In *The Norms of Nature*. Edited by M. Schofield and G. Striker. Cambridge: Cambridge University Press.

1988. "Disunity in the Aristotelian Virtues." In *Oxford Studies in Ancient*

Philosophy. Edited by J. Annas and R.H. Grim. Suppl. vol. Oxford: Clarendon Press.

1990a. "The Scope of Deliberation: A Conflict in Aquinas." *Review of
Metaphysics* 44: 21–42.

1990b. "Virtue, Praise, and Success." *The Monist* 73: 59–79.

Jaffa, Harry. 1952. *Thomism and Aristotelianism: A Study of the Commentary of Thomas
Aquinas on the Nicomachean Ethics*. Westport, CT: Greenwood Press.

Jordan, Mark. 1986. *Ordering Wisdom: The Hierarchy of Philosophical Discourses in
Aquinas*. Notre Dame: University of Notre Dame Press.

1990. *The Alleged Aristotelianism of Thomas Aquinas*. The Etienne Gilson Lecture
Series no. 15. Toronto: Pontifical Institute of Mediaeval Studies.

1991. "Thomas Aquinas' Disclaimers in the Aristotelian Commentaries." In
Philosophy and the God of Abraham: Essays in Memory of James A. Weisheipl, OP.
Edited by R.J. Long. Papers in Mediaeval Studies no.12. Toronto: The
Pontifical Institute of Mediaeval Studies.

1997. *The Invention of Sodomy in Christian Theology*. Chicago: University of
Chicago Press.

Jordan, Winthrop. 1977. *White Over Black: American Attitudes Toward the Negro,
1550–1812*. New York: Norton.

Kant, Immanuel. 1985. *Foundations of the Metaphysics of Morals*. 2nd rev. edn.
Translated by Lewis Beck White. New York: Macmillan.

Kenny, Anthony. 1991. "The Nicomachean Conception of Happiness." In
Oxford Studies in Ancient Philosophy. Edited by Julia Annas. Suppl. vol.
Oxford: Clarendon Press.

1992. *Aristotle on the Perfect Life*. Oxford: Oxford University Press.

Kent, Bonnie. 1989. "Transitory Vice: Thomas Aquinas on Incontinence."
Journal of the History of Philosophy 27: 199–223.

1995. *Virtues of the Will: The Transformation of Ethics in the Late Thirteenth Century*.
Washington, DC: The Catholic University of America Press.

Kerr, Fergus. 1997. *Immortal Longings: Versions of Transcending Humanity*. Notre
Dame: University of Notre Dame Press.

Kilcullen, John. 1988. *Sincerity and Truth: Essays on Arnauld, Bayle and Toleration*.
Oxford: Clarendon Press.

Korsgaard, Christine. 1983. "Two Distinctions in Goodness." *Philosophical
Review* 91: 169–195.

1985. "Aristotle and Kant on the Source of Value." *Ethics* 96: 24–47.

Kraut, Richard. 1989. *Aristotle on the Human Good*. Princeton: Princeton University Press.

Kretzmann, Norman. 1988. "Warring Against the Law of My Mind: Aquinas
on Romans 7." In *Philosophy and the Christian Faith*. Edited by Thomas V.
Morris. Notre Dame: University of Notre Dame Press.

Le Goff, Jacques. 1988. *Medieval Civilization: 400–1500*. Translated by Julia
Barrow. Oxford: Basil Blackwell.

Long, A.A. 1991. "The Harmonies of Stoic Virtue." In *Oxford Studies in Ancient
Philosophy*, Edited by Julia Annas. Suppl. vol. Oxford: Clarendon Press.

Lovibond, Sabina. 1983. *Realism and Imagination in Ethics*. Minneapolis: University of Minnesota Press.

MacDonald, Scott. ed. 1991. *Being and Goodness: The Concept of the Good in Metaphysics and Philosophical Theology*. Ithaca: Cornell University Press.

MacIntyre, Alasdair. 1988a. "*Sophrosune*: How a Virtue Can Become Socially Disruptive." *Midwest Studies in Philosophy* 13: 1–11.

1988b. *Whose Justice? Which Rationality?* Notre Dame: University of Notre Dame Press.

1990. *Three Rival Versions of Moral Enquiry*. Notre Dame: University of Notre Dame Press.

1994. "How We Can Learn What *Veritatis Splendor* Has To Teach." *The Thomist* 58: 171–195.

1996. "Natural Law As Subversive: The Case of Aquinas." *Journal of Medieval and Early Modern Studies* 26: 61–83.

McDowell, John. 1978. "Are Moral Requirements Hypothetical Imperatives?" *Proceedings of the Aristotelian Society*. Suppl. vol. 52:13–29.

1979. "Reason and Virtue." *The Monist* 62: 331–50.

McGinn, Bernard. 1975. "The Development of the Thought of Thomas Aquinas on the Reconciliation of Divine Providence and Contingent Action." *Thomist* 39: 741–752.

McInerny, Ralph. 1982. *Ethica Thomistica: The Moral Philosophy of Thomas Aquinas*. Washington, DC: The Catholic University of America Press.

1992. *Aquinas on Human Action: A Theory of Practice*. Washington, DC: The Catholic University of America Press.

Maritain, Jacques. 1943. *The Rights of Man and Natural Law*. Translated by Doris C. Anson. New York: Charles Scribner's Sons.

1950. *Man and the State*. Chicago: University of Chicago Press.

Mates, Benson. 1981. *Skeptical Essays*. Chicago: University of Chicago Press.

Mavrodes, George. 1984. "Is the Past Unpreventable?" *Faith and Philosophy* 1: 131–146.

Merchant, Carolyn. 1980. *The Death of Nature*. San Francisco: Harper & Row.

Migne, J.-P., ed. 1844–1890. *Patrologiae cursus completus Series Latina accurante. Paris*.

Nagel, Thomas. 1979. "Moral Luck." In *Mortal Questions*. Cambridge: Cambridge University Press.

Nelson, Daniel Mark. 1992. *The Priority of Prudence: Virtue and Natural Law in Thomas Aquinas and the Implications for Modern Ethics*. University Park, PA: Pennsylvania State Press.

Nussbaum, Martha Craven. 1978. *Aristotle's De Motu Animalium*. Text with Translation, Commentary, and Interpretive Essays. Princeton: Princeton University Press.

1986. *The Fragility of Goodness*. Cambridge: Cambridge University Press.

1988. "Nature, Function, and Capability: Aristotle on Political Distribution." In *Oxford Studies in Ancient Philosophy*. Edited by Julia Annas and R.H. Grimm. Suppl. vol. Oxford: Clarendon Press.

1990. "Transcending Humanity." In *Love's Knowledge: Essays in Philosophy and*

Literature. New York: Oxford University Press.

Oakeshott, Michael. 1962. "Rationalism in Politics." In *Rationalism in Politics*. London: Methuen.

O'Neill, Onora. 1989. *Constructions of Reason: Explorations in Kant's Practical Philosophy*. Cambridge: Cambridge University Press.

Pieper, Josef. 1959. *Prudence*. Translated by R. Winston and C. Winston. New York: Pantheon.

Pike, Nelson. 1970. *God and Timelessness*. London: Routledge & Kegan Paul.

Pinckaers, Servais. 1995. *The Sources of Christian Ethics*. Translated from the third edition by Mary Thomas Noble. Washington, DC: The Catholic University of America Press.

Pitkin, Hanna. 1984. *Fortune is a Woman*. Berkeley: University of California Press.

Pocock, J.G.A. 1975. *The Machiavellian Moment*. Princeton: Princeton University Press.

Pohlerg, M. 1970. *Die Stoa: Geschichte einer geistigen Bewegung*. 2 vols. 4th edn. Gottengen: Vardenhoek and Ruprecht.

Porter, Jean. 1986. "Desire for God: Ground of the Moral Life in Aquinas." *Theological Studies* 47: 48–68.

――― 1990. *The Recovery of Virtue: The Relevance of Aquinas for Christian Ethics*. Louisville: Westminster/John Knox Press.

――― 1996. "Contested Categories: Reason, Nature, and Natural Order in Medieval Accounts of the Natural Law." *Journal of Religious Ethics* 24: 207–232.

Rawls, John. 1971. *A Theory of Justice*. Cambridge: Harvard University Press.

――― 1985. "Justice As Fairness: Political Not Metaphysical." *Philosophy and Public Affairs* 14: 223–251.

Reeve, C.D.C. 1992. *Practices of Reason: Aristotle's Nicomachean Ethics*. Oxford: Clarendon Press.

Rist, John. 1969. *Stoic Philosophy*. Cambridge: Cambridge University Press.

Rorty, Amelie O. 1972. "Belief and Self-Deception." *Inquiry* 15: 387–410.

――― 1988a. "The Deceptive Self: Liars, Layers, and Lairs." In *Mind in Action*. Boston: Beacon Press.

――― 1988b. "Persons and Personae." In *Mind in Action*. Boston: Beacon Press.

――― 1988c. "The Two Faces of Courage." In *Mind in Action*. Boston: Beacon Press.

――― 1989. "Socrates and Sophia Perform the Philosophic Turn." In *The Institution of Philosophy*. Edited by Auner Cohen and Marcelo Dascal. LaSalle, IL: Open Court.

Rorty, Richard. 1979. *Philosophy and the Mirror of Nature*. Princeton: Princeton University Press.

――― 1989. *Contingency, Irony, and Solidarity*. Cambridge: Cambridge University Press.

――― 1991a. "Inquiry as Recontextualization: An Anti-Dualist Account of Interpretation." In *Objectivity, Relativism, and Truth*. Cambridge: Cambridge University Press.

1991b. "Non-Reductive Physicalism." In *Objectivity, Relativism, and Truth.* Cambridge: Cambridge University Press.

1991c. "The Priority of Democracy to Philosophy." In *Objectivity, Relativism, and Truth.* Cambridge: Cambridge University Press.

Rorty, R., J.B. Schneewind, and Q. Skinner. 1984. "Introduction." In *Philosophy in History.* Edited by R. Rorty, J.B. Schneewind, and Q. Skinner. Cambridge: Cambridge University Press.

Ruprecht, Louis. 1989. "Nussbaum on Tragedy and the Modern Ethos." *Soundings* 72: 589–605.

Sandbach, F.H. 1975. *The Stoics.* New York: W.W. Norton & Co.

Schneewind, J.B. 1984. "The Divine Corporation and the History of Ethics." In *Philosophy in History.* Edited by R. Rorty, J.B. Schneewind, and Q. Skinner. Cambridge: Cambridge University Press.

1993. "Kant and Natural Law Ethics." *Ethics* 104: 53–74.

1997. *The Invention of Autonomy: A History of Modern Moral Philosophy.* Cambridge: Cambridge University Press.

Schneewind, J.B., ed. 1990. *Moral Philosophy From Montaigne to Kant.* 2 vols. Cambridge: Cambridge University Press.

Sherman, Nancy. 1989. *The Fabric of Character: Aristotle's Theory of Virtue.* Oxford: Oxford University Press.

Shklar, Judith. 1984. *Ordinary Vices.* Cambridge: Harvard University Press.

Slote, Michael. 1983. *Goods and Virtues.* Oxford: Clarendon Press.

Smith, Barbara Herrnstein. 1988. *Contingencies of Value.* Cambridge: Harvard University Press.

Sorabji, Richard. 1980. *Necessity, Cause and Blame.* Ithaca: Cornell University Press.

Stegman, Thomas D. 1989. "Saint Thomas Aquinas and the Problem of Akrasia." *The Modern Schoolman* 66: 117–128.

Stout, Jeffrey. 1988. *Ethics After Babel.* Boston: Beacon Press.

1993. "On Having a Morality in Common." In *Prospects for a Common Morality.* Edited by G. Outka and J.P. Reeder. Princeton: Princeton University Press.

Striker, Gisela. 1988. "Greek Ethics and Moral Theory." Tanner Lectures vol. IX. Salt Lake City: University of Utah Press.

1991. "Following Nature: A Study in Stoic Ethics." In *Oxford Studies in Ancient Philosophy,* vol. IX. Edited by Julia Annas. Oxford: Clarendon Press.

Stump, Eleonore. 1986. "Dante's Hell, Aquinas's Moral Theory and the Love of God." *Canadian Journal of Philosophy* 16: 181–198.

Stump, Eleonore, and Norman Kretzmann. 1988. "Being and Goodness." In *Divine and Human Action: Essays in the Metaphysics of Theism.* Edited by Thomas V. Morris. Ithaca: Cornell University Press.

Taylor, Charles. 1982. "The Diversity of Goods." In *Utilitarianism and Beyond.* Edited by A. Sen and B. Williams. Cambridge: Cambridge University Press.

1985. "What is Human Agency?" In *Human Agency and Language.* Vol. II of

Philosophical Papers. Cambridge: Cambridge University Press.

Thurber, James. 1945. *The Thurber Carnival*. New York: Harper & Row.

Tilly, Maureen A. 1991. "The Ascetic Body and the (Un)Making of the World of the Martyr." *Journal of the American Academy of Religion* 59: 467–497.

Veatch, Henry. 1990. *Swimming Against the Current in Contemporary Philosophy*. Washington, DC: The Catholic University of America Press.

Verbeke, Gerald. 1974. "Fatalism and Freedom According to Nemesius and Thomas Aquinas." *St. Thomas Aquinas (1274–1974) Commemorative Studies*, vol. 1. Toronto: Pontifical Institute of Mediaeval Studies.

Vlastos, Gregory. 1980. "The Paradox of Socrates." In *The Philosophy of Socrates*. Edited by Gregory Vlastos. North Dakota: University of North Dakota Press.

———. 1991. *Socrates: Ironist and Moral Philosopher*. Ithaca: Cornell University Press.

Wadell, Paul. 1992. *The Primacy of Love: An Introduction of the Ethics of Thomas Aquinas*. New York: Paulist Press.

Walzer, Michael. 1977. *Just and Unjust Wars*. New York: Basic Books.

Waterlow, Sarah. 1982. *Nature, Change, and Necessity in Aristotle's Physics*. Oxford: Oxford University Press.

Westberg, Daniel. 1994. *Right Practical Reason: Aristotle, Action, and Prudence in Aquinas*. Oxford: Clarendon Press.

White, Stephen A. 1990. "Is Aristotelian Happiness a Good Life or the Best Life?" *Oxford Studies in Ancient Philosophy*, vol. VIII. Oxford: Clarendon Press.

Wiggins, David. 1980. "Deliberation and Practical Reason." *Proceedings of the Aristotelian Society*. n.s. 74 (1975–1976): 29–51. Reprinted in *Essays on Aristotle's Ethics*. Edited by Amelie O. Rorty. Berkeley: University of California Press.

Williams, Bernard. 1972. *Morality*. New York: Harper & Row.

———. 1973. "Ethical Consistency." In *Problems of the Self*. Cambridge: Cambridge University Press.

———. 1981a. "Conflicts of Values." In *Moral Luck*. Cambridge: Cambridge University Press.

———. 1981b. "Moral Luck." In *Moral Luck*. Cambridge: Cambridge University Press.

———. 1985. *Ethics and the Limits of Philosophy*. Cambridge: Harvard University Press.

———. 1993. *Shame and Necessity*. Berkeley: University of California Press.

Wippel, John F. 1988. "Thomas and the Axiom 'What is Received According to the Mode of the Receiver.'" In *A Straight Path: Studies in Mediaeval Philosophy and Culture*. Edited by R. Link-Salinger, J. Hackett, M.S. Hyman, R. James Long, and C. H. Manckin. Washington, DC: The Catholic University of America Press.

Wittgenstein, Ludwig. 1953. *Philosophical Investigations*. Translated by G.E.M. Anscombe. New York: Macmillan.

Wolf, Susan. 1980. "Asymmetrical Freedom." *Journal of Philosophy* 77: 151–166.

Wolterstorff, Nicholas. 1975. "God Everlasting." In *God and the Good*. Edited by C.J. Orlebeke and L.B. Smedes. Grand Rapids: Eerdmans.

Yack, Bernard. 1989. "How Good is the Aristotelian Good Life?" *Soundings* 72/2: 607–629.

Yearley, Lee H. 1990. *Mencius and Aquinas: Theories of Virtue and Conceptions of Courage*. Albany: State University of New York Press.

Zabzebski, Linda. 1985. "Divine Foreknowledge and Human Freedom." *Religious Studies* 21: 279–298.

Zeller, Edward. 1962. *Stoics, Epicureans, and Sceptics*. Rev. edn. Translated by O.J. Reichel. New York: Russell & Russell.

Index